# Juan Fermín de Aycinena

Juan Fermín de Aycinena
Central American Colonial Entrepreneur,
1729–1796

By Richmond F. Brown

University of Oklahoma Press : Norman and London

Published with the assistance of the Program for Cultural Cooperation between Spain's Ministry of Education and Culture and United States' Universities.

Library of Congress Cataloging-in-Publication Data

Brown, Richmond F. (Richmond Forrest), 1961–
    Juan Fermín de Aycinena : Central American colonial entrepreneur, 1729–1796 / by Richmond F. Brown.
      p. cm.
    Includes bibliographical references and index.
    ISBN 0-8061-2948-4 (cloth: alk. paper)
    1. Fermín de Aycinena, Juan, 1729–1796. 2. Businessmen—Central America—Biography. 3. Central America—History—To 1821. I. Title.
HC141.B75 1997
338'.04'092—dc21   97-3818
                                                                                                           CIP

Text design by Debora Hackworth.

The paper in this book meets the guidelines for permanence and durability of the Committee on Production Guidelines for Book Longevity of the Council on Library Resources, Inc. ∞

Copyright © 1997 by the University of Oklahoma Press, Norman, Publishing Division of the University. All rights reserved. Manufactured in the U.S.A.

        1 2 3 4 5 6 7 8 9 10

For my parents
and in memory of Louis Kirk

Contents

	List of Illustrations	ix
	List of Tables	xi
	Preface	xiii
	Introduction	3
1	The Kingdom of Guatemala	13
2	Friends and Family in Old and New Spain	36
3	Aycinena and the Santiago Elite	57
4	Colonial Entrepreneur	74
5	The Casa de Aycinena at Home and Abroad	101
6	Aycinena and the State	132
7	Aycinena and the Church	158
8	Prestige, Profits, and Persistence	178
9	Epilogue	197
	Conclusion	203
	Notes	209
	Glossary	263
	Bibliography	267
	Index	285

Illustrations

FIGURES

Juan Fermín de Aycinena dispensing alms to the poor	2
Plaza Mayor of Antigua, Guatemala	19
View of Volcano Agua, Antigua, Guatemala	21
Frontispiece of Juan de Goyeneche's *Executoria de la Nobleza del Valle de Baztan*	44
A mule train in early nineteenth-century Mexico	117
Ayuntamiento, Antigua, Guatemala	134
Cathedral of La Merced, Antigua, Guatemala	160

MAPS

1.	The Kingdom of Guatemala	14
2.	Navarre and the Basque Country	38
3.	Northern Navarre, the Baztán Valley	39
4.	Bishopric of Oaxaca, 1786	49

Tables

1. Estimated Population of Central America, ca. 1820 — 16
2. Population of Major Central American Cities, 1750–1800 — 17
3. Lineage of Juan Fermín de Aycinena — 40
4. The Children of Juan Fermín de Aycinena — 70
5. The Wealth of Juan Fermín de Aycinena, 1768–1777 — 75
6. The Aycinena Estate, 1796 — 76
7. Relative Size of Active Dependencies, 1777 — 81
8. Central American Indigo Exports, 1772–1804 — 82
9. Geographic Distribution of Active Commercial Debts owed to Juan Fermín de Aycinena, 1777 — 90
10. Active Dependencies, by Locality — 90
11. Known Haciendas of Juan Fermín de Aycinena — 93
12. Large Debtors of Juan Fermín de Aycinena, 1777 — 98
13. Aycinena's Isthmian Representatives — 107

14.	Aycinena's Representatives outside Central America	110
15.	Wealth of Pedro de Aycinena e Yrigoyen, 1785	120
16.	Public Positions of Juan Fermín de Aycinena	136
17.	Guatemalan Captains General in the Time of Juan Fermín de Aycinena, 1750–1800	143

Preface

This work originated on the fourth floor of Tulane University's Howard-Tilton Memorial Library, otherwise known as the Latin American Library. It was there in the mid-1980s that I had the opportunity to participate in a series of graduate seminars on the history of Central America, masterfully led by Ralph Lee Woodward, Jr. In those vigorous meetings, as we wrestled with the problems of a beautiful but troubled land's past, attempting to uncover the most important determinants of isthmian history, the debate invariably turned to *los que mandan*—those who rule. We talked for hours of presidents, priests, ambassadors and generals, banana men and the CIA, railroad builders and coffee planters. Naturally, much of the discussion focused on the region's most powerful families. It became clear that any treatment of Central America's oligarchs must consider not only the Somoza dynasty of Nicaragua, or the "Fourteen Families" of El Salvador, but also what contemporary observers of the nineteenth century bitterly called "La Familia," the Aycinena family of Guatemala City. Their power became perhaps the most controversial issue in Central American politics in the era of independence and for decades thereafter. How could such a small group exercise so much influence? How could so few people be at the center of so much history? This study hopes to provide the beginnings at least of some answers to those questions. It inquires into the origins, behavior, and significance of one of Central America's most intriguing figures, Juan Fermín de Aycinena e Yrigoyen (1729–96), who founded La Familia in the waning years of Spanish rule. It is my contribution to the ongoing discussion begun so many years ago in the classrooms and study carrels overlooking the oaks and magnolias of uptown New Orleans.

This work was made possible by the assistance of a number of individuals and institutions. The Shell Foundation provided funding that allowed me to carry out research in Guatemala in 1988–89. Earlier grants by the Matilda Geddings Gray Foundation and the Tinker Foundation permitted initial research into the Aycinena family. Two separate grants from the University of South Alabama Research Council allowed me to travel to Guatemala in the summer of 1994 and to Mexico in the summer of 1995. The College of Arts and Sciences of the University of South Alabama helped underwrite some of the costs of maps and illustrations.

In Guatemala, I benefited from the extraordinary kindness of the late Margarita Fortuny Nanne, who permitted me unlimited access to her collection of Aycinena family papers. Ramiro Ordóñez Jonomá, genealogist, attorney, and director of Guatemala's ecclesiastical archives, shared with me his unrivaled knowledge of Guatemalan elite family history. The directors and staff of the Archivo General de Centroamérica (AGCA) provided indispensable services. I am especially grateful to Gregorio Conchoa Chet of the AGCA, who devoted decades of tireless service in support of historical research in his country. Denise G. Brown helped with some of the more tedious aspects of archival work. I gratefully acknowledge the support of the late William Swezey, Steve Elliott, and the professional staff of the Centro de Investigaciones Regionales de Mesoamérica (CIRMA) of Antigua, Guatemala.

In Mexico, the staffs and directors of several archives provided essential services and many kindnesses. I want to acknowledge especially María de Jesus Díaz Nava and Teresa Matabuena of the Acervos Historicos of the Universidad Iberoamericana and Alejandra Cortes Hernández and Juan Robles of the notarial archives of the Federal District. Linda Arnold and John Crider helped me get my bearings at the Archivo General de la Nación (AGN) in Mexico City. Hugo Villafan provided friendship and transportation. In Oaxaca I received extraordinary cooperation from the director of the state notarial archives, Román Fierro Zarate, and especially Gustavo Andrés Santos, who in addition to providing prompt and professional service, sacrificed the use of his own desk for more than a week so that I would have a space to work.

Eugene Wilson, recently retired from the Department of Geography of the University of South Alabama, crafted the maps. Director Guillermo Náñez Falcón and his assistant Richard J. Pérez of the Latin American Library of Tulane University arranged for the photographs from the Sidney David Markman Collection and patiently answered my queries. Lawrence Feldman readily responded to numerous requests for information. And my colleagues Mike Thomason and Tollef Tollefsen provided valuable assistance in preparing the illustrations.

Once again I must thank my adviser and mentor, Ralph Lee Woodward, Jr., for his knowledge, kindness, and patience. Richard Greenleaf and Trudy Yeager, exceptionally talented teachers of Latin American history, provoked many of the ideas explored in this work. Colin MacLachlan and Bill Meneray made several useful comments on an earlier version. A number of gracious colleagues provided encouragement and helped to sharpen my focus over the years: David McCreery, Elizabeth Anne Kuznesof, Steven Palmer, and Regina Wagner gave of their time and knowledge to make this work possible. Detailed and insightful comments from Christopher Lutz and John Kicza have doubtlessly improved the work. John Drayton, Alice Stanton, and Sheila Berg of the University of Oklahoma Press have my profound respect and gratitude for their professionalism and hard work in guiding this study to print.

On a more personal level, I want to acknowledge my enduring debt to my undergraduate mentor, Lawrence M. Bryant, formerly of Spring Hill College, who deepened my love for history and talked me out of law school. I must express my appreciation for the support of my friends and colleagues in the history department at the University of South Alabama. My chairman, George H. Daniels, has nurtured a remarkably supportive environment in which to teach and write. The friendship, support, and constructive criticism of Aaron Fogleman, Lenny Macaluso, Mel McKiven, Mike Monheit, and Dan Rogers are reflected in the pages that follow. Ellen Williams, Jerry Dixon, Debbie Thomaston, and especially Helga McCurry provided invaluable technical assistance. My remarkable Mexicanist colleague Stephen D. Morris carefully read the complete work in several drafts, made invaluable suggestions for its improvement, and allowed me to win a few games of racquetball. Paul J. Dosal and F. Todd Smith provided friendship and encouragement over the years, as did Doyle Stewart and Ford Chambliss. Finally, I thank my family for their love and support. My parents, Richmond P. Brown and Laura G. Brown, and my brothers, Kevin Brown and John Robert Brown, know well the road I and this project have traveled. They provided the company that made the journey bearable.

Juan Fermín de Aycinena

Juan Fermín de Aycinena dispensing alms to the poor, circa 1790. This portrait is located in the home of Margarita Fortuny Nanne, Guatemala City. (Photograph by the author.)

Introduction

Central America staged a deadly morality play in the 1970s and 1980s. For more than a decade an international audience watched in rapt attention, exhilarated (or unnerved) at the sight of a downtrodden people rising up in the quest for justice, horrified (or perhaps reassured) by the brutal response of those in power. The gripping drama of revolution and counterrevolution, acted out by such compelling dramatis personae as death squads and liberation theologians, guerrillas and mercenaries, radical juntas and military governments, well-meaning if impotent "moderate elements," oligarchs, students, workers, peasants, and "Families of the Disappeared," all played out within an international context of lines drawn in the jungle by nostalgic old men and starry-eyed lieutenant colonels poised against bearded tropical revolutionaries and the ubiquitous if unseen hand of the "Evil Empire," was irresistible. Romantic martyrs of the isthmian struggle for justice, the incredible scope of human tragedy, and the obsessions of inveterate cold warriors compelled a broad audience and endowed the isthmus with an importance unique in its history. For a time at least Central America stepped out from its customary place in the shadows.

The end of the cold war, the electoral defeat of the Sandinistas in Nicaragua, and the negotiated end to the brutal civil war in El Salvador have shifted attention away from the isthmus in recent years, returning it to its more accustomed position in the international order. Even Guatemala has embarked on the difficult if hopeful road to reconciliation and thus, perhaps, oblivion. But, while it persisted, Central America's newsworthiness set off an avalanche of publications about the region—works of both popular appeal and scholarly presumptions. Although many of the works spewed forth from the isthmian volcano proved to be of transitory value, the unrest also produced scholarship of lasting importance.[1] And although most of the production centered on the contemporary crisis, there has also been renewed interest in the region's long and troubled history.

Indeed, many of the recent works look to the region's history to understand the origins of today's crises. As the Canadian historian Jim Handy (formerly Central American coordinator for Amnesty International Canada and now perhaps the leading authority on Guatemala's revolutionary experiment of 1944 to 1954) reminds us in the introduction to his 1984 history of Guatemala, "the roots of the current brutal nightmare in Guatemala stretch far back into history. To explain contemporary Guatemala it is necessary to trace those roots back into the depths of colonial society where the underpinnings of the existing society were established."[2] Similarly, the anthropologist Carol Smith, in her preface to an important collection of works treating Indian-state relations in Guatemala, remarks that "while the past must inform our interpretations of the present, the present must also inform our interpretations of the past." In other words, she explains, "history must be reinterpreted by each generation, so as to reflect the concerns and understandings that come from the events and social circumstances that impinge on that generation."[3]

Central America's recent and in some cases continuing upheaval is often linked to stark inequalities in the distribution and control of vital resources. Too much power and too much wealth is concentrated in too few hands. This much seems obvious. But systematic investigations of los que mandan, the elite families who have most benefited from Central America's skewed economic and social structure, have been rare.[4] Among other things, such queries would presumably tell us something of how the skewing came about in the first place. As David McCreery observed in his insightful discussion of the historical literature on Guatemala, "We know more about the despised Indian than we do about the dominant national or regional or local families."[5] The gap is a glaring if paradoxical one.

In Central America, to an extent matched in few other places, the privileged few have exercised, and still exercise, inordinate power. The remarkable resiliency of isthmian elites, giving rise to what some have called a "living museum,"[6] has much to do with Central

America's recent travails. Studying those elites, therefore, is both practical and fundamental to understanding Central American history. Richard Graham, moreover, advises that a focus on elites is perhaps the most time-effective approach for the Latin American historian.[7] As individuals, families, and kinship networks, they wielded an extraordinary influence over politics, the economy, and society, much greater, relatively, than the much more numerous, and infinitely more sympathetic, common people. The Brazilian historian Emilia Viotti da Costa tells us, "It is impossible to understand the history of the powerless without understanding the history of the powerful."[8] Although I would not go so far as to adopt Carlyle's dictum that history is merely the biography of great men, it must be said that great men have done much to shape, or misshape, the history of Central America.

Thus, I set out to study the most important of the isthmian ruling clans in the eighteenth and nineteenth centuries, the Aycinena family of Guatemala City. The Aycinenas were Central America's wealthiest and most prominent family in the late colonial and early republican eras. They alone resided on Guatemala City's *plaza mayor* (central plaza). They alone held a Castilian title of nobility in Bourbon Central America. Given John Kicza's criteria for defining the late colonial elite of Mexico, they were *the* "Great Family" of Central America. As Kicza writes,

> The distinctions that separated the Great Families from the other elements of the upper class in Mexico City were their unparalleled wealth, the diversity of their holdings and investments, the success of their business practices, the honors that they received, their ability to

place their children in the upper ranks of the civil and ecclesiastical administrations, their close alliances with other leading political and clerical figures, their choice of marriage partners, and, as a culmination of these other factors, their longevity at the summit of the social hierarchy.[9]

Kicza's description applies perfectly to the Aycinenas' preeminence in late colonial Central America. It was a stature, moreover, that they maintained well after independence in 1821.[10] Aycinena family members dominated the Guatemalan early independence elite, a dominance that in itself became a central issue in early national politics. Falling from grace in the 1830s, La Familia returned to power under the aegis of the caudillo Rafael Carrera (1840–65) who looked to restore much of the colonial order.[11] And although the Aycinenas' political fortunes declined once again with the onset of the "Liberal Revolution" of 1871, they were able, to a surprising extent, to retain their social and economic position well into the twentieth century. Of the families who made an often-cited 1974 list of Guatemala's "Top Twenty" families, they alone were rooted in the colonial era.[12] Even in the late twentieth century, the Aycinena family remains, in the words of a Guatemalan gentleman working beside me in Guatemala City's Archivo General de Centroamérica, "arriba todavía." Clearly, the Aycinena story can tell us a great deal about the history of Central America.

We cannot comprehend the reasons behind the Aycinenas' remarkable resiliency without first understanding the foundations of the family's early success. An appropriate starting point, therefore, is the dynasty's founding by the Spanish emigrant Juan Fermín de

Aycinena e Yrigoyen. Miles Wortman states flatly that "Juan Fermín de Aycinena held more power than any one man in the history of Central America."[13] Of course, others might argue that this distinction belongs to such Guatemalan caudillos as Rafael Carrera, Justo Rufino Barrios, or Manuel Estrada Cabrera, or perhaps Yankee entrepreneurs like Minor Cooper Keith or Samuel Zemurray. Regardless, Aycinena obviously merits critical study. In an essay outlining research priorities for Bourbon Central America, Mario Rodríguez judged that "[a] figure whose biography is long overdue is Juan Fermín Aycinena, the first marquis of that name and one of the most dynamic entrepreneurs of the eighteenth century."[14] Rodríguez echoed the words of Troy S. Floyd, who wrote in 1961 that "only a monograph could do full justice to the career of Aycinena."[15]

I propose to take up the challenge posed by Floyd and Rodríguez. The story of Juan Fermín de Aycinena offers a marvelous vehicle for understanding the politics, economy, and society of late colonial Central America. It also presents an intriguing case study of Spanish American merchants, a group whose role remains somewhat controversial. The controversy derives from the ambiguous nature of the colonial economy, the ambiguous role of merchants within it, and the ambiguous effects of their activities on it. Were they agents of change or bulwarks of the status quo, or some complex combination of the two?[16]

What is beyond debate is that Juan Fermín de Aycinena constructed a glittering edifice of wealth and power in Central America, a dazzling yet sturdy structure that survived the ravages of independence and beyond. His building blocks were a powerful extended

INTRODUCTION

family network, a mastery of colonial business, and the expert use of church and state. The relative importance of the pillars of his enterprise is difficult to determine with any precision. Each in some way reinforced the others, and their relationship to one another has a somewhat circular quality. They are separated here only for the purposes of analysis, for they fit together in a general strategy of achieving wealth, status, and power.

This study addresses the following questions: How did Juan Fermín de Aycinena gain such extraordinary wealth, status, and power, and so quickly? What use did he make of them? What steps did he take to ensure that his influence would persist beyond his lifetime? What accounts for his uniqueness? And what does his story tell us about late colonial Central America?

The study is based primarily on two sets of archival documents. The first is a relatively large body of privately held Aycinena family papers that belonged to the late Margarita Fortuny Nanne of Guatemala City. Ms. Fortuny Nanne was the principal heiress to what might be seen as the *mayorazgo*, or entailed estate, established by Juan Fermín de Aycinena, her great-great-great-grandfather, in 1796, the year of his death. It is a remarkable collection hitherto untapped—with the limited exception of the Guatemalan diplomat/scholar Enrique del Cid's privately rendered collection of annotated documents.[17] Among the family papers, which hold an even greater abundance of materials for the nineteenth century, the most important documents for this study are a series of inventories detailing Juan Fermín's wealth in 1768, 1771, and 1777. These inventories, conducted on the occasions of his first wife's death, his second marriage, and his second wife's death, respectively, tell us in great detail of Aycinena's household, merchandise, debtors, and creditors. They provide amazing snapshots of the most important and most successful commercial enterprise in late colonial Central America. His first wife's will indicates Juan Fermín's worth on entering marriage in 1755 and his wife's enormous contribution to his estate. An 1811 document summarizes Juan Fermín's holdings at the time of his death. Thus it is possible to gain a sense of the evolution of Juan Fermín de Aycinena's estate, although obviously large gaps remain. Numerous other documents provide commercial records, instructions on estate management, and private family correspondence.

The second set of documents is the extensive collection of *protocolos*, or notarial records, maintained in the AGCA. The records document numerous transactions, personal, commercial, legal, and official, business agreements, credit arrangements, land transfers, and powers of attorney. In some cases, the notarial records helped to identify persons and relationships mentioned in the family papers. These were supplemented by as many other documents as could be found on Juan Fermín de Aycinena in the AGCA, located largely by consulting the useful but incomplete name (*onimástico*) file.

The original research for this project, conducted primarily in 1988 and 1989, was supplemented by additional research in Guatemala in August 1994 and in Mexico City and Oaxaca in the summer of 1995. Especially fruitful in the latter visit were the Yraeta-Yturbe collection of merchant papers housed at the Universidad Iberoamericana in Mexico City and the notarial records of the Federal District and the state of Oaxaca. The Yraeta-Yturbe collection contains perhaps the most complete documentary record of any merchant enterprise in colonial Spanish America (and early republican Mexico as well). It contains the copious correspondence between the Mexican merchant Francisco Yraeta (1731–97) and his family and business associates throughout the Spanish world. Yraeta corresponded with Aycinena (and other members of the Guatemalan merchant community) about once a month. Although it was disappointing not to find correspondence from Aycinena himself, Yraeta's monthly missives to our protagonist provide a much fuller view of commercial relations between Yraeta and the merchants of Guatemala, as well as occasional bits of personal information. Similarly, the notarial records of Mexico City and the state of Oaxaca provided new information on the valuable connections Aycinena enjoyed and maintained in those two crucial areas of his enterprise, before and during his remarkable isthmian business career.

After a brief chapter providing the historical context of the Aycinena story, I analyze the pillars of his success. Chapters 2 and 3 examine the family connections Juan Fermín de Aycinena established, extended, and embellished as a means of securing and enhancing his own and his immediate family's wealth, status, and power. Chapter 2 looks at his Spanish origins and Mexican connections while chapter 3 focuses on his relations with the colonial elite of Guatemala.

Chapters 4 and 5 are devoted to Aycinena's all-important business endeavors and are based largely on the three separate estate inventories (1768, 1771, and 1777) discovered in the Aycinena family papers, notarial records of Guatemala and Mexico, and the Yraeta collection of Mexico City. How did Aycinena acquire such a dominant role in the Central American colonial economy? And how did that dominance contribute to his social prominence and political power?

Chapters 6 and 7 explore Aycinena's use of the Spanish colonial institutional apparatus (state and church) to advance his interests and those of his family. Chapter 6 looks at Aycinena's office holding and his relations with the royal bureaucracy. What kinds of connections aided and abetted Aycinena's ascent? In what respects were his public trusts conducive to his private interests? Where is the elusive intersection of private and public life? Chapter 7 explores Aycinena's dealings with the church establishment. We have no reason to doubt his piety. But we should inquire about how his own interests were advanced by his sustained support of the church. What roles other than spiritual succor did the church play for Aycinena and his family? Was support of the church merely part of the nobleman's legal and social obligations, or were there more immediate and tangible returns?

Chapter 8 addresses the questions raised by Aycinena's acquisition of a noble title, his admission to a Spanish military order (as Knight of the Order of Santiago), and his establishment of an entailed estate in 1796. How did Aycinena manage the tensions created by the competing demands of profits and social prestige? How did he attempt to secure his family's position for succeeding generations? Chapter 9 offers a brief epilogue, followed by a conclusion that summarizes the study's findings.

Chapter 1

The Kingdom of Guatemala

Around 1750, the young Juan Fermín de Aycinena left his ancestral home in the highlands of Navarre to seek his fortune in the Indies. He was about twenty years old. The story goes that he carried only the 1,000 pesos his family had given him for the journey.[1] By 1751 he was in Mexico City, learning the ways of colonial commerce and making valuable contacts.[2] By 1753 he was in business with a cousin in Oaxaca, plying his trade from Acapulco to Santiago de Guatemala.[3] The next year he identified himself as a *vecino* (citizen) and merchant of Oaxaca residing in Santiago de Guatemala.[4] Almost constantly in motion to this point, he would now stay put. Aycinena had found a niche in the Kingdom of Guatemala (see map 1). During the rest of his life he would move just once more, obliged to do so

Map 1. The Kingdom of Guatemala

only by the vagaries of nature and, perhaps, isthmian politics.

By the time he settled in Santiago, Aycinena could boast of a modestly impressive worth of 21,000 pesos.[5] Within two decades, the enterprising emigré from the Kingdom of Navarre had become the wealthiest man in the Kingdom of Guatemala. By 1783, as Marqués de Aycinena, he held the only noble title in Central America and soon afterward was made a Knight of the Order of Santiago. In 1796, the year of his death at the age of sixty-six, he established a mayorazgo to be passed down to his eldest son, along with the family title. His wealth at the time of his death, including homes, haciendas, trade goods, personal property, and outstanding debts owed to him, approached 1.5 million pesos.[6]

The remarkable story of Juan Fermín de Aycinena frames a distinct era in Central America. He lived and worked and prospered, married, married again, and married a third time and fathered more than a dozen children, in the dynamic years between the end of the War of Jenkins' Ear (1749) and the commercially crippling wars of the French Revolution near century's end. The age of Aycinena witnessed the dramatic economic expansion of Western Europe, an expansion that drew Central America, licitly and otherwise, into the international economy via demands for its high-quality indigo. In the second half of the eighteenth century, Central American indigo consistently ranked as the second or third leading Spanish American export product (behind Mexican silver and alternating with Oaxacan cochineal). Annual indigo production in these decades regularly exceeded a million pounds.

Relatedly, the Aycinena era saw the apex of Bourbon reforms under Charles III (1759–88), reforms that opened up colonial trade within the empire and brought about more reliable shipping, especially to formerly peripheral areas like Central America. For Spanish American commerce in general, the period between the establishment of *comercio libre* (free trade) in 1778 and the English blockades of 1796 has been described as a "brief golden age."[7] In a time of unprecedented expansion, Juan Fermín de Aycinena came to control perhaps as much as 25 percent of all Central American commerce.[8] More than any other individual, Aycinena personified the prosperity of late colonial Central America.

POPULATION AND SOCIETY

Although technically part of the viceroyalty of New Spain (Mexico), colonial Central America was administered separately and autonomously as the Kingdom of Guatemala (Reino de Guatemala).[9] The Kingdom encompassed the present-day Mexican state of Chiapas and stretched to the frontier separating Costa Rica and Panama. It contained some 800,000 people in 1778.[10] By the end of the century, the population had increased to about one million (see tables 1, 2). Roughly between 50 and 60 percent of the Kingdom's population resided in the province of Guatemala itself.[11]

The Kingdom of Guatemala was home to a stunningly complex mix of peoples. A small European class (peninsulars and creoles) ruled over a large indigenous population and a rapidly increasing number of *castas*, people of mixed race.[12] Of the million or so inhabitants of Central America in 1800, the best estimates hold that about 580,000 were Indian (58%), 375,000 (37.5%)

TABLE 1
Estimated Population of Central America, ca. 1820

Costa Rica	63,000
El Salvador	248,000
Guatemala	595,000
Honduras	135,000
Nicaragua	186,000
Central America	1,227,000

Source: Ralph Lee Woodward, Jr., "The Aftermath of Independence, 1821–c. 1870," in *Central America since Independence*, ed. Leslie Bethell (Cambridge: Cambridge University Press, 1991), 8.

TABLE 2
**Population of
Major Central American Cities, 1750–1800**

City	Population	Year
Santiago de Guatemala	38,200	1750s
Nueva Guatemala	5,917	1776
Nueva Guatemala	23,434	1793
Quezaltenango	11,000	1800
San Salvador	12,059	1800
San Miguel	5,539	1800
San Vincente	4,087	1800
Granada	8,233	1800
León	7,571	1800
Cartago	8,337	1800
San José	8,326	1800

Sources: W. George Lovell and Christopher H. Lutz, *Demography and Empire: A Guide to the Population History of Spanish Central America, 1500–1821* (Boulder: Westview Press, 1995), 17; and Oakah L. Jones, Jr., *Guatemala in the Spanish Colonial Period* (Norman: University of Oklahoma Press, 1994), 164.

were considered castas, and 45,000 (4.5%) were considered Spaniards.[13] The ethnic situation in colonial Central America was even more complicated than these numbers suggest.

Different parts of the Kingdom experienced varying degrees of social and economic transformation. Predominantly indigenous areas in Guatemala's western highlands, for example, tenaciously resisted or moderated colonial pressures to change. In contrast, urbanization, miscegenation, and commercialization dramatically altered the Hispanicized towns of eastern Guatemala, the indigo region of El Salvador, and the silver mining zone of Honduras. These, in turn, provided a sharp contrast with the cattle ranches and smallholdings of Nicaragua and Costa Rica (which had lost most of their relatively small indigenous populations in the immediate aftermath of the conquest). And the Caribbean coastal areas, what by the eighteenth century had become the Mosquito Coast, was a world even farther apart. There, British loggers and contraband traders established small outposts stretching from present-day Belize to Costa Rica, coexisting with highly mobile and largely miscegenated "native" populations that had absorbed substantial African elements. Those areas that experienced more intensive European settlement and more vigorous extractive economic activity became what scholars have called Central America's colonial "core." Areas of more limited commercial or residential use for Spaniards became the colonial "periphery" and featured a radically different ethnic makeup.[14]

Despite their small numbers, the European class of Central America dominated politics, society, and the economy, especially in the Hispanicized, core areas.[15] There, as in other parts of Spanish America, "colonial establishments" prevailed, representing a marriage of convenience between local elites, ambitious newcomers, and colonial officials.[16] Despite occasional disputes between new arrivals and the well entrenched, "Spanish society in Guatemala was," in Stephen Webre's view, "an immigrant society, founded by immigrants, and continually reinforced through immigration."[17] This was a pattern Aycinena enthusiastically joined, and which served him well.

SANTIAGO DE GUATEMALA

The center of Aycinena's activities from his arrival in Central America around 1754 until the mid-1770s was Santiago de Guatemala (present-day Antigua). Nestled in a deceptively serene and strikingly beautiful valley in Guatemala's southeastern highlands, surrounded by majestic volcanoes, Antigua today is designated a "Monument of the Americas," deservedly famous for its colonial architecture and ambience. It has become something of a minor tourist mecca, a quaint, peaceful island in a violent land. In the eighteenth century, however, Santiago was the administrative, commercial, cultural, and ecclesiastical center of Central America, one of the most important cities in Spanish America. At the time Aycinena arrived there, some 38,200 people lived in Santiago—6,500 Europeans, 6,700 Indians, and

Plaza Mayor of Antigua, Guatemala (colonial Santiago). (The Sydney David Markman Collection, Latin American Library, Tulane University.)

some 25,000 castas.[18] The young Navarran must have been impressed by Santiago's broad streets laid out in the classical grid pattern of Spanish colonial towns. Thirty-eight religious structures, including a magnificent cathedral, testified to the wealth and power of the church establishment. The Kingdom's only university, the University of San Carlos, provided a veneer of learning, a modicum of European culture, and a limited avenue for social mobility and thus was one more inducement attracting the ambitious to the city.[19]

Aside from its physical charms, Santiago was the locus of power in colonial Central America. There, the highest officials of state and church carried out their duties and wrestled for power. There, isthmian trade was registered, taxes were collected, and (since 1739) money was coined. There, private and governmental agencies and individuals waged their battles and settled their differences. In these contests, local interests voiced their concerns through the *ayuntamiento* (municipal council) of Santiago. Composed of the city's leading vecinos, the ayuntamiento governed the surrounding valley as well as the city itself. By the time of the 1761 public auction of *cabildo* (council) seats, if not earlier, it came to be dominated by indigo-exporting merchants tied together by family connections. The Santiago cabildo boasted a number of important functions at the time Juan Fermín de Aycinena arrived in Santiago, making a council seat a desirable post. The council collected taxes (including the *alcabala*, or sales tax, for the entire Kingdom), took in rental income on municipal property, distributed land and Indian labor in the Valley of Guatemala, conducted bids for lucrative concessions (such as the meat and liquor monopolies), supervised guilds and markets, and exercised judicial and police functions. In the second half of the eighteenth century, the ayuntamiento of Santiago faced challenges from two directions: provincial elites determined to preserve their autonomy and independence and Bourbon efforts to limit its own power.

From July until September 1773, a series of earthquakes rocked the Central American capital, heavily damaging or destroying much of the town. The earth-

View of Volcano Agua from the courtyard of the University of San Carlos, Antigua, Guatemala. (The Sidney David Markman Collection, Latin American Library, Tulane University.)

quakes provoked a mighty debate over whether to rebuild or relocate the capital, a debate that dominated the 1770s and deeply divided the colonial aristocracy. Ultimately, the captain general prevailed over the archbishop and the great majority of Santiago's inhabitants who preferred to keep the capital in the present location, and the capital was moved to the site of present-day Guatemala City. Juan Fermín de Aycinena became a central figure in the debate and eventually sided with the Crown and those favoring a new locale. As we shall see, he was amply rewarded for his cooperation. Nueva Guatemala emerged slowly in the late eighteenth century as the new center of wealth, power, and culture.

THE PROVINCES

The Kingdom of Guatemala consisted of several provincial power centers that only occasionally felt the hand of governmental authorities in Santiago. Provincialism and localism prevailed in an era of restricted state power, limited economic integration, and lack of regional identification.[20] As of 1800, Central America consisted of some fifteen separate provinces, governed by eight *alcaldes mayores* two *corregidores* (district magistrates), one *gobernador* (governor), and four intendants. The *alcaldías mayores* were Totonicapán, Sololá, Chimaltenango, Sacatepéquez, Sonsonate, Vera Paz, Escuintla, and Suchitepequez. The *corregimientos* were Quezaltenango and Chiquimula. The *gobierno* (area presided over by a governor) was Costa Rica, and the intendancies, introduced in 1786, were León (Nicaragua), Ciudad Real (Chiapas), Comayagua (Honduras), and San Salvador (El Salvador).[21]

Provincial elites jealously guarded their power and resented intrusions from the capital—economic or political. Antagonisms routinely flared between the merchants (and officials) of Santiago, on the one hand, and the planters of El Salvador, the miners of Honduras, and the cattlemen of Nicaragua, on the other. Just as often, if not more often, the provincial elites feuded with neighboring areas. Thus, in addition to the center-periphery squabbles, mutual regional animosities pitted León against Granada, Cartago against San José, and Comayagua against Tegucigalpa.

Occasionally the menaces of English pirates or Miskito Indians dramatized the importance of unified colonial defense.[22] For the most part, however, the isthmus was only loosely bound together. Costa Rica, for example, was more closely tied to Panama than to the Kingdom's distant capital.[23] A rugged geography, the few roads and navigable waterways, the patchwork of ethnic groups (more than twenty distinct Mayan linguistic groups in Guatemala alone), the relative lack of exportable resources (at least until the eighteenth century), and Central America's minor role in the imperial scheme of things—all promoted the emergence of distinct and discrete power centers.

That situation began to change in the eighteenth century. The expanding political and military power of the Spanish state in Central America and the growing commercial power of wholesalers in Guatemala City began to encroach on provincial autonomy. The eighteenth-century expansion, while bringing great prosperity to some, contributed to rising tensions: it expanded the power of the capital merchants over provincial producers, intensified pressures on land and people, and raised the stakes of success and failure.

Although recent scholarship has questioned its scale and duration,[24] the movement toward the economic and political integration of Central America contributed to considerable unrest in the last decades of colonial rule and darkened the prospects of a peaceful Central American nation after independence.

ECONOMY

Until the indigo boom of the second half of the eighteenth century, Central America held little intrinsic value for the Spanish Crown. For most of the colonial era, it was a remote backwater, cut off from the mainstream of imperial trade, bereft of accessible mineral wealth or any real importance other than its strategic location alongside the sealanes tying Spain to Mexico and Peru. Poor and extremely difficult to defend, royal advisers probably saw Central America as more trouble than it was worth.

Entrepreneurs likely held similar reservations. In the aftermath of conquest in the early sixteenth century, booty capitalists had combed the isthmus in search of exportable commodities that would bring rapid wealth and perhaps allow them to retire comfortably to Spain. Fleeting economic cycles—an Indian slave trade, shipbuilding, gold and silver, cacao and indigo—had all played out by the turn of the seventeenth century. The population decreased, immigration slowed, cities shrank, hacienda complexes grew, and Indian communities could breathe more easily with the diminishing weight of colonial demands. The limited wealth available in Central America's long "century of depression" depended principally on one's intimacy with the state, and particularly on access to the pensions and *encomiendas* (royal grants of rights to collect tribute) doled out by the Crown and its agents.[25]

Central America began to emerge from its depression-induced feudalistic shell only in the late seventeenth and early eighteenth centuries, with the recovery of indigo and silver production and the expansion of illicit trade. In the new era, the extractive economy offered the primary avenue to wealth. Indigo and silver were also the most volatile sectors of the colonial economy, dependent on reliable shipping and international peace, favorable weather, fertile lands and bountiful lodes, and capital and supplies (e.g., salt, mercury). They also required adequate labor.

Although mining and indigo never employed a majority of isthmian inhabitants, they did disrupt subsistence and local production in times of expansion.[26] And because it was often necessary to compel the Kingdom's Indians to participate in the colonial economy against their will, systems of coerced labor (*repartimiento*) and forced trade (*repartimiento de efectos*) played central roles.[27] The miners, planters, and merchants thus depended on the state to support their efforts. Those with wealth used it to secure access to power, which in turn allowed them to protect and further expand their wealth.

STATE

In Central America, the successful and the ambitious struggled mightily to control important offices, or the officeholders themselves, for they were keys to wealth and power.[28] The Central American bureaucracy descended from the captain general of Guatemala and the *audiencia* (high courts) down to the level of provincial officials—corregidores, gobernadores, and alcaldes mayores. Local inhabitants received some voice through town councils—cabildos or ayuntamientos—although these tended to represent the interests of the most powerful members of colonial society and were hardly democratic.

The most powerful and prestigious isthmian official was the captain general. Invariably a Spaniard, in the eighteenth century he tended to be a military figure, reflecting the growing concerns about isthmian defenses in a time of rising prosperity and foreign threats. In addition to his duties as captain general, he also served as governor and as president of the audiencia. In the eighteenth century, the captain general enjoyed a salary of 10,000 pesos.[29]

Santiago/Guatemala City also furnished the headquarters for the audiencia, the Kingdom's highest court of appeals, which also dispensed and oversaw legislative and supervisory duties. As of 1783, the Central American audiencia was composed of four *oidores* (judges), two *fiscales* (Crown attorneys), and an *alguacil mayor* (chief constable). Fourteen other officials had lesser roles. In all, some twenty-two people comprised or supported the audiencia, with a total payroll exceeding 43,000 pesos.[30] No Guatemalan-born individual served as an oidor of the audiencia until after 1806. Judges were usually Spaniards, but about 30 percent of their number were born in the Americas.[31]

A royal audit in 1783 listed some 152 bureaucratic positions in the Kingdom of Guatemala, from the captain general to provincial officials (with a total annual salary of nearly 163,000 pesos).[32] Despite their subordinate stature in the bureaucratic hierarchy, provincial officials were perhaps the most crucial component of the imperial system. Alcaldes mayores and corregidores (and their subordinates, known as *tenientes*) operated at the economic, social, and political intersection of Spanish and Indian Central America. They were responsible for collecting tribute, assigning labor, meting out justice, and providing for defense. Poorly paid and weighted down by the costs of assuming office, frequently and illegally they became business partners of colonial merchants. In some cases, they were merchants themselves who wished to exploit the tremendous business opportunities afforded by their posts. They collected raw materials or domestic products to be exported while retailing the goods supplied by merchants of the capital. Some officeholders even owned properties in the areas they governed.

Supplicants in Spain and America vied aggressively for control over strategic provincial offices in Central America. The most hotly contested colonial posts governed the silver mines of Honduras, the indigo plantations of El Salvador, and such densely populated indigenous regions as Totonicapán, Chimaltenango, or Sololá. Their purchase prices reflected the level of competition to occupy them, which, in turn, was based on the illicit income their proprietor could expect to gain.[33]

CHURCH

Representatives of the Catholic Church were possibly even more fundamental to Central American unity than the servants of the state. Churchmen were both more numerous and more widely dispersed than colonial officials, and they played a relatively greater part in the daily lives of the peoples of Central America.[34]

The roles of church and state in colonial Central America are not easily separated. The conquest was as much a religious crusade as a military and economic enterprise. In the early colony, state-sponsored Catholicism permitted the transfer of Hispanic culture to a new land and a means of incorporating alien peoples into the colonial society and economy. Practices such as the *congregación* provided an instrument of social control over potentially dangerous populations, forcibly relocating villages into nucleated towns and training subject peoples at least superficially in the ways of their new lords.[35] Even in the later colony, the church remained the most tangible representative of Spanish rule in outlying areas.[36] And in the cities, the church's cathedrals, convents, *colegios* (schools), and Hispanic *cofradías* (lay brotherhoods) were the most formidable bastions of European culture.

The church housed a complex of competing agencies and individuals, internally divided and often pursuing divergent ends. The most important cleavage separated the secular hierarchy and the mendicant orders. In a sense, there were two churches: an Indian, nontithing church run by missionary orders in the colonial "periphery" and a tithing Hispanicized church, in the hands of seculars in the colonial "core." The two wings of the church jostled with one another for supremacy. Even the orders competed vigorously among themselves, jealously guarding their parishes from each other and from the encroaching secular hierarchy.

Still, as a whole, ideologically and institutionally, the isthmian church bound together amazingly diverse peoples and filled a broad array of powerful and essential roles. Through its varied agencies, the church ministered to the faithful, converted the heathen, and prosecuted the heretical.[37] Beyond its religious monopoly, the church administered education, hospital care, orphanages, poor relief, and other forms of charity. Church agencies also acquired great wealth: they became large landholders and leading dispensers of credit. Archbishop Cortés y Larraz noted in 1768–69 that the total annual tribute to the church amounted to 192,835 pesos. An additional 265,000 pesos was raised in cofradía income.[38] And this does not include revenues from the sale of indulgences, sacramental fees, *capellanias* (prayer endowments), property rental, and interest income from mortgages and short-term loans.

Like colonial officials, individual clergy, posted throughout the isthmus, were often engaged in business as planters and merchants, using their sacred positions for mundane ends. Because the church and churchmen (and women) had power, they attracted and often served the powerful. Here, too, entrenched and aspiring elites realized that privileged access to church offices and revenues was crucial to their success.

In sum, church and state created a reasonably flexible system of authority, balancing imperial needs with local interests, and endowed the isthmus with a semblance of unity, avenues for redress, and resources for defense, while permitting, if not encouraging, the existence of competing centers of economic and political power. At the same time, the power and resources of church and state might well determine the acquisition and retention of privilege on the part of colonial elites. Undeniably faithful and loyal to church and state, Juan Fermín de Aycinena nevertheless used the wealth, power, and patronage they possessed for his own ends.

BOURBON REFORMS IN CENTRAL AMERICA

As noted earlier, Aycinena's arrival in Central America was exquisitely timed. The half century from 1750 to 1800 witnessed a phenomenal rise in indigo production and exports, in response to the expanding demand from northern Europe's modernizing textile industries. The isthmian economy, especially the merchants of the capital, also benefited from adjustments to the imperial trading system introduced by the Spanish Crown. Those adjustments were part of a broader effort to reform the imperial system.

The Bourbon dynasty that came to power in 1700 resolved to restore Spain's former imperial greatness. In Central America, Bourbon officials faced problems of increasing contraband and foreign territorial encroachments. Corruption and nepotism infested the colonial bureaucracy. The continuing demographic crisis of the indigenous population undermined the tributary base, making tribute an increasingly less viable source of governmental revenue. To make matters worse, an ominous series of natural disasters—epidemics, earthquakes, locusts—plagued the isthmus.[39]

The eighteenth-century monarchs sought to reverse the decline. Although the reforms linked with their name were not as consistent or systematic as is sometimes assumed, proceeding instead by fits and starts, induced and interrupted by war, now retreating, now advancing, the Bourbons did undertake a monumental effort to overhaul the empire and preserve it for Spanish rule. Regardless of their ultimate failure, the reforms accelerated change in Central America and conditioned the environment in which our subject flourished.

In the Kingdom of Guatemala, the Bourbons looked to stimulate commerce, increase royal revenues by taxing the expanded trade, and improve military defenses by devoting much of the new money to isthmian defenses.⁴⁰ Aiming to centralize power, they were determined to strengthen the audiencia and to weaken the cabildo (especially with respect to the control of labor and taxes). In theory, provincial and local officials would be discouraged from their traditional participation in illegal commerce.

Simultaneously, the Bourbons attacked the economic power of the church. Espousing regalism, the Bourbons worried that excessive numbers of clergy and cofradías diverted wealth from the Crown and supported an ideological rival. Because church activities and revenues were largely exempt from royal taxation, the Spanish Crown introduced a series of measures to reduce church economic power. They also sought to reduce the independence of outlying parishes and to restrict the jurisdiction of mendicant orders. Guatemala was made an archdiocese in 1744, creating a seat for an archbishop and giving Santiago authority over the other regions of the isthmus. This permitted the "ecclesiastical offensive" of the second half of the eighteenth century. Beginning in 1754, the audiencia began to transfer the majority of regular *doctrinas* (Indian parishes) to the secular clergy and episcopal control. The number of regular clergy and convents was limited, the Jesuit order was expelled, and most parishes were secularized.⁴¹

The Bourbons attempted to shift Central America away from a tribute-based economy to a market economy. Thus they endeavored to transfer the isthmian tax burden to the non-Indian population.[42] They abolished encomiendas, yet again.[43] They revised collections of the alcabala, the principal tax on non-Indians. The effort to do so illustrates the practical difficulties of reform. The audiencia had collected the tax since the 1660s, but revenues declined in the early eighteenth century as a result of widespread corruption, underreporting, and illicit trade. The Bourbons felt compelled to return collection of the tax to the cabildo of Santiago, which in turn delegated it to Santiago merchants in 1729, represented by the *diputación comercial* (merchant assembly). This was a strategic, if temporary, retreat from the Bourbon attack on local power. The cabildo retained jurisdiction over the tax until the 1760s, when collection was returned to the audiencia.[44] The alcabala was raised in 1766 and again in 1782 (from 2% to 3% to 4%). A general accounting department was established in 1771 to handle the enhanced revenues.[45] The Bourbons altered the isthmian fiscal structure by creating government monopolies on alcohol (1753) and tobacco (1767). Although the new agencies reflected a drive to increase governmental revenues in a time of foreign rivalry and mounting defense costs, they also offered additional opportunities for private individuals to gain access to public resources, and thus to determine who had power and who did not.

In one sense, with the Bourbon efforts to centralize power, the hand of government rested more heavily on Central America than ever before. At the same time, however, internal restrictions on imperial trade were relaxed. Central America was permitted to trade with Havana in 1760. In 1774 Guatemala was allowed to trade by sea with Mexico, New Granada, and Peru.

Imperial free trade followed in 1778 and was implemented in Guatemala in 1781, thus lessening Guatemala's dependence on members of Mexico City's *consulado de comercio* (merchant guild).[46]

Although it was not their intent, the principal beneficiaries of Bourbon efforts to stimulate the isthmian economy were the merchants of Santiago (and later Guatemala City). This was the end result of nearly every imperial commercial reform. In the 1730s, for example, Bourbon intervention in Honduran mining—intensified labor drafts, lowered taxes, a readier supply of cheap mercury, and the installation of a royal mint in Santiago (1739)—spurred the recovery of silver production. But the real winners were the merchants of Santiago, who were able to profit from their control of mercury supplies, credit, provisioning, and transport of the silver to the mint in the capital. Similarly, as noted, indigo exports took off after the end of the War of Jenkins' Ear. As in the case of silver, the greatest beneficiaries were the Santiago merchants, again based on their control of credit, provisioning, and marketing of the dye.

In the last quarter of the eighteenth century, however, with defenses strengthened, commerce expanding, and governmental revenues growing, and with the traditional obstacles to the royal will subdued, the Spanish Bourbons turned against their former allies and now their greatest rivals in Central America, the merchants of Santiago/Guatemala City. The Bourbon dilemma was to limit colonial merchant power while depending on that power to sustain the imperial system itself. It was a dilemma never fully resolved.

From the late 1770s on, the Bourbons took steps to rein in merchant control. They sided with silver miners, cattle producers, and indigo growers in their conflicts with the capital merchants. They ordered the moving and official supervision of the annual fairs to gain favorable prices for the producers. In 1779 the Bourbons attempted to regulate the isthmian cattle trade in favor of the cattlemen. In 1780 they established an exchange bank (the Casa de Rescate) in Tegucigalpa to provide mining credit. And in 1782 they set up the Indigo Growers' Fund (Monte Pío de Cosecheros del Añil) to furnish credit to indigo farmers in the hope of lessening their reliance on merchant financing. To minimize the overwhelming advantage of Guatemala City (in effect, an inland port), the Bourbons attempted to develop Caribbean ports. Trujillo and Omoa were declared tax-free ports in 1784, Santo Tomás in 1789. And in 1786, largely to minimize Guatemala City's administrative power, intendancies were established in El Salvador, Chiapas, León, and Comayagua.[47]

Despite its vigor, the Bourbon effort to circumscribe Guatemalan merchant strength—and more generally, the power of the capital over the provinces—failed. Guatemalan merchants never really lost control over pricing. The Indigo Growers' Fund was poorly funded, and producers defaulted to it as they had to the capital city merchants. The fund was soon bankrupt and planters were once again forced to rely on merchant capital.[48] Similarly, by 1792 the earlier restrictions on tobacco, mining, and the cattle trade had also been abandoned. As if to seal their victory, the Guatemala City merchants received their own consulado de comercio in 1793. Agitation for such an institution had been the merchants' response to what they perceived as an unfair governmental attack directed against them as a class—namely, the Bourbon efforts to protect isthmian producers. It was also an effort to create a judicial organization independent of provincial courts or the Mexican consulado, agencies outside their control.[49] Perhaps more than anything else, the establishment of the consulado demonstrated merchant influence with the makers of colonial policy. Appropriately, the guild's first presiding officer (*prior*) was Juan Fermín de Aycinena.[50]

Although the late colonial era in Central America was marked by several disputes between the members of the new consulado and the cabildo of Guatemala City (the traditional mouthpiece of the colonial elite), the significance of intraelite conflict in the last years of the Kingdom of Guatemala has been exaggerated. The strength of the merchant families that dominated the Kingdom of Guatemala resided, not in any particular governmental body or bodies they controlled, but in the class itself, in their fundamental economic power and the leverage that power gave them with the ultimate authorities in the Spanish imperial system. Only with the collapse of indigo (after 1800) and the imperial crisis (after 1808) did the power of the center over the periphery begin to wane and the tensions attending that shift affect the politics of the capital. But that is part of another story.

What matters for us is that in the last decades of the eighteenth century virtually all areas of the Kingdom of Guatemala were integrated into a single economic framework, dominated by the merchants of the capital city. In part because of, and later in spite of, a series of sweeping imperial adjustments, Guatemala City's merchant princes reigned supreme. Their unquestioned leader was Juan Fermín de Aycinena.

Chapter 2

Friends and Family in Old and New Spain

The image of the rugged and resourceful individual who struggles and prevails against great odds to achieve unusual success is a compelling one. And indeed, in its tale of the poor immigrant rising to become a wealthy nobleman, there is something of a Horatio Alger-like quality to the life of Juan Fermín de Aycinena. But the quest for understanding compels us to probe beyond the mythic character of the Aycinena story. Remarkable though it was, the rise of Juan Fermín de Aycinena has a rational basis rooted in the institutions and practices of his day, and it is the purpose of this study to offer the soundest possible explanation for his unique success.[1]

A crucial part of Aycinena's astounding rise to wealth and power relates to the family connections he enjoyed in Spain and Mexico and those he established in the Kingdom of Guatemala. Although his business talents and his astute manipulation of the apparatuses of church and state obviously contributed enormously to his success, strategic family ties were essential. And though Juan Fermín as an individual reaped the benefits of his enterprise's success, both the enterprise itself and the rewards they brought should be seen in the context of his extended family network.

A large body of scholarship on Latin America posits the central importance of the corporate family both to individual fortunes and to the region's history.[2] The authors of the now-standard history of colonial Latin America insist, for example, that individuals among the colonial elite must be placed in the context of their extended family—linked by blood and marriage—over several generations, with a holistic view of the family's economic and political relations.[3] Individuals acted within the context of extended family needs. Based on this assumption, the social historian Diana Balmori advises turning the conventional approach on its head: "Instead of studying the family through an institution or one of its enterprises, the family should be considered as *the* enterprise."[4]

PENINSULAR BEGINNINGS

The Aycinena family enterprise began in the Spanish Kingdom of Navarre, one of four Basque provinces of northern Spain (see map 2).[5] Incorporated into Spanish territory by Ferdinand of Aragon in 1512, even afterward Navarre maintained substantial autonomy. By the eighteenth century it was the only peninsular region called a kingdom. It alone was governed by a viceroy, who shared power in the Navarran provincial capital of

Map 2. Navarre and the Basque Country

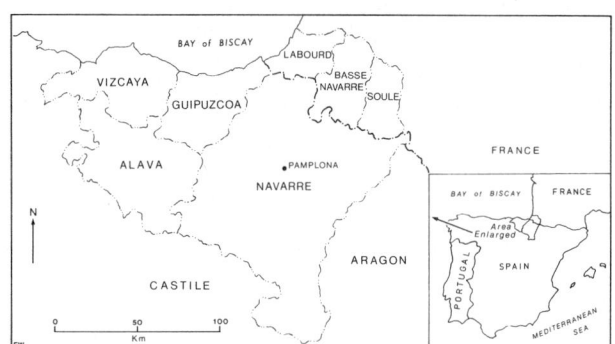

Pamplona with the *consejo real* (similar to an audiencia), a *cortes* (provincial parliament) that met some nine times over the eighteenth century, and the *diputación*, a permanent body that supervised matters normally handled by the cortes in the years when it did not meet. Navarrans jealously guarded their traditional *fueros* (privileges). The kingdom merited such royal deference because of its strategic location adjacent to France and because, in times of need, its nobles and hidalgos invariably lent financial support to the Spanish Crown.[6]

On July 7, 1729, Juan Fermín de Aycinena e Yrigoyen was baptized in San Lorenzo de Ciga, one of fourteen towns in the Baztán Valley, nestled in the western Pyrenees (see map 3).[7] Population figures for the region are difficult to come by. The population of the Spanish Basque provinces as a whole remained about 350,000 throughout the seventeenth century (out of a Spanish population of 7.5 to 8 million).[8] Navarre itself had a population of about 185,000 in the late sixteenth century.[9] Pamplona, the capital and largest city, had a population of about 10,000 in 1637 and

Map 3. Northern Navarre, the Baztán Valley

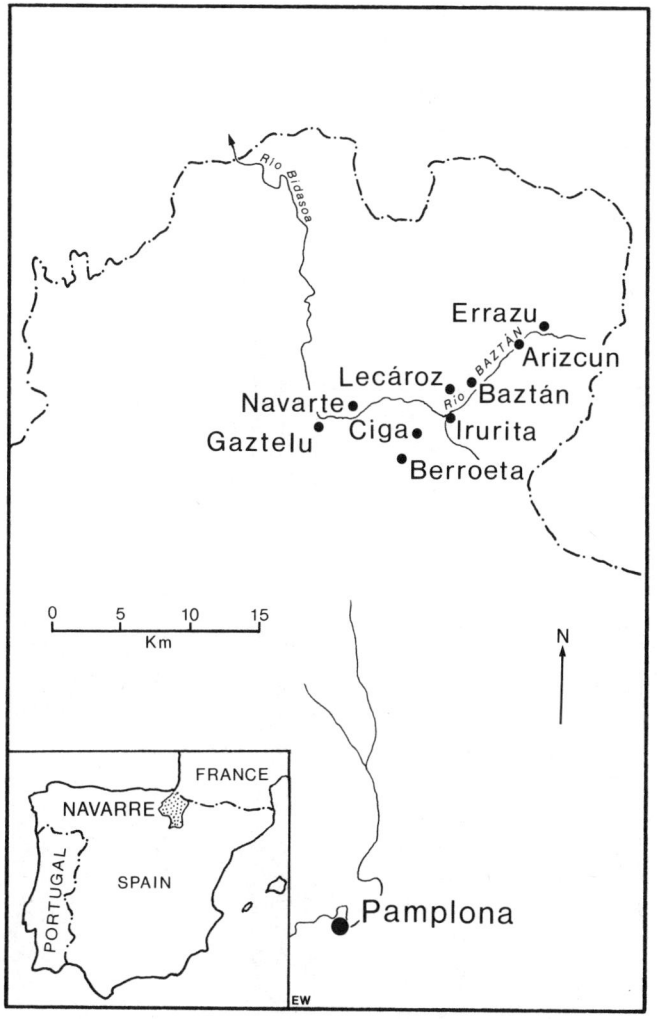

TABLE 3
Lineage of Juan Fermín de Aycinena

Aycinena

Juan de Aycinena = María Martina de Indantea

Miguel de Aycinena (b. 1627, Berroeta [m. 1647, Ciga] = Graciara Lagarrea

Juan de Aycinena Legarrea (b. 1655, Ciga) [m. 1684, Ciga] =

Juan de Alzualde = Catalina de Alzuar

Juan Alzualde (b. 1614, Arrayoz) [m. 1640, Ciga] = Estebania de Ladecoa

Juana de Alzualde y Aldecoa (b. 1655, Ciga)

Yrigoyen

Miguel de Yrigoyen = Juana de Laurraga

Juan de Yrigoyen y Laurraga (b. 1622, Lecaroz) [m. 1646, Ciga] = María Juana de Echandia

Fermín de Yrigoyen y Echandia (b. 1653, Lecároz) [m. 1674, Lecároz] =

Juan de Yturralde Perurena = María de Jauregui

Juan de Yturralde Perurena y Jauregui [m. 1652, Arizcun] = María de Borda

María de Yturralde Perurena (b. 1655, Lecároz)

Juan Miguel de Aycinena Alzualde (b. 1685, Ciga) [m. 1709, Ciga] = Ana Antonia de Yrigoyen e Yturralde Perurena (b. 1689, Ciga)

Juan Fermín de Aycinena e Yrigoyen (b. 1729, Ciga)

Source: AGCA, A1.40, Leg. 4797.

14,000 in 1780. Tudela, the second city, had a population of about 5,000 in 1637.[10] Ciga's population was considerably smaller than that.

Juan Fermín's family roots burrowed deeply in the Baztán Valley (table 3). Both of his parents, don Juan Miguel de Aycinena Alzualde (b. 1685) and doña Ana Antonia de Yrigoyen e Yturralde Perurena (b. 1689), claimed Ciga as their birthplace.[11] Juan Fermín's father's family had established themselves there by the late 1640s. Ana Antonia's forebears came from nearby Lecároz. In Ciga, Juan Fermín's parents owned the *casa de* Aldecoa.[12] The Aycinena *casa solariega* (family home) was established in the Baztán town of Berroeta. Juan Miguel and Ana Antonia were hidalgos and vecinos of note. Juan Miguel would have been among the electors of representatives to the Navarran cortes.

Given such roots and local significance, what prompted the young Juan Fermín de Aycinena to leave his homeland? He (and his family) obviously determined that his ambitions could not be realized in Navarre. For one thing, he was a younger child. Juan Fermín's mother was nearly forty years old at his birth. His sister Graciana married in 1740, when he was but ten or eleven. His nephew Pedro de Aycinena y Larraín, who later joined him in Guatemala, was born in 1741, the son of Juan Fermín's older brother, Juan de Aycinena, and María de Larraín.[13]

The key is to be found in the inheritance practices of Navarre. There, in contrast to Castile, property passed down whole to a single "elected" heir. New casas solariegas were forbidden.[14] And in his testament of 1751, Juan Fermín's father acknowledged the concession of the casa solariega de Aldecoa to Juan Fermín's sister, Graciana Aycinena e Yrigoyen, and her husband, Pedro de Larraín.¹⁵ It stands to reason that his parents had informed Juan Fermín of this decision before they confirmed it in front of a notary and before he left his valley.

Nonelected youth had to seek their fortunes elsewhere. They might move to another village, to a larger city or to bustling trade centers such as Barcelona, Seville, and Cádiz, or even to the Indies.¹⁶ The young Aycinena could behold numerous role models as he left home. Navarran emigrants, particularly natives of the Baztán Valley, had done extremely well in the generations immediately preceding his own. In fact, the Spanish anthropologist Julio Caro Baroja has called the early eighteenth century "the hour of Navarre." From the closing years of the reign of Charles II (1665–1700) through the reign of Philip V (1700–46) Baztaneses practically dominated Madrid.¹⁷

Caro Baroja dates this dominance from the founding of the Real Congregación de San Fermín de los Navarros in Madrid in 1683. Technically a religious brotherhood, the Real Congregación functioned as a mutual aid society supporting families and individuals from Navarre and, most significant, as a powerful lobby acting on behalf of the Navarrese not only in Madrid but also in Seville and Cadiz and throughout the Indies.¹⁸

Madrid-based Baztaneses obtained powerful patronage positions based on their wealth derived from commerce in Spain and America, officeholding, and lucrative *asientos*, or royal concessions. These *hombres de transición* espoused "French" ideas, wrote economic treatises, promoted commerce and industry (especially in their native province) and patronized public, cultural, and religious institutions in their birthplaces. Many confirmed their success with titles and membership in military orders—preferably a marquessate and a place among the Caballeros del Orden de Santiago (Knights of the Order of Santiago).

The Arizcun native Juan de Goyeneche y Echenique (1656–1735) helped initiate the so-called Navarran era, acquiring tremendous power in Madrid via his control of treasury offices. He employed his wealth to stimulate industry and urban renewal in Navarre.[19] His Madrid-born son Francisco Xavier Goyeneche (b. 1690) enjoyed a similar stature. He too became a Knight of Santiago and eventually Marqués de Belzunce (in 1731). Most crucial, in view of its patronage possibilities, was his role on the Council of the Indies. He became general treasurer of the body in 1708, and later its *decano* (senior member). Eventually he joined the Camara Real.[20]

Francisco Xavier's Arizcun-born cousins Tomás and Juan Francisco de Goyeneche e Yrigoyen renewed the ties between Madrid and the Baztán Valley. Tomás (1681–1721) was a Knight of Santiago and served as the *contador mayor* (principal accountant) for the widow of Charles II. His brother Juan Francisco (1689–1744) joined his brother, cousin, and uncle in Madrid and likewise gained admittance to the Knights of Santiago. As of 1711 he administered the sea and land mails (*correos maritimos y terreste*) of Spain. Elected prefect of the Real Congregación de San Fermín de los Navarros in 1729, he served as treasurer on the Consejo Real (Royal Council) while also acting as a member of the Navarran Consejo Real. He crowned his rise to eminence with the title Marqués de Ugena (Marqués y Señor de las Villas de Ugena y Torrejoncillo). A businessman (*hombre de negocios*) as well as a royal con-

Frontispiece of Juan de Goyeneche's *Executoria de la Nobleza, Antiguedad, y Blasones del Valle de Baztan* (Madrid, 1685), an antiquarian genealogy of the elite families of the Baztán Valley, which he dedicates to his children and forbears. The illustration depicts the towns and villages of the Valley. (Courtesy of The Hispanic Society of America, New York.)

cessionaire (*asentista*), on his death in 1744 he was worth 17,524,967 *reales de vellón* (about 876,250 pesos).[21] As we shall see, the Marqués de Ugena played an important supporting role in the fortunes of Juan Fermín de Aycinena.

The influence of the Goyeneche dynasty was rivaled by that of the Uztáriz family. Gerónimo de Uztáriz (1670–1732) also came from Arizcun. He served on His Majesty's Royal Council as secretary of war and navy in the 1720s, in which capacity he wrote his famous reformist tract, *Teória y práctica del comercio y de la marina* (1724).[22] In 1729 he was secretary of the Council and Camara of the Indies, where he directed policy toward New Spain. In subsequent decades, his family's merchant firm, the Casa de Uztáriz, became linked closely to the Cinco Gremios of Madrid and emerged as the preferred trading house of Charles III (1759–88).[23] The firm conducted considerable business with the Casa de Aycinena of Guatemala.

We must be careful, at this point, not to exaggerate the importance of this group of extraordinarily influential Navarran financiers and asentistas for our story. How closely Juan Fermín's family was linked to these Baztán notables remains to be determined. At the very least, tangential connections are suggested by the recurrent coincidence of surnames figuring in Caro Baroja's study and those shared by Juan Fermín's forebears: Iturralde, Yrigoyen, Borda, Echandía, Jauregui, and Aldecoa. If he and his immediate kin did not benefit directly from such ties, they were at the very least indirect beneficiaries of their power and patronage.

In addition to the success of Navarrans at the Spanish Court, the exploits of Navarrans in the Indies issued a similar call to nonelected youth. *Indianos*, those who returned home to live off the fruits of their labors and, no doubt, to entertain listeners with their tales of fortune and misfortune, of conquests military, commercial, and sexual, excited the imaginations of Navarran youth. Pious works, scholarships, and chaplaincies funded by the faithful, the grateful, and the conspicuous testified to the opulent possibilities of life in America. The gleaming walls of public buildings and church edifices, newly built or embellished through the largesse of transplanted native sons, deeply impressed Iberian youths facing genteel poverty or restricted prospects at home. For the ambitious and adventurous, joining prominent and successful family members in the New World represented an obvious option.

CÁDIZ

Juan Fermín almost certainly spent some time prior to embarking for America—weeks, months, perhaps even a year or more—in the Andalusian port city of Cádiz. By the eighteenth century Cádiz was the center of Spain's American trade, since 1717 housing the Casa de Contratación. In the 1700s Cádiz was a thriving entrepôt of about 70,000 people. The *comerciante*, or merchant community, perhaps 15 percent of the population, was the "soul of the city."[24] As was the case in Madrid, Navarrans figured prominently among the merchants of Cádiz. The Navarrese (and the other immigrants from northern Spain) were especially noteworthy for the strength of their corporate families and endogamous marriage practices.[25] They not only provided Juan Fermín with essential connections at the start of his career, they furnished long-term commercial relations essential for his business success.

In Cádiz, Juan Fermín would have joined his merchant brother Pedro de Aycinena e Yrigoyen and perhaps other relatives.[26] There, he was exposed to the practices of colonial trade. There, he learned that success for the aspiring merchant usually entailed travel to the Indies, either for specific transactions or to establish a short-term or possibly permanent residence. Young merchants had to pay their dues. A 1729 document rendered by the elders of the Cádiz consulado stressed that the "young or unsuccessful comerciantes were the ones who usually had to acquire experience and fortune and therefore the ones who had to travel more to America."[27]

MEXICAN INTERLUDE

Juan Fermín de Aycinena did not embark for the New World without preexisting contacts and probably did not go alone. He had family members waiting for him on his arrival. And, indeed, he made his trip shortly before, or possibly in the company of, his brother, Pedro de Aycinena e Yrigoyen. In Cádiz on September 25, 1750, Pedro accepted goods worth 2,320 pesos on consignment from the Cádiz merchant Francisco Trelles. He redeemed the obligation in Mexico City, paying Trelles's Mexican agent, Juan José Fagoaga, the required amount in April 1751.[28] In February 1753, Juan Fermín referred to his brother as a Spanish merchant residing in Veracruz.[29] Pedro remained in Veracruz until the late 1750s, when he became part of the Mexico City merchant community—one of the vaunted *almaceneros* (wholesalers or long-distance traders). Mirroring his brother's success in Guatemala, Pedro flourished in Mexico City, realizing tremendous wealth as an importer of European goods and a reexporter of South American cacao. He obtained high office in the Mexico City Consulado de Comercio before returning to Spain around September 1783.[30]

Pedro de Aycinena e Yrigoyen was just one of many Navarrans active in Mexican commerce. The more successful among them joined the Basque (Bascongada) party of the Mexico City Consulado de Comercio.[31] A shared place of origin meant that Juan Fermín and his fellow Navarrans in Mexico City enjoyed a common background, mutual acquaintances, and even ties of blood, all of which would have provided Juan Fermín with some entrée into the community and at the same time given his Mexico City cohorts a reasonable assurance of his trustworthiness.[32]

It is perhaps curious that Juan Fermín established himself in Mexico City while his brother remained in Veracruz. In terms of family strategy, Juan Fermín (or his kin) perceived that he was more likely to further the enterprise of the family by setting up in the capital of New Spain rather than remaining in Veracruz—the colony's principal port of entry. As he arrived in Mexico City around 1750, Juan Fermín most likely entered the service of an established Mexican merchant, presumably a family member. Such a man might have been Juan José de Barreneche e Yrigoyen, a native of Ciga, Navarre, and a vecino of Mexico City.[33]

An even likelier contact was Pedro Angel de Yrigoyen y Dutari, probably a cousin. Yrigoyen y Dutari had recently established himself in the Mexican capital after years of fruitful political and commercial activity in Puebla and Oaxaca. About this time, Juan Fermín definitely established links with Pedro Angel's cousin and his own first cousin, Pedro Bernardo de Yrigoyen. A

Map 4. Bishopric of Oaxaca, 1786

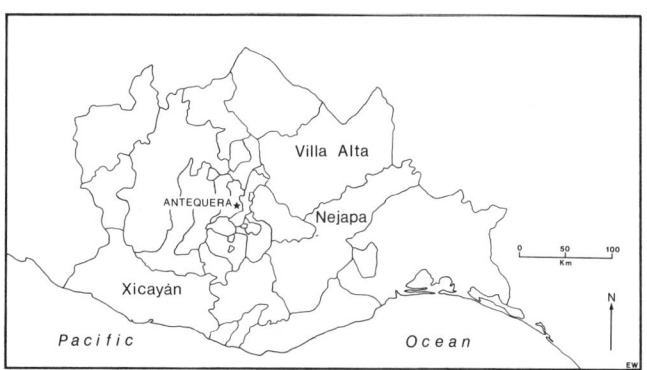

vecino of Oaxaca, Pedro Bernardo was in Mexico City in late 1750 and throughout much of 1751 settling legal matters.[34] Back in Oaxaca by January 1752, Pedro Bernardo de Yrigoyen named his Mexico City cousins, Pedro Angel de Yrigoyen and Juan Fermín de Aycinena e Yrigoyen, as his estate executors.[35]

Juan Fermín joined Pedro Bernardo in the Oaxacan capital of Antequera (today Ciudad Juárez de Oaxaca) by early 1753, probably after the death of Pedro Angel de Yrigoyen in April 1752.[36] (See map 4.) It turns out that Juan Fermín's relatives were well established there. Oaxaca had long held importance as a way station in the commerce between Mexico City and Santiago de Guatemala.[37] The period from 1750 to 1820 has been called Oaxaca's golden age. And, indeed, there are striking parallels between the Bishopric of Oaxaca and the Kingdom of Guatemala. Expansion of cochineal and textile production began in the 1740s and took off in subsequent decades. The scarlet dye was Mexico's second most important export, and Oaxaca held a virtual monopoly on its production until the nineteenth century.[38] As with the indigo merchants of Santiago de Guatemala, the cochineal trade came to be dominated by a relatively few well-connected peninsular merchant/officials who displaced the local elite from power.[39]

Juan Fermín's relatives were prominent among these usurpers. They had held a privileged place in Oaxaca for decades by the time he arrived there in the early 1750s. Established as merchants and cabildo members of Antequera, they also held lucrative provincial posts. These positions, because of their capacity for monopolizing the lucrative cochineal and textile trades, were viewed as the most desirable in all of New Spain.[40] Merchants centered in Antequera financed the officeholders or occupied the offices themselves, usually without ever leaving the Oaxacan capital.

The alcaldías mayores of Villa Alta and Nejapa were especially sought after. Few Spaniards lived in the regions, and there were virtually no independent merchants. Through tribute mechanisms, the alcaldes mayores (or more often their tenientes) would advance funds to Indian communities which they would require to be repaid in cochineal dye or textiles. The Indian communities were compelled either to produce these commodities themselves or to purchase them with the funds advanced by the alcaldes mayores. Because the "purchase price" of the cochineal and textiles was well below the "market price" they commanded in Mexico City or Spain, the alcalde mayor and his merchant financiers enjoyed extraordinary profits.

Juan Fermín's relatives became rooted in Oaxaca at least by the 1730s. Three figures played the key roles: Miguel Yrigoyen y Echenique and the aforementioned

Pedro Angel de Yrigoyen y Dutari and Pedro Bernardo de Yrigoyen. Teniente Coronel Miguel Yrigoyen y Echenique was probably the oldest of the three. A native of Errazu, Navarre, he arrived in Oaxaca by the mid-1730s, after years of military service to the Crown. He channeled some 70,000 pesos from Veracruz merchants to a Oaxacan official in 1734.[41] As of 1740, Yrigoyen e Echenique was alcalde ordinario *de primer voto* (of first vote) in the Antequera municipal council.[42] At least as early as 1742, he was alcalde mayor of Nejapa.[43] In this capacity, he acquired the hacienda Aranjuez in 1745.[44]

In 1744, Miguel de Yrigoyen y Echenique found himself in the awkward position of having claims to two Oaxacan alcalde mayor posts at one time.[45] He relinquished the post of Villa Alta to his nephew Pedro Angel de Yrigoyen, then a businessman in Puebla. Pedro Angel in fact had already served one term as alcalde mayor of Villa Alta, from 1731 to 1738. His second appointment lasted from 1745 to 1749.[46] Pedro Angel was a native of Errazu, like his uncle, and the son of Pedro de Yrigoyen and María de Dutari. His father was the older brother of Miguel de Yrigoyen e Echenique. Juan Angel's brother, Juan Lorenzo de Yrigoyen y Dutari, was an eminent priest in Pamplona.[47] After his second term in Oaxaca, sometime between 1750 and 1751, Pedro Angel relocated to Mexico City.[48] He died on April 6, 1752.[49] A few months later, Pedro Angel's teenage daughter, Juana, married her father's cousin and fellow Oaxacan officeholder, Pedro Bernardo de Yrigoyen.[50]

Pedro Bernardo de Yrigoyen arrived in Oaxaca at least by the early 1740s. In 1743, calling himself a vecino of Antequera, Pedro Bernardo received a five-year lease on *diezmo* ("tithe") collections for Tututepeque, Xamiltepeque, and Huazalotulan. The tithe amounted to 1,260 pesos per year, to be paid in cattle and cotton. His profits would come from any amount exceeding the mandated collection.[51] The next year, however, he acquired an even more lucrative sinecure. In October 1744 Navarran native Miguel de Ibarra ceded him the post of alcalde mayor of Jicayán.[52]

Thus, by late 1744, no fewer than three of the most sought after political positions in all of New Spain were in the hands of three Yrigoyens, an uncle and two nephews, at the very same time. Obviously, to acquire these posts, the Yrigoyens had powerful patrons at the Spanish court.[53] In 1742 Miguel de Yrigoyen y Echenique conceded powers to pursue honors and offices at the Spanish courts to don Juan Francisco de Goyeneche e Yrigoyen, the Marqués de Ugena[54] (the Spanish asentista worth some 17 million reales de vellón). In fact, the Goyeneche and Echenique families were closely intertwined.[55] Pedro Angel de Yrigoyen y Dutari and Juan Francisco de Goyeneche e Yrigoyen were cousins.[56]

The Yrigoyens' family-oriented approach to imperial officeholding is illustrated by a Christmas Eve transaction in 1744. On that date, Pedro Angel de Yrigoyen, alcalde mayor–elect of Villa Alta, contracted a debt of 70,000 pesos with the Veracruz merchant house of Gaspar Saenz Rico; 50,000 pesos came from Saenz Rico himself and another 20,000 came from Manuel Arechaga, Saenz Rico's son-in-law and partner in Mexico City. Pedro Angel's guarantors and cosigners (*fiadores y llanos pagadores*) were Colonel Miguel de Yrigoyen e Echenique, alcalde mayor of Nejapa, and Pedro Bernardo de Yrigoyen, alcalde mayor–elect of Jicayán.[58] In this transaction, the Veracruz firm looked to acquire exclusive rights to two of the most lucrative commodities in Spanish America—Oaxacan textiles and cochineal.

Alas, Miguel de Yrigoyen y Echenique died in June 1746, unable to realize fully the extraordinary possibilities of his family's control of Oaxacan offices. His spouse, María Luisa de Veitia, died a few months later. Both named Pedro Bernardo de Yrigoyen as their executor and sole heir. It was perhaps a dubious task. Yrigoyen y Echenique left large debts (63,791 pesos) to the Veracruz merchant firm of don Gaspar Saenz Rico e Hijo (as well as some 8,000 pesos to the Jesuits). These debts (temporarily at least) cost his heir the hacienda Aranjuez and in 1751 compelled a trip to Mexico City to resolve the matter legally.[58] There he encountered his cousin, Juan Fermín de Aycinena.

Pedro Bernardo de Yrigoyen remained an important Oaxacan businessman and official until his death around 1760. He continued to be Juan Fermín's principal Oaxacan associate until then. Ironically, in 1757 he called himself a Guatemalan businessman living in Oaxaca.[59] This had to do, no doubt, with his young cousin's extraordinarily good fortune in Santiago de Guatemala.

ON TO SANTIAGO

In 1754, Juan Fermín de Aycinena moved on to the Kingdom of Guatemala as a merchant traveling on behalf of his cousin and partner, Pedro Bernardo de Yrigoyen. He arrived on the last leg of a business trip that took him first to the Pacific port of Acapulco. In Acapulco, he probably acted as a purchasing agent for his cousin in the acquisition of Asian goods. He would then have overseen their trek across Mexico and ultimately to Santiago, where they would be used to reinforce standing commercial relationships. He would have exchanged Asian and European goods for Guatemalan indigo, which would then be routed through his cousin in Antequera and on to Mexico City and then perhaps Veracruz and Spain—along the same channels as Oaxacan cochineal and textiles.

From Antequera in February 1753, before commencing his journey, Juan Fermín conceded rights to effect a will (*poder para testar*) jointly to his brother in Veracruz, to his cousin in Antequera, and to Antonio Salgado, a vecino and businessman of the city of Guatemala.[60]

Whether or not Juan Fermín (or his cousin) intended his presence in Santiago to be permanent, it turned out that way. In July 1754 he extended powers of representation to Pedro Bernardo in Oaxaca, signaling his intention to remain in Central America.[61] Within the year, any further thoughts of relocating vanished. On March 15, 1755, Aycinena married Ana María Carrillo y Gálvez (1730–68). Ana María was the only child of extremely prominent Santiago natives (who happened to be first cousins). Irrespective of her other charms, she brought to the marriage a dowry exceeding 178,000 pesos.[62] And not only did Juan Fermín gain access to great wealth, he was now linked to the most powerful family network in the Kingdom of Guatemala, with all the social, political, and commercial benefits thus implied.

An obvious question is why Ana María's family would place such a valued "family asset" in the hands of an upstart merchant from Navarre. His Navarran roots undoubtedly helped.[63] More tangibly, Juan Fermín could boast of wealth exceeding 20,000 pesos (likely received from his cousin Pedro Bernardo),[64] several years experience in long-distance trade, and, most important, well-established family and business ties in Mexico and Spain.

The exalted status of Aycinena's family in Oaxaca and their connections in Mexico City, Cádiz, and Madrid were the strongest arguments in his favor. The Guatemalan merchant community would have been well aware of the prominence of the Yrigoyens and other Navarrans in Oaxaca. Antonio Salgado was probably Aycinena's first Santiago contact. Cayetano Pavón (who preceded Juan Fermín to the Kingdom of Guatemala by about a decade) had spent a considerable time in Oaxaca before moving on to Central America, and he maintained relations there well afterward.[65] An especially helpful Oaxacan/Guatemalan connection was the Larrazábal/Obregón family.

The peninsular Simón de Larrazábal y Barroeta (1686–1737) came to Central America under the sponsorship of the Navarran-born merchant/official Pedro Carrillo y Mencos in the 1720s. In 1725 Larrazábal married his sponsor's niece, Francisca Antonia Varón de Berrieza.[66] They established themselves in Oaxaca, and in 1728 Simón acquired the extremely lucrative alcabala concession for Antequera and Cuatro Villas for nine years (after a "bid" of 15,000 pesos).[67] Simón died in March 1737.[68] His widow then married the Madrid native Francisco de Obregón in September of that same year. Obregón held lucrative posts of his own: he was alcalde mayor of Mitla and treasurer of the Santa Cruzada (sale of indulgences) in Oaxaca. In these capacities, he established financial ties with Miguel de Yrigoyen y Echenique.[69] Obregón died in 1748, widowing Francisca for a second time.

By 1749 Francisca returned to her birthplace in Santiago de Guatemala.[70] From her twenty-five years among the elite of Antequera, she would have been intimately familiar with Juan Fermín's Oaxacan relatives. In Santiago she would have been an effective spokesperson on his behalf as he courted her niece, Ana María Carrillo y Gálvez. The exact nature of their relations is unknown, but on her death in 1759 Aycinena became the legal guardian of her minor children.[71] Regardless of these imponderables, one thing is beyond doubt: marriage vaulted Aycinena to the apex of Guatemalan society.

CONCLUSION

Juan Fermín de Aycinena benefited directly and indirectly from the family ties he enjoyed in Spain and Mexico. These ties helped smooth his path to New World success, providing him with immediate connections who supervised his training, gave him business experience, and furnished him with capital and letters of introduction. They, in turn, were able to do so because of the extraordinary power Navarrans enjoyed, for a time at least, at the Spanish court in the first half of the eighteenth century. In a sense, Aycinena's family connections extended to the highest levels of the Spanish state. Through his marriage to Ana María de Carrillo y Gálvez, the young Navarran also established no less important ties in his adopted city.

Chapter 3

Aycinena and the Santiago Elite

Central America's indigo boom in the second half of the eighteenth century attracted an ambitious group of Spanish immigrants to Santiago de Guatemala. Historians have argued that these peninsulars effected a commercial and, in a limited sense, even a social revolution in Central America, usurping the power of the colonial establishment. Unlike earlier immigrants, who were absorbed by the local power structure, the eighteenth-century cohort overwhelmed it.[1]

This picture of dramatic change in eighteenth-century Central America, although substantially accurate, overlooks significant continuities and exaggerates the extent to which the new migrants departed from established practice. Certainly the new arrivals helped to facilitate Central America's renewed entry into the international economy and as by-products of this, helped integrate the Kingdom of Guatemala and spread the hegemony of the capital—meaning, of course, their own commercial dominance of the provinces. The eighteenth-century emigrés were able to "usurp" the position of the creoles more rapidly and more thoroughly than previous generations because of the dramatic expansion of international commerce, which yielded greater wealth and allowed them greater resources to apply to the task.

Still, in many respects, what took place was the continuation of an old pattern: the incorporation of Spanish immigrants into the existing structure of power in the Kingdom of Guatemala. Although some powerful creole families may have suffered a decline in their fortunes, much of the old creole establishment persisted in altered form (or at least with altered surnames). The political and economic realities of Central America's colonial status and the demographic realities of a small group of Europeans amid a "sea of Indians" and various admixtures mitigated the potentially volatile jealousies between creoles and peninsulars.[2]

The ruling class of Santiago de Guatemala at the time Juan Fermín de Aycinena arrived there in the early 1750s exhibited "a confusing, tightly woven, and intertangled system of kinship ties."[3] Given the small size of Santiago's European population, this was perhaps inevitable. Even still, the extent of elite endogamy in late colonial Guatemala is astounding. The parents of Ana María Carrillo y Gálvez offer a perfect example.

A few months after Juan Fermín de Aycinena was baptized in Ciga, Navarre, Pedro Carrillo y Varón married his first cousin, Manuela de Gálvez y Varón, in

Santiago de Guatemala. The marriage took place on October 27, 1729. The intimate kinship of the newly betrothed apparently dictated a secret marriage.[4] The "just causes" for the secrecy were not spelled out, but presumably they had to do with the closeness of kinship. The laws of church and Crown forbade marriages within four degrees of kinship or between ritual kin.[5] Yet churchmen and colonial officials who were relatives of Pedro and Manuela attested to the marriage. Fathers Francisco Xavier de Paz and Francisco Navarro and then or future magistrates Francisco Zeage and Cristóbal de Gálvez gave their familial, official, and sacramental approval.

The marriage of Pedro Carrillo y Varón and Manuela Gálvez y Varón typified the practices that created and preserved the elite of eighteenth-century Santiago. The story of the families they united, representing perhaps the most dominant families among that elite, epitomizes the society that Aycinena joined and came to lead.

THE VARÓN DE BERRIEZA CONNECTION

Ana María Carrillo y Gálvez's grandmothers, Francisca Rosa Varón de Berrieza y López de Ramales and María Manuela Varón de Berrieza y López de Ramales, were sisters. They were daughters of Juana Antonia López de Ramales and José Varón de Berrieza.[6] José Varón de Berrieza (1632–96) came to Central America from Burgos eventually to become "perhaps the most powerful financial figure of his day."[7] He began his career as a soldier in the Indies fleet and arrived in Central America among the retinue of Captain General Carlos de Mencos (1659–67). In 1661 Varón de Berrieza became *justicia mayor* (principal justice) and *juez de milpas* (judge of plantings) of Soconusco. A year later he was named justicia mayor in Totonicapán, and his public career continued to blossom. In 1667 he became treasurer of the Real Hacienda as well as captain of the calvary in Sonsonate. In 1673 he was elected alcalde ordinario of Santiago. In 1677 he became chancellor and registrar of the Real Audiencia. In 1679 he became treasurer of the Santa Cruzada. Finally, in 1690 he was named alcalde mayor of Zapotitlán and Suchitepequez.

In short, Varón de Berrieza acquired a series of lucrative offices that provided the key to his and his descendants' dominance in the Kingdom of Guatemala. Probably the most important of these offices was treasurer of the Santa Cruzada, which he held from 1673 to 1689. The Santa Cruzada, which was responsible for selling indulgences to fund religious conquest, brought in enormous revenues and often shielded illicit trade from appropriate taxes.[8] Eventually charged with serious misdeeds, Varón de Berrieza defended himself primarily by implicating his fellow Guatemalan merchant/officials in similar activities. After a prolonged legal struggle, he was convicted of smuggling Peruvian wine and Guayaquil cacao into Guatemala. "A heavy fine was imposed on the culprit, which his widow paid out of his estate shortly after his death."[9]

Varón de Berrieza's conviction did not loosen his isthmian kin's grip on local power. In the 1698 mass sale of Santiago cabildo seats, no less than four prospective regidores were his sons-in-law; Bartolomé de Gálvez Corral, Tomás Cilieza y Velasco, Bernardo de Mencos, and Francisco Navarro. The Council of the Indies ultimately refused to approve the unusually low bids and the regidores departed their offices. Despite their displacement (at a time when the cabildo held limited attraction anyway), the episode signified the family clique's efforts to dominate local politics. The roster of regidores is mostly important as an index of Santiago's social and economic elite at the turn of the century and a commentary on their ambitions for power. As Stephen Webre explains, the power resided in the group itself, not the institution, which, in this case, it failed to control.[10]

THE CARRILLO FAMILY

In 1665 José Varón de Berrieza married Juana Antonia López de Ramales. She was the daughter of Pedro López de Ramales, another Burgos native who came to Guatemala with Captain General Carlos de Mencos. The descendants of Varón de Berrieza and Juana Antonia (and their spouses) became integral components of the eighteenth-century oligarchy of the Kingdom of Guatemala. Two of their daughters would be the grandmothers of Ana María Carrillo y Gálvez.[11]

María Manuela Varón de Berrieza's first marriage to Francisco Navarro ended with his death in 1700. She married the Navarran Pedro Carrillo y Mencos in 1705.[12] Carrillo y Mencos, a Knight of Santiago, was alcalde mayor of Escuintla and Guazacapán from 1693 to 1703.[13] In 1707 Carrillo identified himself as a vecino of San Vicente, in the heart of indigo country, where he likely collaborated with his powerful relatives in Santiago.[14] Later, the Navarran moved to Santiago and served as alcalde ordinario of the ayuntamiento in 1720 and its *síndico procurador* (city attorney, the cabildo's spokesman before the audiencia) in 1728. Perhaps his crowning moment came in 1728, when the Council of the Indies awarded him the alcabala concession for the entire Kingdom of Guatemala. Although the cabildo and merchants of Santiago objected to giving the concession to a single individual and prevailed on the Crown to grant it to the cabildo instead, the fact that Pedro Carrillo received the concession in the first place gives some idea of his influence with the Spanish court—after all, this was still "la hora Navarra."[15]

Carrillo combined officeholding with commercial pursuits. His estate inventory illustrates the workings of colonial business and the connection between politics and wealth. A merchant financier and wholesaler, he owned wholesale and mercantile stores in Santiago and at the time of his death had various quantities of indigo dispersed throughout his commercial network in Oaxaca, Puebla, Veracruz, Mexico City, and Cádiz. His associates included the Gaspar Saenz Rico firm of Veracruz, which obviously invested in more than cochineal and whose practices dated to the early decades of the eighteenth century.[16]

Don Pedro died on November 24, 1729, at nearly eighty years of age. His sole heir was his son, Pedro de Carrillo y Varón.[17] Pedro the younger would become the father of Ana María Carrillo y Gálvez a few months later. Following in his emigrant father's footsteps, Carrillo y Varón became alcalde ordinario of the Santiago cabildo in 1734 and again in 1737. Endowed with wealth, social status, political power, and commercial connections throughout Central America, Mexico, and Spain, Pedro's promising future ended abruptly with his death in 1743. His cousin and widow, Manuela de Gálvez y Varón, assumed management of their estate.[18]

THE GÁLVEZ CORRAL FAMILY

Manuela de Gálvez y Varón came from an equally privileged background. Her parents were Francisca Rosa Varón de Berrieza (1670–1756) and Bartolomé de Gálvez Corral (1659–1715). Gálvez Corral had immigrated from Málaga by the 1680s. Some time before 1686 he was the corregidor of Atitlán.[19] He was married in 1688 and returned to Spain briefly in 1689. He came back to Guatemala holding the *futuro* (future claim to royal office) on the alcalde mayor post of El Salvador, an office he assumed from 1699 to 1703.[20] In the meantime, he became treasurer of the Santa Cruzada, "one of the most lucrative offices in the land in terms of both its legitimate yield and its opportunities for graft."[21] Bartolomé had acquired the office from his brother-in-law, don Juan Antonio Varón de Berrieza. Before then, recall, it had been the property of Bartolomé's father-in-law, José Varón de Berrieza, with somewhat unfortunate consequences. Bartolomé had better luck: at the time of his death in 1715, his estate was worth more than 400,000 pesos.[22] Accumulated at a time when Central America was only beginning to emerge from nearly a century of commercial isolation and economic depression, this was an amazing fortune, the product of trade and politics.

The children of Bartolomé and Francisca Rosa made strategic matches that widened or strengthened family connections within Guatemala. Manuela, of course, married her first cousin, Pedro Carrillo y Varón, in 1729 and became Juan Fermín de Aycinena's mother-in-law in 1755.[23] The principal heirs to the power of Bartolomé de Gálvez Corral in Central America were his younger sons, Cristóbal Marcos de Gálvez Corral y

Varón and Manuel de Gálvez Corral y Varón.[24] They were perhaps the dominant figures in Santiago de Guatemala at the time Juan Fermín de Aycinena arrived there.

Cristóbal Marcos de Gálvez Corral was born around the turn of the century and lived until 1784. His longevity probably accounts, in part, for his assumption of family leadership. In a sense, he was both a predecessor and a contemporary of Juan Fermín de Aycinena. In 1733 Cristóbal married Luisa Gonzaga Cilieza Velasco y Varón (1704–71). Naturally, Luisa was his first cousin, the daughter of María Varón de Berrieza y López de Ramales and Tomás de Cilieza y Velasco. Yet another son-in-law of José Varón de Berrieza, Tomás had taken part in the short-lived Santiago cabildo of 1698 and had since become a prominent landholder and indigo producer in El Salvador.[25]

Like his father (and grandfather), Cristóbal de Gálvez Corral held a variety of colonial offices. He seems to have been much more active than his father in municipal office holding. This was due in part to the resurgence of the cabildo's prestige with its recovery of alcabala collections in 1729. Although he never became a permanent seat holder (leaving that to his younger brother, Manuel, in 1742), Cristóbal did serve as alcalde ordinario of Santiago in 1732 and again in 1763.[26] More important, perhaps, he exercised a number of the cabildo's fiscal charges. From at least 1751 until 1757 he was accountant of the *renta de alcabalas* (sales tax revenue), supervising, in effect, the cabildo's collection of the important tax. This position was in practical terms similar to the one denied Cristóbal's uncle, Pedro Carrillo, in 1728. In 1761 Gálvez Corral was accountant of tithes of the Cathedral of Guatemala.[27] Over his long life, he controlled some of the most lucrative sources of government revenues, secular and religious, in the Kingdom of Guatemala.

Cristóbal de Gálvez Corral enjoyed great control over offices in the indigo-producing regions of El Salvador. For much of the eighteenth century, Gálvez and his family either directly occupied the post of alcalde mayor of El Salvador or exercised extraordinary control over the position through the financial obligations (*fianzas*) of officeholders to his family. Gálvez Corral practically owned the Salvadoran alcaldía mayor in the 1730s and again in the 1760s.[28] He held the Salvadoran post personally from 1734 to 1737, before giving way to his younger brother, Manuel, who wielded it from 1737 until 1741.

Two decades later, in the wake of the legal proceedings against controversial Alcalde Mayor Bernabé de la Torre Trassierra (1757, 1771–73), proceedings instigated in part by Gálvez Corral relatives, the family reasserted its dominance over the position. Cristóbal gained control of the office for a period of ten years beginning in 1761. Delegating it initially to relatives, he occupied the post himself in 1765, before giving way to his son-in-law a year later. He acquired the Salvadoran concession in part as compensation for the loss of the lucrative post of *contador real* (royal accountant) of the Santa Cruzada in 1751, which had been temporarily suspended.[29] Gálvez Corral eventually turned over the post of alcalde mayor to his son-in-law, Manuel Fadrique y Goyena, in 1766, financing his kinsman's office holding to the tune of 40,000 pesos.[30] And even though the deposed Bernabé de la Torre was eventually reinstated in 1771, kinsmen of Gálvez Corral, including Fadrique y Goyena, regained control over the position soon thereafter.[31] Cristóbal de Gálvez Corral was probably the most powerful man in Central America at the time Juan Fermín de Aycinena arrived in the isthmus.

Cristóbal's younger brother, Manuel de Gálvez Corral y Varón (1715–63), shared in his power and status. Manuel became a general in the Spanish army. Following Cristóbal, he served as alcalde mayor of San Salvador from 1737 to 1741. In 1742 Manuel purchased a permanent seat on the cabildo of Santiago. He was elected alcalde ordinario of Santiago in 1753 and 1757. In the meantime, Manuel also served as corregidor of Quezaltenango beginning in 1745.[32]

Manuel converted his family connections and his control of municipal and provincial offices into an incredible landed patrimony. Between 1750 and 1755 he acquired a series of estates in Escuintla that he consolidated into a hacienda exceeding 314 *caballerías* (roughly 13,188 hectares). He acquired yet another Escuintla hacienda, San Nicolás de la Majada, in 1758. Earlier, in 1753, he had purchased a cattle hacienda named La Culebra near the Mixco valley. And in El Salvador, he owned an indigo hacienda, San José de la Bermuda.[33]

In 1755 don Manuel married Josefa Nicolasa de Gálvez y Cilieza. The marriage was yet another example of the endogamy typical of the eighteenth-century Santiago elite. Several years younger than her spouse, Josefa Nicolasa was not only the daughter of Manuel's brother, Cristóbal, but also the child of Manuel's first cousin, Luisa Cilieza. The marriage took place on March 6, little more than a week before that of Juan Fermín de Aycinena and Ana María Carrillo y

Gálvez, another of Manuel's nieces (a sacrament for which Manuel served as a witness).[34] After her uncle/cousin/husband's death in 1763, Josefa married her impecunious first cousin, Nicolás de Obregón y Gálvez, in 1769 (formerly the ward of Juan Fermín de Aycinena).[35] The unfortunate Josefa Nicolasa, childless and dependent on her father, thus provided a marital link not only between her father and her uncle but also, through her second marriage to her first cousin, Nicolás Obregón, to her father's sister, Francisca Antonia Gálvez y Varón, and to the Larrazábal/Obregón family formerly of Oaxaca. In effect, her marriages brought full circle the Gálvez Corral family network.

In brief, the children and grandchildren of Bartolomé de Gálvez Corral controlled a variety of strategic offices, engaged in lucrative commercial pursuits, acquired abundant landholdings, and made a number of propitious marriages, all of which helped to ensure their exalted place in the Kingdom of Guatemala. At the time Juan Fermín de Aycinena made his appearance in Santiago, the Gálvez Corrals and associated families dominated Central American government, society, landholding, and commerce. Once he joined them, their dominance afforded the young Navarran powerful allies in his struggle for wealth, status, and power in late colonial Central America.

JUAN FERMÍN'S SUBSEQUENT MARRIAGES

Ana María Carrillo y Gálvez died in June 1768, at the age of thirty-seven. In subsequent years, Juan Fermín de Aycinena would marry twice more. Each marriage extended his family network and helped further consolidate his social position. All this prompted Miles

Wortman to write of the "fortuitous deaths" of Juan Fermín's first two wives.[36] Even apart from its callous phrasing, however, Wortman's assertion is wrong; Aycinena would certainly have remained at the summit of Central American society by virtue of his "fortuitous" first marriage and his commercial success. This is not, however, to deny Wortman's central point: Aycinena helped himself immensely through his wise choice of marriage partners.

On May 6, 1771, Juan Fermín married María Micaela Josefa Brigada de Nájera y Mencos (1747–77). The marriage cemented Aycinena's ties with another powerful landholding and office-wielding creole family. María was one of nineteen children of José Delgado de Nájera and María Felipa Mencos Varón. A scion of one of Central America's oldest families, José Delgado de Nájera had been a fixture on the Santiago cabildo at least since 1742. His son Ventura José Nájera y Mencos (1733–1808) became a prosperous indigo merchant and municipal officeholder. With the transfer of the Central American capital in the 1770s, Ventura joined his brother-in-law Juan Fermín de Aycinena in a venture to build a municipal slaughterhouse. Ventura's brother, Francisco Xavier José de Nájera y Mencos (1741–1811), was a treasury official in Santiago as of 1777.[37]

Widowed again in 1777, Juan Fermín de Aycinena married a third and final time in July 1781.[38] His last wife was Micaela Piñol y Muñoz (1761–1820). This marriage reflected a slightly different "family strategy" than his first two: although it somewhat deepened his ties to old Santiago, perhaps more significant, it widened his connections to encompass the family network of a fellow peninsular merchant. Micaela Piñol y Muñoz was some three decades younger than her husband and the daughter of José Piñol y Sala and his creole wife, Teresa Muñoz y Barba. José Piñol, like Juan Fermín, was an extraordinary emigrant success story. The Barcelona native had established a commercial firm with two brothers in Cádiz around 1720. He arrived in Guatemala in 1752, not too long before his future son-in-law. He came to Central America as the factor of the Spanish slave trade monopoly (Real Asiento de Negros). He also became a major indigo exporter: in 1760, a vessel belonging to his family's company carried over 200,000 pesos worth of indigo, roughly one-third of Central American exports for the year.[39]

The merging of these two merchant families created an exceptionally powerful alliance. The alliance was strengthened by subsequent marriages as well. In 1788 Vicente Aycinena y Carrillo (1766–1814), Juan Fermín's oldest son, married Juana Nepomucena María Piñol, another daughter of José Piñol (in the process, father and son became brothers-in-law). In 1791 María Bernarda Aycinena y Nájera, Juan Fermín's daughter from his second marriage, married Tadeo Piñol y Muñoz, the son of José Piñol (making father and daughter sister- and brother-in-law). These marriages inextricably linked the fortunes of the Aycinena and Piñol families and helped to create the basis of Guatemala's postindependence elite. Other marriages of his children played a role in consolidating Aycinena's family and commercial networks (see table 4).

The 1796 marriage of María Micaela Aycinena y Nájera to Manuel José Pavón y Muñoz, son of Cayetano Pavón, a wealthy merchant from Extremadura, created another formidable commercial link. And the 1794 marriage of Juan Fermín's daughter María Josefa

TABLE 4
The Children of Juan Fermín de Aycinena

First Marriage: Ana María Carrillo y Gálvez (1730–68)
  Vicente Anastasio (1766–1814)
  m. 1788, Juana N. María Piñol y Muñoz (1763–1832)
  José Alejandro (1767–1826)
  m. 1799, Mariana J. Micheo y Nájera Mencos (b. 1782)
  Maria Francisca (died at birth, 1768)

Second Marriage: María Micaela Josefa Brigada de Nájera y Mencos (1747–77)
  Juan de Aycinena y Nájera (b., d. 1772)
  María Josefa (b., d. 1773)
  María Bernarda (1774–1835)
  m. 1791, Tadeo Piñol y Muñoz (d. 1810)
  María Clara (b., d. 1775)
  María Josefa Sebastiana (1776–98)
  m. 1794, Juan Bautista Marticorena (d. 1824)
  María Micaela (b. 1777)
  m. 1796, Manuel José Pavón y Muñoz (b. 1765)

Third Marriage: Micaela Piñol y Muñoz (1761–1820)
  María Teresa de la Santisima Trinidad (1784–1841)
  Miguel (178?–1832)
  Juan Fermín (1788–1822)
  m. 1819, Antonia María Piñol y Aycinena
  Mariano (1789–1854)
  m. 1824, Luz Batres
  Ignacio (1790–1816)
  María Ignacia (b., d. 179?)
  José María (1792–1816)

Sources: AGCA, A1 3.10, Leg. 1907; Enrique del Cid F., *Origen histórico de la Casa y Marquesado de Ayzinena* (Guatemala City: published privately, 1969); Ramiro Ordóñez Jonomá, "La Familia Varón de Berrieza," *Revista de la Academia Guatemalteca de Estudios Genealógicos, Heráldicos e Históricos* 9 (1987): 523–826.

Sebastiana Aycinena Nájera to yet another incredibly successful Navarran merchant in Guatemala, Juan Bautista Marticorena, brought new talent into the family and renewed ties to the Peninsula.

THE PENINSULA REVISITED

D. A. Brading detected the curious practice by which peninsular immigrants in colonial Mexico sponsored the subsequent emigration of Spanish nephews who joined them as business associates and, surprisingly often, as sons-in-law.[40] Juan Fermín de Aycinena faithfully partook of at least part of this tradition. Pedro de Aycinena Larraín and Pedro de Beltranena Aycinena left Navarre to join their uncle in Guatemala, providing trusted associates in his isthmian enterprises, helping to preserve or extend his peninsular connections, and widening his kinship ties and connections in Central America.

Like Juan Fermín de Aycinena, Pedro de Aycinena y Larraín came from Ciga, Navarre. Born in 1741, he was the son of Juan Fermín's elder brother, Juan de Aycinena. He became an extremely prominent figure in late colonial Guatemala, owing much, no doubt, to his uncle's influence. For much of his time in Guatemala, Pedro de Aycinena y Larraín and his cousin Pedro de Beltranena Aycinena served as their uncle's principal *cajeros* (business subordinates).[41] He would hold a number of important municipal offices (some of which he inherited from his uncle). And his marriage to Francisca Barrutia y Echeverría helped to reinforce Aycinena connections with another important Santiago merchant, Francisco Ignacio Barrutia.

Pedro José de Beltranena e Aycinena (d. 1821) came from Irurita, Navarre, the son of Martín de Beltranena and Ana María de Aycinena, Juan Fermín's sister.[42] He arrived in Guatemala sometime in the 1760s.[43] In 1778 Pedro married María Josefa Ana Filomena de Llano y Nájera (1753–1805), the daughter of the peninsular Manuel Eugenio de Llano and Josefa Francisca Xaviera Nájera y Mencos (the sister of Juan Fermín's second wife).[44] Thus, like their uncle, both Navarrans married into the local elite, widening or reinforcing the crucial web of influential isthmian connections. They became integral to the family enterprise.

CONCLUSION

Juan Fermín de Aycinena inserted himself into the Santiago elite through marriage. These ties were amplified with the marriages of his children and nephews. At the same time, the marriages helped to refurbish the Guatemalan ruling class by reestablishing ties with the metropolis. After all, Central America remained a Spanish colony, and continual reinforcement of ties to the Spanish court (to obtain desired offices) and to Spanish capital and long-distance trading networks (to infuse wealth) was required for the elite to maintain their dominance. Although the eighteenth-century immigrants to Central America achieved special prominence, this was not anything very new: the family network Aycinena joined reached back to at least the 1660s, well before the indigo boom drew peninsulars to the isthmus. The network had been fashioned through the absorption by marriage of immigrants into creole families, through privileged access to strategic offices, and through participation in long-distance trade. The practices, we might add, were not always licit. Perhaps the most striking thing that emerges from an exploration of Juan Fermín de Aycinena's enterprise of the family in Central America is the continuity of power, prestige, and wealth that runs in a straight line from José Varón de Berrieza, Pedro Carrillo y Mencos, Bartolomé de Gálvez Corral, and Cristóbal and Manuel de Gálvez Corral y Varón to Juan Fermín de Aycinena. What took place was the "renovation" of the creole oligarchy.[45] Aycinena was not an exception to the age-old pattern but a brilliantly successful participant in it. He was aided immensely, no doubt, by the fact that he made these crucial family ties at a time of unprecedented economic growth that led, for merchants involved in overseas trade, to a period of unique prosperity.

Chapter 4

Colonial Entrepreneur

Juan Fermín de Aycinena flourished at the crossroads of colonial commerce. He advanced goods and cash to isthmian producers (silver miners and indigo planters) in exchange for export commodities, which he would then distribute through his imperial commercial network. But this was typical of colonial merchants.[1] It was not so much the kinds of activities Aycinena engaged in that set him apart from his merchant colleagues as their scale. The amount of capital he was able to employ, the extent of his trading network, and the degree to which he diversified and vertically integrated his enterprises separated Aycinena from his contemporary merchants.

Aycinena's multiple roles in the isthmian economy—banker, wholesaler of European and Asian

TABLE 5
The Wealth of Juan Fermín de Aycinena, 1768–1777 (in pesos)

	1768	1771	1777
Mercantile goods	207,714	125,457	148,009
Household	72,997	74,802	63,803
Dependencies	812,635	1,049,458	1,337,359
Active	589,830	758,288	1,014,997
Doubtful	127,450	87,662	65,076
Lost	95,355	202,508	257,186
Total assets	1,093,346	1,249,717	1,549,171
Debts	161,515	215,056	281,160
Total wealth (minus debts)	931,831	1,034,661	1,268,011
Wealth (adjusted for lost dependencies)	836,476	1,012,153	1,010,825
Wealth (adjusted for lost, doubtful dependencies)	**709,026**	**924,488**	**945,749**

Sources: Aycinena Family Papers, Estate Inventories of 1768, 1771, and 1777.

goods, indigo exporter, and, ultimately, shipowner, mine owner, and indigo planter—rendered him uniquely successful. Tables 5 and 6 document that success.

CAPITAL FORMATION

Aycinena's marriage to Ana María Carrillo y Gálvez launched him toward his great wealth. He "received as a dowry, 178,912 pesos and 4 reales, comprised of money, mercantile goods, jewelry, gold and silver furnishings, and dependencies (credit accounts)." For his part, Aycinena brought to the marriage some 21,000 pesos.[2]

TABLE 6
The Aycinena Estate, 1796

Assets	
Goods, haciendas, houses	1,186,313
Capital and interest	17,442
Dependencies	1,500,696
Active and current	705,020
Doubtful	213,384
Lost	582,292
Accounts due ("Por pagar")	17,864
Total assets	2,722,315
Liabilities	
Censo (long-term loans) and *usura* (interest)	207,269
Dependencies	312,134
Depósitos (short-term loans)	8,882
Total liabilities	526,286
Total wealth (assets minus liabilities)	2,196,029
Wealth (adjusted for lost dependencies)	1,613,737
Wealth (adjusted for lost and doubtful dependencies)	1,400,353

Source: Aycinena Family Papers, "Resumé del Caudal de Juan Fermín de Aycinena, 1796."

Law and practice gave Juan Fermín control over the dowry, which remained technically the property of Ana María and the future inheritance of her legitimate descendants (or else her natal family).³ Susan Socolow, in her masterful examination of merchant career patterns in late colonial Buenos Aires, suggests "that it was not goods which were prized" in such dowries, "but rather social and business connections which the bride brought to the marriage."⁴ Certainly marriage into Guatemalan society provided Aycinena with immediate business connections. In his case, however, the material benefits of the dowry were obvious. Aycinena inherited, in effect, the venerable family enterprise launched by Pedro Carrillo y Mencos earlier in the century. From the beginning, he could tap into and continue business relationships previously established by the Carrillos. Together with the relationships developed by his own family members in Spain and America, these provided invaluable assets to the young merchant.⁵

WHOLESALE TRADING

Aycinena asserted his commercial presence in Central America through his role as a wholesale trader. A substantial portion of the wealth counted in each inventory of the Aycinena estate consisted of trade goods (*generos de mercancia*). In 1768, 207,714 pesos (nearly 25 percent of his total adjusted wealth) were tied up in merchandise. In 1771, the amount was 125,457 pesos (12 percent). And in 1777, goods accounted for 148,009 pesos (14.6 percent). The percentage made up by goods is significantly lower in the later years. Perhaps this reflects a slightly different pattern of investments, the tying up of the Casa's resources in other kinds of endeavors (mining or indigo), or the acquisition of real property. But we should keep in mind the fluid nature of business. The contents of Aycinena's wholesale store were constantly in flux and varied, perhaps greatly, from year to year and even seasonally, ebbing and flowing with the cycles of commerce. The inventories are helpful snapshots of a colonial enterprise at specific moments, giving a sense of the scale of the enterprise and the kinds of goods imported. They provide less of a sense of motion. There is little doubt, however, that Aycinena was the dominant importer in late colonial Guatemala. An inventory of alcabalas paid on European imports by Guatemalan merchants from 1783 to 1790, for example, reveals that Aycinena accounted for some 22.5 percent of the taxes paid by all importers (47,761 pesos out of a total of 212,205).[6]

The trade goods counted in the 1768 inventory provide a sense of the kinds of products Juan Fermín imported for distribution throughout his isthmian network. The Aycinena store stocked luxury items, essentials, and articles of everyday use. It supplied thread, buttons, twine, ribbons, braids, tapestries, and chintz. Sombreros of all qualities, other types of hats, shoes, petticoats, reams of paper, cinnamon, floor cloth, bedspreads, *huipiles* (Indian women's blouses), stirrups, blankets, garnets, and rosary beads also filled his shelves. The great majority of his goods, however, were textiles: Italian velvets, taffeta from France and Spain, fine linen from Brittany, English flannel, Chinese silks, damasks from China and Valencia, Belgian lace, English serge, cottons from Rouen, India, and China, and cheesecloth.[7]

FINANCE

Aycinena used his access to capital and goods to insert himself into the heart of isthmian production. He expanded his role and asserted his dominance over crucial sectors of the Central American economy through advances of goods and cash in credit arrangements. In a region chronically short of specie, credit was crucial to the conduct of business. As early as November 1755, Aycinena assumed the role of financier.[8] Apart from the sheer volume of the wealth represented in the estate inventories cited earlier, their most striking aspect is the proportion of Aycinena's wealth represented as dependencies, or outstanding debts due him. This, of course, was not unusual for colonial merchants.[9]

One way to gauge the importance of commercial advances for Aycinena is to look at active dependencies in relation to his total wealth (adjusted for lost and doubtful dependencies) (see table 5). In 1768 Aycinena had 589,830 pesos recorded in active dependencies. His adjusted wealth was 709,026 pesos. Thus active dependencies made up about 83 percent of his adjusted wealth. In 1771 he had 758,288 pesos distributed throughout his commercial network in active dependencies. His total wealth adjusted for both lost and doubtful dependencies was 924,488 pesos. Thus active accounts represented 82 percent of his wealth adjusted for lost and doubtful dependencies. In 1777 the picture is even more striking. Aycinena had some 1,014,997 pesos invested in the colonial economy by way of active and current dependencies. Yet his wealth (adjusted for lost and doubtful dependencies) amounted to only 945,749 pesos. In effect, 107 percent of his adjusted wealth was tied up in active dependencies.[10] These numbers reveal an extremely aggressive and perhaps by 1777 an overextended colonial merchant.

The percentage of active debts in relation to the total debt gives us some idea of the soundness of Aycinena's investments. That percentage is as follows: 72.58 percent for 1768, 72.25 percent for 1771, 75.89 percent for 1777, and 46.98 percent for 1796. In turn, the percentage of debts lost, or written off, is as follows: 11.7 percent in 1768, 19.3 percent in 1771, 19.2 percent in 1777, and 38.8 percent in 1796. The accretion is obvious. Such an accretion was perhaps inevitable over the long haul, because debts once written off remained a permanent part of the portfolio. It is unclear if debts considered lost (by 1796) reflected any compensation gained through foreclosure or other legal proceedings. The shift of "doubtful" debts into the "lost" category is also a clearly discernible pattern. However, this shift was probably offset by the exchange of debts for real property.

Our most complete view of Juan Fermín's investment portfolio comes from the inventory of 1777, which provides a tabular summary of all active dependencies. Of the 191 active accounts recorded in 1777, all but a handful were individual accounts. These ranged in size from the two and a half pesos of Matías de Landaburu of Cádiz to the more than 39,000 pesos owed by Juan de Taranco of San Vicente. These are cumulative totals and may or may not reflect long-term relationships. Ironically, Matías de Landaburu was probably one of Juan Fermín's most consistent peninsular contacts. The larger accounts likely involved longer-term relationships. In most cases, the larger debtors were indigo planters. Table 7 presents the relative size of the accounts.

Aycinena lent to virtually all comers: high churchmen, humble priests and nuns, convents and monasteries, colonial officials such as audiencia judges and

TABLE 7
Relative Size of Active Dependencies, 1777

Amount (in pesos)	Number	Percentage
0–99	30	15.7
100–499	41	21.5
500–999	17	8.9
1000–4999	59	30.9
5000–9999	21	11.0
10000+	23	12.0
	191	100.0

Source: Aycinena Family Papers, Inventory of 1777.

alcaldes mayores (and possibly captains general), as well as merchants and planters, artisans, bird tenders, and even one gentleman styled as "el pobre" (the poor one). Anyone who could conceivably repay the money or credit advanced was apparently seriously considered. His guidelines for determining who deserved credit and who did not are unknown (records of those denied credit are not available). Nevertheless, anyone commercially active in colonial Central America was likely to borrow, at one time or another, from Juan Fermín de Aycinena. As the estate inventories make clear, he was eager to lend.

Indigo

At least as early as the 1770s, Aycinena's principal field of investment was indigo. Not only for Aycinena but also for eighteenth-century Central America in general prosperity seeped from the indigo plant. In the eighteenth century the isthmus was known as the producer of the world's finest indigo, a dye much in demand in the expanding textile industry of northern Europe.[11] Floyd estimates that Central America exported some 24 million pounds of indigo between 1772 and 1800.[12] According to Wortman, the greatest profits came in the 1780s, when the finer grades of indigo predominated.[13] Table 8 presents Wortman's figures.

The indigo trade tended to fall into the hands of those who possessed the commercial contacts to dispose of the dyestuff—a phalanx of Guatemala City merchants with Cádiz connections, cemented by family ties. Floyd identifies 138 merchants who participated in the indigo trade from 1778 to 1785, of whom 20 were major exporters. These twenty merchants accounted for more than 60 percent of exports in those years, nearly 2.5 million of the total 4.05 million pounds. Juan Fermín de Aycinena clearly dominated this group: from 1778 to 1785, he exported some 666,737.5 pounds of Central American indigo, or about 16 percent of total

TABLE 8
**Central American Indigo Exports, 1772–1804
(annual average, in pounds)**

1772–76	561,000
1777–81	834,000
1782–86	884,000
1787–91	1,016,000
1792–96	1,035,000
1797–1801	1,006,000
1802–1804	637,227

Source: Miles Wortman, *Government and Society in Colonial Central America, 1680–1840* (New York: Columbia University Press, 1982).

exports. His nephew Pedro de Beltranena exported another 143,637.5 pounds. Together, Aycinena and Beltranena sent abroad 810,375 pounds between 1778 and 1785. They alone accounted for more than 20 percent of Central American indigo exports in those years.[14]

Despite the potential profits, producing indigo was a risky undertaking. Favorable weather and freedom from insects were essential to a planter's success. The indigo planter depended on the state to provide him with an adequate labor supply.[15] He relied on merchant financing to fund his production. He paid wages to workers who cleared and planted his land and who harvested and manufactured his indigo. He also had to provide for support personnel. Vats for steeping and beating and other equipment had to be maintained or replaced. Sorting the indigo into grades and wrapping it in *zurrones* (cowhide cases) for transport was also time-consuming and costly. Larger planters acquired mules (which had to be fed and periodically replaced) whose drivers also had to be paid.[16]

Once it had been harvested, congealed, sorted, and wrapped, indigo was transported by mule to the capital, usually in January and February. The arduous trip took about six weeks from San Miguel and about a month from San Salvador. From there the dye traveled to the Golfo Dulce. The mule trains had to reach the Caribbean by May to escape the wet season on land and to reach ships that had to depart the Caribbean by June, before the onset of hurricane season.[17]

The exchange of indigo took place at annual trade fairs, the most important of which was that of Santiago and later Guatemala City. The capital city fair was held in February. A variety of provincial fairs, frequented by small-scale producers, took place in the months immediately preceding the fair in the capital. The fairs at Chalatenango (November 1) and San Miguel (November 22) and even the major provincial fair at Apastepeque (November 1) were considered to be "poor man's fairs." At the indigo fairs, wholesale merchants and planters bargained over grades and prices of indigo and planters selected trade goods from the merchant stores and arranged for cash advances for the year to come. Commonly, the planter pledged his future crop as payment for the money and goods advanced. The customary agreement was that the merchant would receive the mortgaged indigo at one real or one-half real per pound less than the "fair price," which would be set by the pricing assembly (made up equally of delegates representing planters and merchants). The real or half real was the merchant's interest on his annual loan. For any part of the planter's debt left unpaid after one year, the merchant charged 5 percent interest. Prices at the Guatemala City fair had to be one real per pound higher than the provincial fairs to account for transport costs. Still, merchants refused to be bound by the Apastepeque prices. Once the fair price was set, the wholesaler adjusted the planter's debt accordingly. The merchant then supplied the planter with goods and money for another year.[18]

The merchants of Guatemala were not content to rely solely on the market or their financial leverage over planters to determine their fate; they also established strategic ties with Salvadoran officials. The alcalde mayor or corregidor controlled labor, dispensed credit, collected tribute, distributed goods, and compelled reluctant consumers to participate in the colonial economy through forced trade (the repartimiento de efectos). The official ties Aycinena established in the region will be dealt with more thoroughly in a subsequent chapter. Here, I focus on his ties to planters.

Aycinena maintained dozens of long-term relationships with Salvadoran planters. Pedro de Souza is one example. In 1760 Souza was a merchant working the provinces of San Salvador and León. As of October 1760 he owed Aycinena 1,061 pesos from the previous year. In October he contracted a new debt, 2,714 pesos in cash and goods worth 2,734 pesos, bringing his total debt to 6,508 pesos.[19] A decade later, in March 1770, Souza had established himself as a vecino and indigo planter in San Vicente. His social mobility was likely a product of his commercial relations with Aycinena. As of 1770 Souza owed Juan Fermín more than 15,318 pesos; 7,586 pesos of this amount had been carried over from previous advances, while the new advances came to 6,240 pesos in cash and 1,491 pesos worth of trade goods. He obtained the advance to develop indigo production on his haciendas near Santiago Nanualco, San José el Obrajuelo, and San Pedro Martir. Souza pledged to pay off the debt by January 1771, in indigo: 13,826 pesos worth at one-half real more than the Apastepeque prices (to cover the old debt and the cash advance); and 1,491 pesos worth of indigo at the Santiago prices (to cover the advance of trade goods). To secure the loans, Souza obligated his "person and haciendas."[20] As of 1777 the Salvadoran owed Aycinena more than 30,000 pesos, making his estates dangerously liable to forfeiture.

Aycinena maintained another long-term relationship with José Rodríguez. On February 4, 1767 (presumably during the indigo fair), Rodríguez had received cash and goods from Aycinena worth 8,475 pesos. He was to pay that debt in indigo at the 1768 fair. But as of February 29, 1768, his *apoderado* (agent), don Francisco de Cañas, had paid only 670 pesos; Rodríguez still owed 7,815 pesos. At this point Rodríguez refinanced his loan with Aycinena. He committed to pay Aycinena the 7,815 pesos plus 391 pesos in common interest, bringing his total to 8,206 pesos. He agreed to pay the debt by the time of the 1769 fair.[21]

Whether he did so is unknown. On March 22, 1769, shortly after the Santiago fair, Rodríguez pursued a different kind of transaction. He arranged to acquire an indigo hacienda named La Joya near San Vicente. The plantation belonged to the estate of Antonio Pereyra. Along with the property, Rodríguez assumed Pereyra's debt of 17,000 pesos to Juan Fermín de Aycinena. In addition, he contracted a new loan for 5,000 pesos, in money and goods. Aycinena also assumed Rodríguez's debt of 4,000 pesos to Gertrudis Pereyra. An additional debt of 3,000 pesos came with the estate in church obligations (censo). In all, in acquiring the hacienda, Rodríguez assumed a debt for 29,000 pesos, 26,000 of which was owed to Aycinena. In return, he agreed to pay off the debt to Aycinena in indigo within three years. If the debt was not completely met after three years, Rodríguez agreed to pay Aycinena 5 percent interest annually on the debt that remained. As collateral, Rodríguez pledged the hacienda La Joya as well as another estate, San Francisco Barillas.[22] As of 1777, however, Rodríguez's obligation to Aycinena had mounted to a total of 29,337 pesos. Not long thereafter, he forfeited La Joya to the Guatemala City merchant.

Souza and Rodríguez were just two of Aycinena's long-term Salvadoran associates. These two particular associations evolved very similarly. Both moved from retailing to planting, largely with the support of Aycinena. Both debtors enlarged their substantial debts rather than retire them. In Rodríguez's case for certain and probably in Souza's case as well, Aycinena acquired the estates pledged as collateral. While their stories may have been atypical, the fates of Souza and Rodríguez indicate the difficulty some planters had in remaining solvent and their vulnerability to the merchants of the capital.[23]

Mining

Although ultimately not on the scale of his involvement with indigo, Aycinena also participated actively in the colonial mining economy, at least early on. He did so for perhaps obvious reasons. The mining regions provided a market for his imports, allowed him to diversify his mercantile enterprise, and provided valuable specie that permitted him to purchase in volume.[24] Although Honduran silver had experienced an impressive recovery in the first half of the eighteenth century, expansion stagnated in the second half of the century. Floyd estimates that total annual production stalled at about half a million pesos.[25]

Numerous structural problems frustrated Bourbon attempts to reform the mining industry: labor shortages, supply scarcities, insufficient capital, outmoded technology, and official corruption. Floyd points out that the lack of governmental support for the Honduran mining industry might have been offset if private capital were available. But indigo was simply more lucrative, less risky, and therefore a more attractive investment, and it diverted much of the needed capital. In general, merchants refused to make long-term investments in mining.[26]

Juan Fermín de Aycinena diverged at least partly from this pattern. As late as the mid-1760s, Aycinena invested substantially in Honduran mining. In 1765 the supervisor of the Casa de Moneda in Santiago reported that Aycinena had deposited a "certain amount" of gold from Tegucigalpa.[27] In April 1766 Luis Francisco de Oliver of Tegucigalpa acknowledged that Aycinena had supplied him with 5,090 pesos in trade goods. Oliver may have been a miner or a retail merchant working the mining regions. At any rate, he promised to make good the debt within one year in minted silver (*plata acuñada, moneda corriente*) delivered to the capital.[28] As in El Salvador, Aycinena maintained substantial financial relations with Honduran officials.

Such precautions could not protect him from the general hazards of investing in Honduran mining. Aycinena's experience with the Landa brothers of Tegucigalpa made this clear. Juan Lucas de Landa and his brother Miguel owned the Mina del Nuevo Bastán in Yuscarán. The name of their mine site hints perhaps that they were countrymen of Juan Fermín. On March 17, 1766, Juan Lucas de Landa delegated power of attorney to Aycinena, who was to provide him with the necessary supplies of mercury.[29] The following year, on January 26, 1767, the partnership was sealed in spectacular fashion. The Landa brothers contracted a debt with Capt. Juan Fermín de Aycinena of 84,719 pesos and 3 1/2 reales. Miguel Landa stated that the loan was to enable them to develop their mine holdings. They pledged to pay the debt in silver (*barras de plata*) within two years.[30] They were unable to do so. As early as 1768, Aycinena estate records show their debt of more than 80,000 pesos as doubtful. By 1771 the debt, now exceeding 90,000 pesos, had moved into the lost column. Aycinena absorbed their mine holdings. He had moved, almost by no choice of his own, from financier (*aviador*) to mine owner.[31] Although he dabbled in subsequent mining ventures, an ironworks in Chiquimula, for example, Aycinena's early experience with mining seems to have discouraged him from making subsequent major investments in the sector.[32] Indigo simply paid off much more handsomely, and absorbed the bulk of his investments.

Investment Preferences

To gain a clearer picture of Aycinena's investment preferences, it is helpful to look again at the 1777 inventory, which provides a complete list of active dependencies but does not include lost and doubtful dependencies and thus excludes the enormous Landa debt (see tables 9 and 10). Predictably, the majority of Juan Fermín's "investments" recorded in 1777 were to be found in the indigo-producing regions of El Salvador. More than 40 percent of his loans considered to be still active and collectible were located in El Salvador. If we add the more than 213,000 pesos represented by *tintas* (dyes) en route to or consigned in Mexico or Peru, the percentage of wealth invested in indigo climbs to over 60 percent. Most of the more than 50,000 pesos owed by Mexican merchants presumably had to do with indigo as well, and inflates the importance of the dye even more.

TABLE 9
Geographic Distribution of Active Commercial Debts Owed to Juan Fermín de Aycinena, 1777
(rounded to the nearest peso)

Place	Number	Amount	Percent of Total Amount
El Salvador	57	416,706	41.0
Nicaragua	17	17,119	1.6
Honduras	14	12,609	1.2
Guatemala	69	121,968	12.0
Costa Rica	5	8,482	0.8
Mexico	8	57,641	5.6
Peru	3	6,705	0.6
Spain	1	128	—
Indigo	1	213,411	21.0
Chests	1	110,108	10.8
Undetermined	15	50,121	4.9
Totals	191	1,014,998	99.5

Source: Aycinena Family Papers, Inventory of 1777.

TABLE 10
Active Dependencies by Locality

Place	Number	Amount (pesos)	Percent of Total
EL SALVADOR			
San Vicente	24	201,741	19.87
San Miguel	15	145,657	14.35
San Salvador	6	3,492	
Alotepeque	1	656	
Apastepeque	2	14,453	1.40
Santiago Nanualco	1	36,151	3.56

TABLE 10 (continued)
Active Dependencies by Locality

Place	Number	Amount (pesos)	Percent of Total
Zacatecoluca	1	3,847	
Santa Ana	1	350	
Chalatenango	1	671	
Sonsonate	3	6,505	
Tejutla	2	3,183	
NICARAGUA			
León	9	12,839	1.20
Granada	4	1,609	
Segovia	1	1,176	
Castillo San Juan	1	306	
Nicaragua	1	1,189	
HONDURAS			
Tegucigalpa	2	1,759	
Comayagua	4	2,533	
Olancho	4	4,704	
Yuzcarán	1	2,841	
Gracias	2	316	
Castillo del Golfo	1	456	
GUATEMALA			
Guatemala City	51	82,679	8.1
Villanueva Petapa	9	9,837	
Quetzaltenango	1	200	
Totonicapán	2	11,264	
Esquipulas	2	1,596	
Amatitlán	1	92	
Chimaltenango	1	1,203	
Sumpango	1	456	
Jocotán	1	6,339	
Gotera	1	8,302	

TABLE 10 (continued)
Active Dependencies by Locality

Place	Number	Amount (pesos)	Percent of Total
COSTA RICA	5	8,482	
Cartago	2	4,454	
Nicoya	3	4,028	
MEXICO			
Mexico City	4	41,022	
Oaxaca	2	2,106	
Puebla	2	14,513	
PERU			
Lima	3	6,705	
SPAIN			
Cádiz	1	128	
OTHERS			
Indigo	1	213,411	21.0
Chests (Cajas)	1	110,108	10.8

Source: Aycinena Family Papers, Inventory of 1777.

FROM FINANCE TO PRODUCTION

Ultimately, Aycinena moved beyond importing, exporting, and banking into other branches of colonial enterprise as well. As early as 1773 he became a shipowner, obtaining from Father Manuel Lorenzo García the merchant vessel *La Fama*. By 1788 he was owner of a frigate in the Cádiz trade, the *Nuestra Señora de los Dolores*, which departed from Omoa on August 21, 1788, "bound for Cádiz with 324,159 pounds of indigo."[33] In the same year he extended powers to his cousin in Cádiz to arrange the sale of another vessel, *La Baztanesa*.[34] By the early 1770s, we recall, he had gained direct ownership of mines near Tegucigalpa. He also came to acquire an immense landed patrimony (see table 11). The great majority, if not all, of these properties were situated in the indigo-producing regions of El Salvador. Rather than through purchase or inheritance, he acquired almost all of the estates through foreclosures.

Aycinena acquired the San Miguel indigo plantation Yaguatique from Father Benito de Castilla in the late 1770s. Castilla had bought it for some 18,000 pesos and added "200 head of cattle, 100 mules, and 250 horses," which increased its value to 36,000 pesos. To acquire the estate and to make it a functioning enterprise, Castilla had borrowed 32,630 pesos at 5 percent

TABLE 11
Known Haciendas of Juan Fermín de Aycinena

Estate	Place	Year Acquired
Yaguatigue	San Miguel	by 1781
Miraflores	San Salvador	1784
Cerro de la Avilla	San Vicente	1780–1785
La Concepción	San Vicente	1780–1785
San Juan de Vista	San Vicente	1780–1785
Archichiquitos	San Vicente	1780–1785
Los Naranjos	San Vicente	1780–1785
Buenaventura	unspecified	by 1791
Buena Vista	unspecified	by 1791
San Marcos	unspecified	by 1791

Sources: Wortman, *Government and Society*, 127–28, 310 n. 28; Protocolo de Manuel Laparte, 1796; Libro de Reales Cédulas, 1784; Ordóñez Jonomá, "La Familia Varón de Berrieza," and Aycinena Family Papers, Estate Instructions of Vicente Aycinena, 1791.

annual interest from Aycinena. He pledged to pay 4,000 pesos a year except when afflicted by war or locusts, when he would owe 3,000 pesos annually. Beset by locusts in 1774 and 1775, he was unable to make his installments, and in 1776 he owed the usual 4,000 pesos plus 4,894 pesos for three years of interest. Unable to meet his obligations, he lost his hacienda to Aycinena some time after 1777. As Wortman tells us, Aycinena claimed five more haciendas worth some 156,000 pesos between 1780 and 1785.[35] As of 1783 Aycinena had acquired from Juan Taranco three indigo plantations in the vicinity of San Vicente—Cerro de la Avilla, La Concepción, and San Juan de Vista—in payment of a debt totaling 80,000 pesos.[36] Aycinena gained the hacienda Miraflores from the heirs of Manuel Andino y Arce in September 1784. Worth some 35,563 pesos then, by 1796, Aycinena had enhanced its value to 57,991 pesos with the addition of new houses, obrajes, and livestock.[37]

The connection between commerce and landholding, between merchants and landlords, has engaged many eminent scholars. Traditionally, the acquisition of land was seen as reflecting the obsessions of aspiring feudal lords, but more recent studies have rejected that view.[38] In his landmark study of Bourbon Mexico, Brading argued that merchants resisted becoming tied down in production, preferring short-term loans to permanent investments to preserve their liquidity, "their saving strength."[39] Nevertheless, many merchants did move into land, which Brading saw as an effort to move toward less risky activities.[40] Noting that numerous merchants became *hacendados* (estate owners), Kicza deduced that merchants sought to protect their wealth by acquiring land as soon as possible.[41] John Tutino argued that the shift from commerce to land represented a shift to perhaps less profitable but more reliable investments. Long-distance trade was simply too risky to sustain merchant fortunes over the long term.⁴² The more recent studies reveal the dilemma of the colonial entrepreneur: the need to retain liquidity (and thus flexibility) to meet the exigencies of a volatile imperial economy while rooting (and thus protecting) their wealth and position in land, an investment that inevitably eroded flexibility.

Aycinena's Central American experience sheds additional light on merchant attitudes toward land and on the question of how, or why, a financier decided to become a planter. Obviously, important differences separated Mexico and Guatemala. Mexican merchants tended to acquire estates that could provision some of the largest urban markets in the Western Hemisphere. Guatemala City, especially in the first years of its existence, hardly compared to Mexico City, or even to Guadalajara or Puebla. And at any rate, the estates Aycinena acquired were not useful for this end. His were Salvadoran indigo plantations, geared toward producing an export commodity that he himself marketed.

In Central America, it must be emphasized, plantation ownership exposed the merchant to the hazards of production, compounding the normal risks of long-distance trade.⁴³ Aycinena knew well the difficulties faced by planters. And he had no desire to disrupt an extraordinarily profitable relationship with them. Why should he take on the risks of production when he already enjoyed the real benefits of the indigo trade? To do so was an extraordinary step. Yet it was a step he took nevertheless. Why? And why then?

Aycinena acquired all of his estates after 1777. Thus a gap of almost twenty-five years separates his arrival in Central America from his acquisition of land. Most of the estates were acquired within a brief time—between 1780 and 1785. The long delay, giving way so abruptly to a flurry of takeovers, indicates that a remarkable confluence of circumstances propelled Aycinena's move to the land.

From 1779 to 1783 war between Spain and Great Britain disrupted Spanish American trade and exposed Central America to armed attacks. A British invasion temporarily captured the fortress of Omoa guarding the Honduran coast. The British also captured an entire shipment of indigo. Acting out of patriotism and economic necessity, Aycinena personally furnished 30,000 pesos to help recover the fortress at Omoa. Even with its recovery in 1780, long-distance trade remained extremely difficult. With the war's outcome unclear, sealanes practically shut down, and the recurrent threat of British invasion, the future remained uncertain.

A series of Bourbon reforms in the late 1770s and early 1780s compounded the uncertainty. The war added to the usual difficulties of indigo planters. Shortly before the war broke out, a locust infestation severely hampered production, preventing many Salvadoran planters from producing a crop and redeeming their advances of cash and goods. They became especially vulnerable to merchant financiers. Coming to their assistance, Guatemalan Captain General Matías de Gálvez instituted several measures favoring the planters at the expense of the merchants. In 1779 Gálvez assumed personal control of indigo prices. In 1781 he established an indigo planters' fund and decreed that all indigo had to be purchased in El Salvador. If the state was to side with planters, Aycinena may well have reasoned, now was the time to become a planter.

As of 1777 Aycinena had some 1,014,997 pesos tied up in active dependencies—an amount that exceeded his actual wealth. He was dangerously exposed at a volatile time. He was probably still reeling from the tremendous losses suffered during the earthquakes that rocked Santiago in 1773 and the expense entailed in relocating first to Villa Nueva and then to the new capital. He had been forced to write off many, if not most, of the expenses he incurred in financing the alcalde mayor of San Salvador, Bernabé de la Torre (1771-73), amounting to 143,000 pesos.[44] At the end of the 1770s, then, Aycinena's ability to tolerate heavy indebtedness and to roll over planters' debts in years of crop failure was dramatically eroded. In such circumstances, foreclosure was a reluctant, drastic, but perhaps inevitable step.

The planters who forfeited their estates were by far Aycinena's biggest debtors (see table 12). Foreclosure meant the complete breakdown of relations with those planters. Aycinena may have deemed that the foreclosures were necessary to maintain the integrity, or even the viability, of his credit network. A failure to foreclose in such circumstances would have been an abdication of his responsibilities to the numerous other participants in his credit system. And if his credit system were to fail, the basis of his extraordinary power in the Central American economy would have crumbled as well.

In short, the combination of an abrupt and unfavorable shift of government policy toward merchants, wartime disruptions, crop failures, and defaulting

Table 12
Large Debtors of Juan Fermín de Aycinena, 1777
(in pesos)

Amount	Debtor	Place	Estate Affected
32,558	Benito Castilla	San Miguel	Yaguatique
17,772	Micaela Vásquez Coronado	San Miguel	
11,084	Juan Cáceres	San Miguel	
13,410	Francisco Becerril	San Miguel	
10,024	Antonio Bolaños	San Vicente	Archichiquitos and Los Naranjos
37,579	Lucía Guete	San Miguel	
10,522	Rafael Villalta	San Vicente	
12,279	Francisco Cornejo	Apastepeque	
11,014	Matías de Manzanares	Totonicapán	
13,214	Francisco Molina	San Vicente	
39,648	Juan Taranco	San Vicente	Cerro de Avilla, La Concepción, and San Juan de Vista
13,072	Antonio Merino	San Vicente	
29,337	José Rodríguez	San Vicente	La Joya
36,151	Antonio and Miguel Andino	Santiago Nanualco	Miraflores
21,080	José Joaquín de Figueroa	San Vicente	
30,212	Pedro Souza	San Vicente	
12,677	María Antonia de Guaria	Mexico City	
11,814	Pedro de Aycinena	Mexico City	
10,532	Francisco Yraeta	Mexico City	

Source: Aycinena Family Papers, Inventory of 1777.

debtors, together with his own vulnerability, seems to have pushed Aycinena toward landholding in the early 1780s. Still, we should not disregard completely the idea that Aycinena saw potential benefits in landholding, or that at least he comforted himself in making virtues of neccessity. Control of production eliminated middlemen and allowed for vertical integration of his commercial enterprises. By the late 1770s Aycinena might well have determined that his enterprise was ready to branch into new areas, confident that he could entrust his estates to experienced family members and tested associates.

More personal factors may also have come into play. Since 1773 Aycinena had been physically in limbo, first while the future of the capital was being debated and then while Guatemala City was being constructed. By the late 1770s, a time of war, locusts, economic crisis, and reform, twice widowed and nearing fifty years of age, Aycinena seems to have embarked on a new era. In 1780 he tooks steps to acquire a noble title (granted in 1783). About the same time, he sought to gain entry into the Knights of Santiago. These honors required the possession of land.[45] Landownership itself may have reflected Aycinena's aspirations to become a Spanish grandee. The prolixity with which he became a landholder, however, bespeaks a great reluctance to do so.

CONCLUSION

Aycinena's complex business enterprise evolved perhaps less according to a well-defined blueprint than by astute responses to conditions as they arose. He could not predict the outbreak of war, the eruption of volcanoes, the destruction of earthquakes, the arrival of locusts, the visitations of epidemics. He could not determine beforehand which of his debtors would remain solvent and which would collapse. He could not control changes in government policy, at times favorable to him and his fellow merchants and at times directed against them. Unreliable transportation, the vagaries of nature, chronic shortages of labor and currency, and the ever-present threats of war and piracy challenged any entrepreneur in colonial Central America. John Kicza has determined that "success at the higher levels of colonial commerce was predicated on continual innovation, expansion, and diversification."[46] This was a formula Aycinena applied with devotion and with unique results.

Chapter 5

The Casa de Aycinena at Home and Abroad

The power of the colonial merchant derived from his strategic placement at the intersection of colony and metropolis. In an era of rejuvenated mercantilism and expanding commerce, the supplier of colonial commodities to the peninsula and the distributor of European and Asian goods in the Indies occupied a powerful seat. Ready access to suppliers and buyers in distant markets distinguished the prosperous long-distance trader from his less successful cohorts. The commercial success of Juan Fermín de Aycinena depended, therefore, not only on his command of capital and goods and wise investments but also on the strength of his "corporate structure" and the great reach afforded by his trading network.

In her study of Cádiz merchants, Paloma Fernández-Pérez explains that "colonial trade had created a complex international web of owners, sellers, buyers, agents and correspondents."[1] Colonial merchants operated at the outer reaches of that web, but they also spun similarly complex, overlapping webs of their own.

THE FAMILY ENTERPRISE

The success of Aycinena's business depended on a broad network of subordinates and associates who were, by and large, family members or fellow Navarrans. Perhaps because formal companies were discouraged by the lack of institutional protections and Castilian inheritance laws, the primary economic unit in colonial Spanish America was the extended family.[2] Poor transportation impeded communication and thwarted supervision, thus leaving many important decisions in the hands of subordinates. The chronic scarcity of specie meant that the colonial economy operated on credit. As Kicza points out, "An economy based on credit meant an economy based on trust, or at least on enforceable guarantees."[3] Trust was best assured, if not guaranteed, by reliance on kin.

Thus Juan Fermín de Aycinena first arrived in Guatemala acting on behalf of his Oaxacan cousin, Pedro Bernardo de Yrigoyen. True enough, his 1755 marriage to Ana María Carrillo y Gálvez gave Aycinena a degree of independence highly unusual for a young merchant. But he did not abandon his original family sponsors. And, as we shall see, he dealt with family members stationed throughout the Hispanic world in what may be fairly described as an eighteenth-century, family-centered version of a multinational corporation.

He incorporated family members into his Guatemalan enterprise. The Aycinena estate inventories of 1768, 1771, and 1777 identify the principal cajeros of the Casa de Aycinena for those years. The Casa was represented at the 1768 proceedings by Juan Fermín himself and his cajeros Pedro de Aycinena, Pedro José de Beltranena, Antonio Bergaña, and Manuel Maldonado. In 1771 the cajeros were Pedro de Aycinena, Pedro José de Beltranena, and Juan de Beteta. And in the 1777 inventory the attending cajeros were Pedro José de Beltranena and Tomás Beteta.[4]

Early on, Aycinena's principal business associates were his peninsular nephews, Pedro de Aycinena y Larraín and Pedro de Beltranena e Aycinena.[5] As of 1768, for example, Aycinena's nephews were responsible for 207,715 pesos of store goods belonging to their uncle.[6] After several years in their uncle's employ, however, Juan Fermín's nephews seem to have set out on their own, or at least to have begun to act increasingly in their own name rather than as representatives of the Casa de Aycinena. They both flourished. Pedro de Aycinena y Larraín stated in his testament of 1791 that he brought more than 140,000 pesos to his marriage to Francisca Barrutia.[7] Pedro José de Beltranena enjoyed even greater success. He appears in Floyd's 1968 study as the third leading Guatemalan indigo exporter from 1778 to 1785.[8] It is not clear to what extent Beltranena was by this time an independent agent. He supervised the affairs of the Casa de Aycinena in his uncle's absence at least as late as 1780. When Juan Fermín began to take an annual month-long vacation at the baths of Escuintla at the beginning of each year, Beltranena spoke for the company.[9] Individual ventures and a continuing relationship with the Casa de

Aycinena were not incompatible. And roles within the firm no doubt altered over time. Once Juan Fermín had secured himself at the summit of Guatemala society, his nephews could step out on their own. But they were comforted in the knowledge of their uncle's ability to assist them in times of need.

As noted, one of Juan Fermín's cajeros in 1768 was Antonio Bergaña, a native of Fitero, Navarre. He and his fellow Navarran Juan de Gortari began commercial relations with Aycinena as early as 1765, when they established a company to trade with Peru, dealing in amounts close to 50,000 pesos.[10] Thereafter they took on roles of increasing intimacy and importance within the Casa de Aycinena. Gortari hailed from Almendro, in the Baztán Valley, and was probably a relative of Aycinena.[11] As of 1771, he administered Juan Fermín's mines at Tabanco (probably acquired from the brothers Landa).[12] Antonio Bergaña was for many years the Casa's principal agent in the Pacific trade, operating between the isthmian ports of Realejo, Nicaragua, and Acajutla, El Salvador, and those of Callao, Peru, and Acapulco, Mexico. As early as 1773 he was *maestre* (supervisor of goods) of Aycinena's merchant vessel *La Fama*.[13] As the Casa de Aycinena expanded and diversified and as its subordinates demonstrated their loyalty and ability, their roles grew with it.

In 1781, the merchants Luis Pérez and Pedro Juan de Lara were granted rights to represent the Casa in all commercial matters in the Valley of Guatemala. They may have assumed these duties in place of Pedro de Aycinena and Pedro de Beltranena.[14] They, in turn, were supplanted by José García Goyena, a native of Tafalla, Navarre. García Goyena became a close commercial associate of the Casa de Aycinena in the 1780s. He was the cousin of Manuel Fadrique y Goyena, who was the son-in-law of Cristóbal de Gálvez Corral, the powerful uncle of Ana María Carrillo y Gálvez. Fadrique y Goyena served as the alcalde mayor of El Salvador for much of the 1760s and 1770s. José García Goyena arrived in Guatemala sometime in the 1770s.[15] His illegitimate son, Rafael, was born in 1766 in Guayaquil, suggesting indirectly that José was long active in the Pacific trade. It was a field in which he maintained a continuing interest.[16] García Goyena looked to use his expertise in the Pacific trade to join the merchant elite of Guatemala City. In 1778 he launched a short-lived partnership with Mariano Nájera, Juan Fermín's brother-in-law.[17] As of February 1787, however, García Goyena was handling affairs of the Casa in the absence of Juan Fermín.[18] And on November 27, 1789, Aycinena gave him powers to represent the Casa in Guatemala City and all its provinces.[19] Last, instructions in 1791 from Juan Fermín's eldest son, Vicente de Aycinena y Carrillo, to the various hacienda managers in his father's employ assigned García Goyena the role of primary intermediary between the managers and the family itself. García Goyena continued his intimate relations with the Casa de Aycinena until his death in 1796.[20]

As the estate instructions from Vicente de Aycinena y Carrillo indicate, Juan Fermín's oldest sons took on an increasingly prominent role in the Casa de Aycinena as they matured. Vicente and José, born in the mid-1760s, began to exercise increasing commercial responsibilities by the early 1790s. During their father's sojourn to Escuintla at the beginning of each year, they ran the company in his stead, taking over this task from García Goyena at least as early as February 1791.[21] This gave them needed experience and introduced them to the many Aycinena correspondents, which prepared them for eventual leadership of the Casa. The idea that the sons of successful merchants should leave trade for supposedly loftier pursuits did not seem to be shared by the Marqués de Aycinena.

Finally, as Aycinena's enterprise grew beyond its mercantile and banking activities to include landholding, he came to depend on a number of hacienda managers. These were named in the previously cited 1791 instructions of Vicente de Aycinena.[22] The estate managers were Felipe Mariano de Vidaurre, Manuel Rodrigo López, Francisco Rivera, Manuel Juares, Benito Domínguez de Castilla, Miguel Beltran, José Sarmiento, and José Ambrosio Marín. Castilla, for one, seems to have been a former owner of one of the Aycinena estates.[23]

ISTHMIAN AGENTS

No merchant could be everywhere at once. Yet from Costa Rica to Chiapas (and beyond), Aycinena's goods had to be distributed, his debts collected, and lawsuits filed and pursued on his behalf. Because of the scale and scope of his Central American business endeavors, Aycinena had to employ agents outside the Casa de Aycinena. He came to depend on a wide range of contacts throughout the various regions of his far-flung operations. The numerous transactions empowering agents on his behalf offer a graphic picture of Aycinena's isthmian network (see table 13).

In some cases, Aycinena delegated powers for a single task, such as the collection of a specific debt. Thus, on May 9, 1765, Juan Fermín, along with Juan

Table 13
Aycinena's Isthmian Representatives

Place	Agent	When Named
San Salvador	Antonio Corleto	Nov. 1770
	Juan Antonio Rosales	Jan. 1773
	Anselmo Quirós	Dec. 1790
San Vicente	Ignacio de Villa Aliva	Apr. 1768
	Antonio Molina	May 1769
	José de Figueroa	Jan. 1773
	Vicente Rodríguez del Camino	Nov. 1780
San Miguel	Francisco Solórzano	July 1768
	José de Avila	Nov. 1780
	Pedro de Castro	Apr. 1790
	Justo Orcie	Sep. 1790
	Antonio Orcie	Sep. 1790
	Vicente Rodríguez	Sep. 1790
	Rafael de San Juan	June 1796
Sacatecoluca	Martín de Iturburra	July 1797
Sonsonate	Francisco de Guevara y Donge	Jan. 1776
Nicaragua	Domingo Cavello (gov. 1766–76)	June 1769
	Juan José Granados	May 1790
León	José Antonio Lacayo	Aug. 1765
	Francisco Icana	June 1780
	Pedro de Lara	Aug. 1780
	J. V. Ycasa	Jan. 1791
	Pedro Brea	Jan. 1791
	Manuel Murillo	May 1797
Granada	Andrés de Araujo	Nov. 1776
	José Antonio de Vargas	Nov. 1776
Cartago	Juan Manuel de Casasola	June 1768
Nicoya	Mateo Espinosa	Feb. 1776
Comayagua	Pablo Nieto	Jan. 1791
	J. M. Bustillo	April 1791
Tegucigalpa	Pedro de Mártir de Zelaya	Oct. 1777
Gracias a Dios	Miguel Machado	June 1768

TABLE 13 *(continued)*
Aycinena's Isthmian Representatives

Place	Agent	When Named
Tuxtla	Sebastián de Olachea	May 1765
Chiapas	Ignacio de Coronado	Dec. 1786
Villanueva	Miguel José Equizabal	Apr. 1774
Guatemala City	Miguel Pasqual Saraliqui	Sep. 1776
	Luis Pérez	June 1781
	Pedro Juan de Lara	June 1781
	Juan José Medina	June 1781
	José García Goyena	Nov. 1789
	Mariano Barrutia	Oct. 1790
Chiquimula	Felisiano Dávila de Lugo	Apr. 1769
	Francisco Xavier Riviero	unspecified
Esquipulas	Ignacio Matheu Gutiérrez	Feb. 1767
Gotera	Joaqin Luceno	Mar. 1768
San Antonio	Antonio Bergaña	Feb. 1769

Source: AGCA, A1.20, Protocolos, 1750–1800.

José Ganuza, Juan Tomás Micheo, and other creditors of the estate of the deceased Miguel Ignacio de Irisarri, appointed Sebastián Olachea of Tuxtla to pursue those debts.[24] In other circumstances, he delegated his *poder cumplido* (complete power, full powers of representation), which denoted the establishment of a lasting business connection. On August 5, 1765, for example, Aycinena conceded full powers to Father José Antonio Lacayo of León and Granada.[25] Similarly, in November 1770 Aycinena appointed Antonio Corleto of San Salvador

> to represent me in all rights and actions, receipts, demands, and expenses, contracted with any persons, of

any rank, quality and condition, judicial and extra-judicial [in that province], involving all monies, jewelry, gold and silver items, slaves, livestock, dyes or other products, goods or anything that I owe or am owed.[26]

Transactions such as these created the superstructure that supported the Aycinena commercial network throughout the isthmus, crafted to monitor the exchange of goods, cash, and credit and generally to watch over the Casa's interests. Aycinena thus maintained agents in San Salvador, San Vicente, San Miguel, Sonsonate, León, Granada, Cartago, Nicoya, Comayagua, Tegucigalpa, Gracias a Dios, Ciudad Real (Chiapas), Chiquimula, Esquipulas, Sumpango, Gotera, Chiquimulilla, Villanueva, Vera Paz, and Sacatecoluca.[27]

BEYOND THE ISTHMUS

Because of the importance of overseas trade to the creation of wealth in colonial Central America, long-distance connections were just as crucial, perhaps more crucial, than the contacts Aycinena established within the isthmus itself. Table 14 provides a partial list of the commercial connections Aycinena developed outside Central America to sustain his business enterprise. As in Central America, some of these connections were established to pursue a specific transaction—to sell a ship or to seek honors—and some involved a general concession. Some *apoderados* (ones legally designated to act on behalf of another) were individuals with which he did substantial business, and others were more ancillary relationships, established to safeguard his interests in commercial transactions.

TABLE 14
Aycinena's Representatives outside Central America

Place	Agent	When Named
Oaxaca	Pedro Bernardo de Yrigoyen	July 1754
Mexico City	Francisco Ignacio de Yraeta	Dec. 1787
	Gabriel de Yturbe e Yraeta	May 1797
Acapulco	Antonio Bergaña	May 1773
Havana	Juan Tomás de Jáuregui	Dec. 1767
Callao	Antonio Bergaña	June 1769
Lima	Juan Miguel Aguerrevere	Aug. 1771
	Isidro de Aborea	Aug. 1771
	Juan de Orobioquita y Aguirre	Aug. 1771
Cádiz	Matías de Landaburu	Oct. 1765
	Juan Baptista Uztáriz	Oct. 1765
	Sebastián Pinto	Oct. 1765
	Juan Antonio de Uzelaz	Dec. 1772
	Fermín de Elizalde	July 1788
	Francisco Xavier de Goenaga	July 1788
Madrid	Francisco Gomez de Cor	Apr. 1771
	Tomás Pres de Arroyo	Apr. 1771
	Domingo Sánchez Barrera	Apr. 1771
	Tomás de Arzú	Apr. 1789

Source: AGCA, A1.20, Protocolos, 1750–1800.

Through his peninsular origins and his stopovers in Mexico City and Oaxaca, Aycinena established commercial relations that would serve him his whole career. The growth of his enterprise entailed a corresponding growth in the scope of his commercial network. As table 14 indicates, Aycinena's commercial network extended throughout the empire.

Libranzas and Consignments

Long-distance trade entailed a mutual dependence binding merchants throughout Spain and the Indies. Such relationships were often long in the making, as trust developed over years of doing business emboldened merchants to take on bigger risks and to place more and more confidence in distant cohorts. But a single disaster could destroy relationships built up over decades. Thus the wise merchant did not commit himself to one supplier or buyer in any given market. It was much more prudent to keep a variety of contacts. Much as Salvadoran planters sought (at times unsuccessfully) to maintain relationships with several merchant financiers, the merchants themselves sought to keep their options open.

Long-distance trade was filled with risk, vulnerable to wars and weather, and subject to dramatic market shifts. Compounding the dangers, long-distance trade was conducted on credit. Two devices colonial merchants employed to minimize the dangers were *libranzas* (bills of exchange) and consignments. In Bourbon Mexico, according to Brading, "the usual method of payment between merchants was the bill of exchange, a preference strengthened of course by the bandit-infested nature of New Spain's territory."[28] A libranza could change hands several times before it was paid by the person on whom it was drawn. Brading cites a 1796 document in which the consulado (of Mexico) explained the use of libranzas to the new viceroy.

> The *libranza* ... was only employed in internal trade; it was frequently issued for very small sums; and it often

served as a form of currency. It lacked, therefore, the formality of the international instrument. On the other hand, it appears to have been a true bill of exchange, in that it involved three parties—the drawer of the note (*librante*), the recipient (*libritario*) and the payor (*manditario*).[29]

Libranzas were also a principal means by which credit and goods were exchanged in Central America.[30] Despite the assertion that libranzas were recognized only internally, in practice their employment spanned imperial borders.

Another innovation in response to the shortage of cash and the dangers of hauling valuable goods over long distances to uncertain markets was the practice of consignment. A merchant would consign goods to a colleague in another city to be sold there. This was not an actual sale, in which ownership of the goods changed hands. In effect, consignees rented out their facilities and marketing ability in exchange for goods supplied by the distant partner. The goods would be marked up sufficiently to yield a profit both to the supplier and to the consignee. The consignee would strive to keep the supplier current on the latest prices and general market conditions, so that the most favorable sales could be realized. If the goods could not be sold, they could be returned to the original supplier. More often, alternative arrangements would be made to cut losses.

A Mexican Associate: Francisco Yraeta

The relationship between Aycinena and the prominent Mexico City merchant Francisco Ignacio de Yraeta illuminates the nature of colonial business transactions.³¹ Born in 1732 in Anzuola, Guipuzcoa, Yraeta migrated to New Spain at the age of twelve. He stayed there for four years and at sixteen departed for the Philippines. The young Francisco became an agent of a Manila merchant firm, for which he made eight separate trips to Acapulco. In 1758 Yraeta relocated to New Spain for good. In 1763 he married María Josefa de Ganuza, the twenty-two-year-old daughter of the Navarran-born Mexico City merchant Pedro de Ganuza. Yraeta entered into commerce under Ganuza's auspices as early as 1767, if not before, and inherited control of the family firm on Ganuza's death in 1769. Juan Fermín de Aycinena was just one of many commercial connections Yraeta inherited from his father-in-law.³²

Yraeta became a major Mexico City importer. In 1771 he imported goods valued at more than 47,000 pesos, and in 1773 his imports exceeded 72,000 pesos. In 1777 his combined importations from Europe (95,892 pesos), the Philippines (12,468 pesos), and Peru (6,506 pesos) came to more than 114,000 pesos.³³ Yraeta had regular dealings with several Guatemalan merchants, with whom he corresponded on a monthly basis. He was especially important as a broker for the Guatemalans at the port of Acapulco, entrepôt of the Asian trade.

In 1770, shortly after taking over from his father-in-law, Yraeta established a company with the Guatemalan merchant José Fernández Gil which lasted from 1770 until 1785. Afterward, Yraeta maintained informal relations with Fernández Gil until at least 1793. However, Yraeta's most important relationship in Guatemala was probably with Aycinena (given that Aycinena was the most important merchant in Guatemala). As of 1771 Yraeta owed Aycinena some 22,811 pesos.[34] In 1777 his debt was 10,532 pesos. They corresponded regularly, exchanging information on commercial conditions, personal matters, and imperial politics. Aycinena even had his Mexico City friend play the lottery for him.[35]

On December 29, 1787, Juan Fermín appointed Yraeta his principal representative in Mexico City.[36] The value of this connection was confirmed when Yraeta became Mexican representative of the Royal Philippines Company at about the same time and, in 1789 and 1790, when he served as consul of the Mexico City Consulado de Comercio.[37]

In at least one instance the relations between Aycinena and Yraeta transcended commerce. In 1776 New Spain's viceroy, Antonio María Bucareli, assigned Yraeta the commission of depositario charged with the collection of money for the construction of Guatemala City.[38] Aycinena had been given a similar commission by the captain general of Guatemala. The lines between public responsibilities and private endeavors often blurred. The Aycinena-Yraeta relationship lasted nearly three decades. In a sense it extended beyond the deaths of the two principals, for on June 28, 1796, in the name of their family, Vicente and José Aycinena y Carrillo gave full powers to Francisco Ignacio de Yraeta.[39]

Yraeta and Aycinena also enabled others to do business in either New Spain or Guatemala. Armed with libranzas, acquaintances of Yraeta could do business in Guatemala by drawing on his line of credit with Aycinena. And people in Mexico City (or Puebla, for example) known to or acting under the patronage of Aycinena could do the same by drawing on Aycinena's account with Yraeta. Aycinena and Yraeta would keep running totals of their transactions with each other and with the many merchants, or others in need of cash and credit, who used them as branch banks. Periodically, the principals would settle up and then start a new balance.[40]

Aycinena's Yraeta connection also yields several examples of the practice of consignment. Aycinena consistently entrusted substantial amounts of Central American indigo to his Mexico City associate. Yraeta would hold the indigo until the Mexico City market yielded an acceptable price, or perhaps route it to regional production centers like Puebla or Querétaro or send it on to Veracruz (and eventually Spain). Once he sold the indigo, he could then send Aycinena his share of the proceeds or an equivalent amount in European or Asian goods.

A common arrangement was for Yraeta to sell Aycinena's indigo in Mexico City or elsewhere in New Spain and then to remit Aycinena's profits from the sales to Acapulco, where they would be invested in Asian goods via the dominant Mexico City trader there, Gabriel Pérez de Elizalde. Thus, in February 1778, Yraeta sent 10,303 pesos of Juan Fermín's indigo profits to be employed by Pérez de Elizalde in the fair at Acapulco.[41] Aycinena maintained a separate relationship with the Navarran-born Pérez de Elizalde.[42] In the 1778 transaction Aycinena's ties with him detoured through Mexico City via Yraeta, which offers just one example of the interdependence and interconnections typical of intercolonial trade.

Such linkages did not always guarantee good relations. In the mid-1770s Yraeta charged that Pérez de Elizalde was monopolizing the Acapulco fair,[43] and in the late 1770s challenged Pérez de Elizalde for dominance there. But he ultimately realized the futility of such a course and took steps to patch things up with his rival in 1780.[44]

Pérez de Elizalde (and eventually Yraeta) also became involved in a bitter commercial dispute pitting him against Aycinena and several Guatemalan merchants. That conflict had to do with a large shipment of Ceylonese cinnamon the Guatemalans purchased at Acapulco from Pérez de Elizalde. The nearly 30,000 pesos worth of *canela* was supposedly in good condition when it departed Acapulco in early 1782. But when the crates were opened in Guatemala City in December 1782, the cinnamon's color and odor repelled the astonished Guatemalan wholesalers. They sought immediately to determine what had happened and, more important, to recoup their rather substantial losses. Presumably, the cinnamon was "bad" when they purchased it, and thus Pérez de Elizalde was liable; in the Guatemalan's view he should seek redress in Manila, where he had been defrauded. They demanded that Pérez de Elizalde give them a credit for the bad cinnamon.

Pérez de Elizalde countered that the cinnamon was in good condition when it left Acapulco and that the fault rested with the *arriero* (muleteer) the Guatemalans hired to transport the spice to Central America. The arriero traveled in the hot season and was delayed by rains and lack of funds to pay the various taxes applied en route. He was detained in Antequera for several months. In all, it took some ten months for the spice to make it from Acapulco to Guatemala. It was Pérez de Elizalde's contention that the cinnamon was mishandled and damaged in transit, and thus the problem was between the Guatemalan merchants and their arriero.

Juan Fermín de Aycinena was an interested party in the dispute. He perhaps hoped to use his prestige and his long ties to Pérez de Elizalde to sway the Acapulco magnate, but without success. The case then came before the consulado de comercio of Mexico City in 1783. Aycinena appealed to his friend Francisco Ignacio Yraeta to act on his behalf. Even this did not work. Pérez de Elizalde and associates prevailed, winning the original case and all subsequent appeals. The case was finally settled in 1788.[45]

The case illustrates a number of things about long-distance trade. Commerce was risky. Transit was hazardous. Valuable goods were subject to loss or damage

A mule train crossing the jungle in early nineteenth-century Mexico. From Carl Nebel, *Voyage pittoresque et archéologique dans la partie plus intéressante du Mexique* (Paris, 1836). Courtesy of the Latin American Library, Tulane University.)

along the way. Even relations of long standing could not prevent or resolve disputes. And regardless of the merits of the case, Mexican merchants seemed to have an advantage in the consulado tribunal in Mexico City. This no doubt gave further impetus to Guatemalan demands for a consulado of their own.

Mexico City

As the Yraeta and Pérez de Elizalde examples show, ties in New Spain were vital to the Casa de Aycinena. This was especially the case prior to the introduction of comercio libre in 1778, but Mexican ties were important afterward as well. It is difficult to say how much of Aycinena's long-distance trade was with Spain and how much with Mexico, Peru, or other parts of the Indies. The 1777 inventory summarized in chapter 4 shows some 5.6 percent of Aycinena's active commercial debts in Mexico and less than 1 percent in Peru. But these figures surely undervalue his overseas trade. In that same year, he had over 213,000 pesos worth of indigo distributed in his commercial network in New Spain and Peru.

Mexico City merchants dominated the European trade via Cádiz, and the Asian trade via Manila and Acapulco. If Aycinena was to gain access to these goods in substantial supply, he had to maintain relations with the powerful merchants of Mexico City. As in Central America, family contacts provided the base on which other less intimate but important connections rested.

Juan Fermín's most obvious Mexico City connection was his brother Pedro de Aycinena. They did business with one another on a regular basis. In 1768

Pedro owed Juan Fermín 1,479 pesos, plus the value of consigned goods worth 20,941 pesos. In 1771 Pedro's debt to his brother was 13,234 pesos, and in 1777, 11,814 pesos.[46]

Pedro de Aycinena e Yrigoyen ascended in the Mexican business community at almost precisely the same time Juan Fermín rose in Guatemala. Pedro arrived in Mexico around 1750, probably in the company of his brother. He remained in Veracruz for several years (perhaps taking part in voyages to Spain). He appears in colonial records as a buyer at the Jalapa fair in 1757 and 1758.[47] In 1761 he was in Mexico City, and at least as early as 1768 he had joined the consulado de comercio, as a member of the Basque party.[48] As of 1764 Pedro was an apoderado of the Veracruz firm Saenz Rico, Hijo y Compañía.[49] In 1772 he was a deputy of the consulado for the Jalapa fair. And from 1777 to 1779 he served as consul of the consulado (one of the three officers elected annually), the first two years as *consul moderno*, the last year as *consul antiguo*.[50]

Pedro de Aycinena's prominence in the consulado derived from his power in trade. He was one of Mexico's leading cacao importers in the 1760s and 1770s, dealing with suppliers in Caracas and Guayaquil.[51] But he by no means limited his activities to cacao. In 1765 he imported 13.6 percent of *all* goods brought into Mexico City. The following year his share was 21.45 percent. In four separate years, Pedro's imports exceeded 100,000 pesos. In 1766 they exceeded 220,000 pesos. In 1777 Pedro probably set a record, bringing in 570,168 pesos worth of goods from Europe and Asia.[52]

In 1783, having reached the pinnacle of New World success, Pedro de Aycinena e Yrigoyen decided to return to Cádiz.[53] This may have been a response to the changes brought by imperial free trade, which undermined Mexico City's role. Another possibility is that he went home to join or replace family members in Cádiz—to direct imperial trade at the "home office." Or he may have decided to enter retirement or semiretirement. At any rate, Pedro was now among the wealthiest Spanish merchants. An estate inventory in 1785 set his worth at more than 755,000 pesos (see table 15).[54]

Pedro de Aycinena e Yrigoyen operated in Mexico City and returned to Cádiz in the company of his (and Juan Fermín's) nephew, Fermín de Elizalde e Aycinena. Like his uncles, Fermín came from Ciga, Navarre.[55] For many years, he served as Pedro's primary cajero, first in Mexico City and then in Cádiz. In this respect, he mirrored the roles played by his cousins, Pedro de Aycinena y Larraín and Pedro de Beltranena, in Guatemala.

Another nephew of Juan Fermín and Pedro de Aycinena e Yrigoyen in Mexico was Juan Angel de Aguerrevere. A vecino of Villa de Texes, he was born

TABLE 15
Wealth of Pedro de Aycinena e Yrigoyen, 1785

Initial capital	53,470
Final capital	854,007
Passive	98,539
Liquid	755,468

Source: Antonio García-Baquero González, *Cádiz y el Atlántico (1717–1778): El comercio colonial español bajo el monopolio gaditano* (Seville: Escuela de Estudios Hispano-Americanos, CSIC, Excelentísima Diputación Provincial de Cádiz, 1976), 1:511–13.

in Irurita, Navarre. His brother, Juan Miguel de Aguerrevere, was then a merchant in Peru. On February 27, 1775, Juan Angel ceded powers to draw up a will. In this transaction he provided information not only about his household, executors, and heirs but also about the familial nature of colonial commerce.

Gravely ill, Juan Angel named as executors Josefa Antonia de Mier (his wife), Leonardo Nafarrate, and Rafael Abad. He was to be buried at a place of their choosing; if they were not available, then his uncle Pedro de Aycinena would make that decision. Juan Angel noted that he and his wife had five children: Isabel, Juan José Tomás, Ana María, Blanca, and the youngest whose name he could not recall! ("y la mas chiquita que se me ha olvidado su nombre").

He had a better recollection of his business matters. Aguerrevere stated that he had entrusted 2,151 pesos to Rafael Abad for employment in the next trade fair at Jalapa. His poder detailed other obligations as well. He declared that his brother in Peru, don Juan Miguel de Aguerrevere, had given him 2,000 pesos for his personal use and another 6,000 for business purchases. And he acknowledged the financial support of relatives in Guatemala. He declared that don Juan Fermín de Aycinena and don Pedro de Beltranena (his uncle and cousin, respectively), "desirous of his well-being," had promised him 3,000 pesos, which they would employ in indigo on his behalf. He directed his executors to pursue the transaction.[56]

To be sure, Aycinena's ties in Mexico City extended well beyond family. At the same time, however, he seems to have dealt almost exclusively with members of the Basque faction in the Mexico City consulado (of which his brother was a prominent figure). Felipe

Gandiaga is a good example. In 1766 Gandiaga was deputy to the Jalapa fair. He was elected consul moderno of the consulado in 1766 and consul antiguo in the following year. Gandiaga imported more than 40,000 pesos worth of European goods into Mexico in 1766 and 1773.[57] A considerable amount of his business was with Juan Fermín de Aycinena: in 1768 Gandiaga owed Juan Fermín 4,815 pesos and had been consigned twenty-five zurrones (1 zurrón = approx. 220 lb.) of indigo from Aycinena; as of 1771, he owed 18,530 pesos.[58]

Another Bascongada associate was Juan Bautista Aldasoro. A native of Placencia, Guipuzcoa, he too obtained high office in the Mexico City consulado—consul moderno in 1769 and consul antiguo in 1770.[59] A major importer, Aldasoro brought in more than 108,000 pesos worth of European goods to Mexico in 1769 and more than 73,000 pesos worth in 1773. His relationship with Aycinena lasted many years and took various forms. In 1762 Aycinena and other cabildo members in Santiago de Guatemala appointed Aldasoro their agent in soliciting more than 30,000 pesos from the Mexican church establishment.[60] They also did business of a more conventional nature. Aldasoro received fifteen zurrones of indigo from Juan Fermín in 1768; in that year, Aycinena owed the Mexico City magnate more than 5,500 pesos.[61]

Still another Mexico City consulado connection was Pedro de Ganuza. A native of Bustos, Navarre, Ganuza's trade links extended from Mexico City to Cádiz, Manila, Lima, Guayaquil, and Guatemala. His cousin, Juan José de Ganuza, was a "merchant priest" in the Guatemalan capital.[62] As early as 1756, Aycinena redeemed libranzas from Domingo Micheo, drawn on Pedro de Ganuza.[63] Aycinena's relationship with the Mexico City merchant persisted until his death in 1769. On Ganuza's death, his affairs came under the management of his son-in-law, Francisco Ignacio de Yraeta, who, as noted, renewed the ties with Aycinena.

The Provinces

Although the merchants of Mexico City were obviously his most important connections in New Spain, Aycinena also maintained substantial relations with other merchants in the viceroyalty. These were important both in their own right and because they lined the commercial highways linking Santiago to Mexico City and, ultimately, Veracruz, Acapulco, Cádiz, and Manila.

Oaxaca was especially important in this regard as it straddled the Camino Real between Mexico City and Santiago. Of course, there was Aycinena's cousin Pedro Bernardo de Yrigoyen in Oaxaca.[64] Members of the Larrazábal family, including Feliciano Larrazábal, remained important figures in Oaxaca through the end of the century.[65] Fernando Sinande was another connection in the dye-rich province of Oaxaca. Sinande's wife, Francisca Xaviera de Larraínzar, was the sister-in-law of Pedro Angel de Yrigoyen, who acted as her guardian in arranging her marriage.[66] Having established himself in Antequera, Sinande became Juan Fermín's primary commercial conduit between Guatemala and Mexico City after the death of Pedro Bernardo de Yrigoyen around 1760.[67] In 1780 Francisco's widow briefly assumed the intermediary role her husband performed for Aycinena and his contacts in Mexico City and Acapulco.[68] Eventually, that role was taken over by the important Oaxacan trader Alonso Magro.[69]

Aycinena sustained several relationships in Puebla. On the whole, his ties there seemed to be more substantive than those in Oaxaca. Puebla was an important manufacturing center whose wares Aycinena may have acquired in exchange for indigo. Thus Aycinena consigned some forty zurrones of indigo to Francisco José Larrasquito in 1768. In 1771 Larrasquito owed Juan Fermín more than 14,000 pesos.[70] In 1777 Francisco José's kinsman, José Ignacio Larrasquito, had a debt with Juan Fermín of more than 5,600 pesos. Similarly, in 1771 Juan Fermín owed Poblano Eugenio González Maldonado 14,164 pesos. José Ojeda y Estrada owed Juan Fermín 8,862 pesos in 1777.[71] Ojeda y Estrada maintained relations well into the 1790s, regularly drawing credit from Aycinena's account with the Mexico City merchant Francisco Yraeta.[72]

Finally, in Veracruz, Aycinena continued his family's long-standing ties with the Saenz Rico family (which in turn had connections with the Uztáriz house in Cádiz). The Aycinena estate inventories indicate an ongoing relationship with Antonio Saenz de Santa María and the commercial firm of Sr. Saenz Rico, Hijo y Compañía. The relatively modest sums involved, however, seem to indicate that they were primarily intermediaries between Aycinena and Spanish houses.[73] We recall the importance of the Saenz Rico company in the fortunes of his relatives in Oaxaca. The relationship persisted with Pedro de Aycinena e Yrigoyen acting as their apoderado in Mexico City.

Peru

The Casa de Aycinena also dealt substantially with the Viceroyalty of Peru, if not on the scale of its business with New Spain. Even before intercolonial trade was legalized, Central American indigo was exchanged for Peruvian cacao, wine, and textiles. Juan Fermín's primary agent for the Peru trade was Antonio Bergaña. An agreement of May 1765 consigned dyes to the care of Bergaña and fellow cajero Juan de Gortari. The indigo was to be shipped to Lima on the *Nuestra Señora de la Soledad*, which had arrived from Peru, and was to return via the Salvadoran port of Acajutla.[74] In 1768 Bergaña and Gortari registered an active dependency of 49,288 pesos and 3/8 reales as representatives of the Casa. This probably involved goods consigned to them en route to or already in Peru. In May 1770 Francisco Yraeta mentioned Aycinena's "dependent" Juan de Gortari in Peru.[75] In 1771 Antonio Bergaña, also in Lima, owed the Casa de Aycinena 38,828 pesos.

Not surprisingly, Aycinena's connections in Peru were among the commercial aristocracy there. That aristocracy was unusually dominated by Basques and Navarrans.[76] In the early 1770s Aycinena's most important link in Peru was probably his Lima nephew, Juan Miguel de Aguerrevere, to whom he extended powers of representation in August 1772.[77] Aguerrevere's Navarran cousins, Antonio and José Matías de Elizalde, operated in Lima as the Hermanos Elizalde. Antonio Elizalde was a wholesaler and banker who served on the cabildo of Lima and eventually joined the Knights of Santiago. His brother José Matías collaborated in his business and exercised other public charges.[78] Juan Bautista de Yrigoyen, probably a relative, was another

Peruvian connection. Perhaps Aycinena's most powerful Lima connection was Isidro de Abarca, the Conde de San Isidro, who served as prior of the Mining Tribunal of Lima.[79] The Aycinena estate inventories document other relationships with Peruvian traders, including the Marqués de Negreiros, Sebastián de Urrutia, Miguel de Olavide, Father Manuel Lorenzo García (formerly of Realejo, Nicaragua, and the owner of the vessel *La Fama*), Juan José Anbelaez, Antonio Rodríguez, and José de Zaldumbide.[80]

The Peninsula

Finally, almost by definition, colonial entrepreneurs depended on ties with the metropolis. Despite Bourbon reforms that diluted its power, Cádiz remained the center of Spanish colonial trade in the eighteenth century.[81] Aycinena had several commercial associates in the port. The dominant traders there were the Cinco Gremios of Madrid and the closely related Casa de Uztáriz. Consolidated in 1686, the so-called Five Guilds of Madrid acquired the leading economic role in Castile and enjoyed a privileged position at court as financiers. They also gradually established a secure trading position in the Indies trade. By 1778, the Cinco Gremios had three representatives in Jalapa, and as of 1784, they established a trading factory in Mexico City.[82]

Aycinena had substantial relations with representatives of the Cinco Gremios in Guatemala. In the 1750s their Central American agent was Domingo Micheo e Uztáriz, with whom Aycinena did business via Pedro de Ganuza.[83] A native of Gaztelu, Navarre, Domingo Micheo married Guatemalan Leonor María

Josefa de Equizabal y Gálvez in 1759. In 1760 he claimed a worth of some 94,500 pesos.[84] In the 1760s the Cinco Gremios were represented by Domingo's cousin Juan Tomás de Micheo y Barreneche of Saldias, Navarre. He also married into the Guatemalan elite, taking as his wife Juana María Petrona de Nájera y Mencos (who was the sister of Juan Fermín's second wife). Worth some 100,000 pesos in 1774, Juan Tomás returned to Spain after the 1773 earthquakes.[85] Juan Antonio de la Peña supplanted Micheo in the 1770s. A Burgos native, he had arrived in Guatemala in 1767. In 1776 he married Ana Eudocia de Obregón y Gálvez, cousin (and benefactress) of Ana María Carrillo y Gálvez. In 1772, de la Peña, who was serving as corregidor of Nicoya, obtained from Aycinena 4,334 pesos in goods and cash to develop his office. As of 1777 de la Peña had a debt with Aycinena of 2,475 pesos.[86]

The Navarran Casa de Uztáriz was closely linked to the Cinco Gremios and gained increasing influence in the second half of the eighteenth century.[87] Together with the Cinco Gremios, the Casa de Uztáriz led the Bourbon thrust to recapture the Spanish American trade for the metropolis. In 1762 they became managers of the royal silk factory in Talavara. In exchange they gained rights to dispatch several ships to the Indies: three as of 1762 (to Veracruz, Havana, and Peru). By 1770 they had eight ships in the Indies trade. The Casa sent its surplus silks to America (occasionally with mercury as well) to exchange for Mexican bullion, Oaxacan cochineal, and Guatemalan indigo.[88] The Casa de Aycinena was apparently well connected to the Casa de Uztáriz. In 1765 Juan Fermín conceded powers of representation in Cádiz to his fellow Navarran (and the future Conde de Reparaz) Juan Bautista Uztáriz.

Aycinena had another account with Cristóbal Xavier de Uztáriz in the late 1770s.[89]

Still other Aycinena connections in Cádiz are detailed by agreements extending powers of representation or by the estate records. In 1765 Aycinena extended powers to Matías de Landaburu, an extremely important Cádiz merchant.[90] Another 1765 apoderado was Sebastián Pinto de Rivera, who in 1768 owed Aycinena 19,791 pesos. Other links included Isabel Jacobs y Pellaert, Pedro de Aguirre, Francisco Ignacio Sagasti, and the Irish-born George Crimin (who Aycinena owed 8,786 pesos).[91]

Aycinena's dealings with the Casa de Uzelas are instructive. Juan Antonio de Uzelas owed the Casa de Aycinena 29,309 pesos in 1768; Aycinena owed Uzelas 10,592 in 1771. Cementing their ties, Aycinena conceded powers of representation to Uzelas in 1772. But relations with Cádiz merchants did not always proceed smoothly. In April 1790 Pedro de Aycinena y Larraín had a suit pending before the consulado of Seville regarding some 30,000 pesos worth of indigo for which he had not been paid by the Casa de Uzelas. For this reason he conferred his powers of attorney on his cousin, Juan Miguel Aguerrevere.[92]

The appeal to Aguerrevere affirms that, as in the Indies, Aycinena's Cádiz ties were built on the strategic placement of trusted family members. We noted that Pedro de Aycinena e Yrigoyen had returned to Cádiz in 1783. But numerous other connections, family or otherwise, predated his reestablishment there. Juan Francisco de Aycinena was a Cádiz merchant as of 1776.[93] Juan Miguel de Larraín also operated out of Cádiz.[94] Another contact was Juan Vicente Marticorena, who in 1778 purchased more than 13,375 pounds of indigo.[95]

The Cádiz merchant Jorge de Araurrenechea e Yrigoyen was a childhood acquaintance of Juan Fermín de Aycinena, most likely a cousin. Born in Ciga in 1730, he joined the consulado of Cádiz in 1753. The following year, at about the time Juan Fermín was establishing himself in Santiago de Guatemala, he married Paula García Bustamante, further rooting himself in Cádiz.[96] In 1768 Araurrenechea had a dependency with Aycinena of 2,034 pesos, while at the same time Aycinena owed him some 2,000 pesos, "the proceeds of various Castilian goods" he had consigned to Aycinena.[97] As of 1771, Arraurrenechea owed 1,507 pesos.

Juan Fermín's nephew Juan Miguel de Aguerrevere had returned to Cádiz by the late 1770s or early 1780s. Born in Irurita, Navarre, in 1739, he joined the consulado of Cádiz in 1765 and sometime thereafter migrated to Lima. He remained in Peru well into the 1770s. Having reestablished himself in Cádiz, in 1782 he married María Ignacia Cadalso Garay, the daughter of the wealthy Cádiz merchant Diego Cadalso and María Francisca Garay. His new bride brought a dowry of 116,000 pesos.[98] Juan Fermín de Aycinena extended powers to pursue honors to his wealthy and well-connected nephew in October 1779. In 1788 he asked his nephew to sell his merchant vessel, *La Baztanesa*.[99]

Juan Miguel's cousin Fermín de Elizalde relocated to Cádiz in 1783. In January 1784 he wrote to his Mexican merchant friend Francisco Yraeta from Puerto de Santa María.[100] His patron, Pedro de Aycinena e Yrigoyen, died around 1785. Fermín de Elizalde continued to be a major Cádiz player. In 1789 he married Manuela Cadalso, who was the sister of María Ignacia Cadalso, the wife of his cousin Juan Miguel de

Aguerrevere e Aycinena. Family politics, it seems, operated more or less the same on either side of the Atlantic.

Fermín de Elizalde e Aycinena and Juan Miguel de Aguerrevere e Aycinena—cousins and perhaps half-siblings—followed remarkably similar career paths. As young men, they had left Navarre for Cádiz and eventually set up in the New World. Aguerrevere went to the viceregal capital of Lima, while Elizalde went to the viceregal capital of Mexico City. Having served their time in the Indies, they returned to Cádiz in middle age, where they remained deeply involved in colonial trade, but now from the other side of the Atlantic. They could do so because other family members or similarly trustworthy connections had taken their place in the colonial capitals.[101]

CONCLUSION

To a perhaps startling degree, Spanish American trade at all levels operated along family lines. The ties detailed in this chapter provide strong evidence of the workings of an empirewide, family-based, commercial consortium, the extent of which has not been sufficiently appreciated. Other Aycinena ties no doubt existed in Cuba, Chile, Ecuador, and Venezuela.[102] Based on his study of Mexico City, Kicza detected "the existence of an ongoing commercial relationship between relatives at both ends of the major trade conduit between Spain and Mexico" but admitted that "its precise nature—especially the locus of power—remains hidden."[103] He was speaking of the great consulado merchants of Mexico City who dealt with family firms in Cádiz and whose independence was possibly in question. This does not seem to be the case with Juan Fermín de Aycinena. Still, the presence of other Aycinenas in Mexico City (Pedro) and in Cádiz (Juan Francisco, Pedro) and other relatives in Peru (Aguerrevere and Elizalde) suggests a high degree of coordination the structure of which is difficult to determine. As for the locus of power, it seems clear that much, if not most, of the power rested with Juan Fermín de Aycinena. His dominance of the isthmian indigo market at a time of rising demand for the commodity placed him in an especially favorable position. His ability to select among wholesalers in Mexico, Spain, and Peru further strengthened his negotiating position. The enormous extent of his trading network (which may have extended even outside legitimate channels) gave Aycinena the wherewithal to distribute trade goods in exchange for profitable export commodities much in demand abroad, namely, indigo. The scale of his long-distance exchanges reinforced his leading position at home, which in turn gave him the means to further embellish his imperial trade network. His was a most enviable position.[104]

Chapter 6

Aycinena and the State

"For all these services and personal merits," proclaimed Charles III of Spain on June 19, 1783, "I have conferred on you the title of Marqués or Conde de Ayzinena."[1] With this gesture, don Juan Fermín de Aycinena e Yrigoyen the Navarran immigrant became the only nobleman in the Kingdom of Guatemala. One can imagine the festivities that greeted the news—Te Deums, High Masses, sumptuous banquets. The marquessate crowned Aycinena's unique success in late colonial Central America. Obviously, his achievements were due in large measure to his financial prowess. But they were also built on his expert use of the machinery of colonial government.

PILLAR OF THE EMPIRE

Although it is sometimes said that Aycinena "purchased" his Castilian title, that is not strictly the case.[2] Titles rewarded extraordinary services rendered to the Crown. Historically, this meant military service, such as the conquest of new lands that enlarged the realm. But Charles III had altered the criteria for ennoblement to include commercial activities that enriched the monarchy.[3] There is little doubt that Aycinena, in this respect, rendered bountiful service to his king. From 1773 to 1780 alone, according to the title, his trading house generated more than 107,000 pesos in tax revenue for royal coffers.

But Aycinena's contributions to the Spanish state in Central America encompassed more than just "tithing" at the royal altar. The catalog of Juan Fermín's merits and services presented in his successful application for a title provides a useful—if unsurprisingly laudatory—outline of his public career up to 1780.[4] He served his sovereign in a variety of colonial offices, mostly in municipal government. Shortly after his marriage to Ana María Carrillo y Gálvez in 1755, he became an *alférez* (standard-bearer) in Santiago. In November 1757 he became a lieutenant of the Santiago battalion of the colonial militia and shortly thereafter, a captain of the same body. In January 1758 Aycinena became the cabildo's síndico procurador, which duties he was said to have discharged with "the greatest zeal in the critical circumstances of grain shortages and viral epidemics afflicting Santiago."[5] In 1759 he was elected alcalde ordinario (one of two annually elected magistrates), where he reputedly carried out "an upright administration of justice, stamping out vagabondage and other threats to the public order." Aycinena graduated from these annually elected positions with the purchase of a permanent place on the Santiago ayuntamiento (*regidor perpetuo*) in the mass sale of cabildo seats in 1761. Significantly, Juan Fermín's bond covering the expenses of his *residencia* (the review of his term in office) was furnished by fellow regidores and then or future kinsmen, Francisco Barrutia, Pedro Loaiza, and Ventura Nájera.[6] Along with his new seat, Aycinena became the cabildo's depositor general (public trustee), an office he held until 1780.

When a series of earthquakes heavily damaged Santiago de Guatemala in 1773, Aycinena eventually allied himself with the Crown and the captain general, who were determined to transfer the capital to a new location against the strident opposition of the church,

Ayuntamiento, Antigua, Guatemala. (The Sidney David Markman Collection, Latin American Library, Tulane University.)

many prominent Guatemalan families, and indeed the majority of the town's inhabitants. Wortman relates that "Aycinena served as the general administrator of supplies to the new city during its construction."[7] To facilitate his task, he was given control of ten years of alcabala revenues, to be used to build the new capital (rather than be remitted to the Crown). Beyond this, he personally financed the building of aqueducts to furnish the new city with water. "After completing the water commission, he discharged other lesser posts" and as of 1780, was "currently ... building a slaughterhouse with his brother-in-law Ventura Naxera."[8] Floyd says that Aycinena "supported the government's order to locate in the new capital with such fervor and financial aid that he was given the right to erect a mansion near the main plaza and certain privileges in connection with locating his own store and warehouses."[9] And indeed, in return for his numerous services, Juan Fermín was rewarded with the choicest plot of land in the new capital—allowing him the only private residence on the central plaza. His place in colonial society could hardly have had a more impressive monument, with the possible exception of his noble title.

Finally, during the American Revolutionary War, which after 1779 engaged Spain and Great Britain in hostilities on the Caribbean coast of Central America, Aycinena provided 30,000 pesos to finance the military campaign of Matías de Gálvez to recapture the strategic Omoa fortress on the Gulf of Honduras.[10] In light of his contributions, the title (supported, of course, with appropriate additional donations to the Crown) appears to have been more than justified.

PILLAR OF ENTERPRISE

Yet if Juan Fermín de Aycinena was a faithful and generous servant of the Spanish state in the Indies, the state served him perhaps just as generously. Throughout his time in Central America, Aycinena assiduously pursued intimate access to political power, through direct control of important offices (see table 16) or influence over important officeholders. For Aycinena and his fellow colonials, the bureaucratic apparatus of

TABLE 16
Public Positions of Juan Fermín de Aycinena

Year	Position
1755	Alférez in Santiago
1757	Lieutenant of the Santiago battalion
1758	Captain of the Santiago battalion
1758	Síndico procurador of the ayuntamiento
1759	Alcalde ordinario
1761	Regidor perpetuo
1761	Depositor general
1762	Administrator of Crown rum monopoly
1769	Administrator of alcabala revenues
1776	General administrator of the *traslado* (transfer)
1784	Alcalde ordinario of Guatemala City
1794	Prior of the consulado de comercio

Source: AGCA, A1.23, Leg. 4633; Woodward, *Class Privilege and Economic Development: The Consulado de Comercio of Guatemala, 1793–1871* (Chapel Hill: University of North Carolina Press, 1966), 11; and Domingo Juarros, *Compendio de la historia del reino de Guatemala, 1500–1800* (Guatemala City: Editorial Piedra Santa, 1981), 198.

the state was one more instrument to be employed in the service of individual or family enterprises.

Some historians have commented on the civic-mindedness of the Guatemalan elite in assuming the responsibilities of government.[11] True enough, some of the positions they occupied were at times onerous and tedious and thus were in some ways undesirable. True also, the offices brought a modicum of social distinction, implicit in a variety of perquisites, including the right to a certain style of dress, conspicuous positions in public processions, and preferred seating at official and religious events. Yet it strains credulity to assert that busy merchants would interrupt their commercial activities from a sense of civic duty or the desire for public recognition alone. While not denying the importance of public-spiritedness, or the prestige that attached to such posts, we should be careful to consider as well the practical and material benefits of officeholding.

Colonial offices could be quite useful, especially offices that yielded access to governmental revenues or conferred the power to make decisions affecting the personal or financial well-being of the officeholder—land apportionment, labor allocation, public contracts (for example, to supply beef or alcohol), and tax collections. Public revenues were often used for private ends.[12] Central America was no exception to this pattern.[13]

Chapter 3 dealt at some length with the kinship network Aycinena joined in Guatemala, many of whose members commanded great wealth and power in the Kingdom. They held their exalted place in part because of their access to lucrative public offices. Bartolomé de Gálvez Corral and his sons, Cristóbal and Manuel, for example, acquired municipal and bureaucratic offices that either generated revenues themselves or facilitated profitable economic activities. Aycinena joined in the "family tradition" of public officeholding. One difference, however, is that he did not seem to be as interested in acquiring the kinds of offices pursued by his predecessors—provincial offices such as alcalde mayor or corregidor posts or graft-rich sinecures such as the Santa Cruzada. This may have had to do, in Aycinena's day, with the unprecedented level of economic integration of the isthmian provinces into the web of power centered in Santiago. The phenomenal expansion of isthmian commerce after midcentury, especially in indigo, provided readier access to more "legitimate" means of enrichment for ambitious colonials. In this respect, a greater specialization of roles in the colonial economy and polity may have become the norm. Moreover, it might be pointed out, most crucial offices were already safely in family hands. In Aycinena's case, direct control of provincial offices was not required to amass wealth and exert power. It was possible, in effect, for Aycinena to direct his affairs from the relative comfort of Santiago.

Nevertheless, as the documents supporting his request for a noble title demonstrate, Aycinena held numerous public offices, again primarily at the municipal level. The Santiago cabildo, reorganized in 1761, provides a succinct index of the closely integrated power structure Aycinena joined through marriage. The cabildo was especially noteworthy for its dominance by merchants involved in the indigo trade and for its control by individuals tied closely to Aycinena. Apart from Aycinena himself, the cabildo of 1761 included two first cousins of his first wife (Simón Larrazábal and Nicolás Obregón), a future father-in law (José de Nájera) and brother-in-law (Ventura Nájera), the future father-in-law of a daughter from his second marriage (Cayetano Pavón), the father-in-law of his peninsular nephew Pedro de Aycinena (Francisco Barrutia), and others with slightly looser family ties (Manuel González Batres, Pedro Ortíz de Letona, Pedro de Loaisa, Fernando Palomo, and Juan Tomás Micheo).[14] For some nineteen years, from 1761 until 1780, Aycinena served as a regidor perpetuo and as depositor general of the cabildos of Santiago or Guatemala City. His post of depositor general, for example, made him the public trustee, or the receiver of property involved in litigation.[15] The position had obvious advantages for a man who would become Central America's leading creditor. Immediate benefits included the right to manage sequestered properties at a small profit. But among the other advantages was some measure of control over the disposition of properties on which he himself had liens. In this respect, Aycinena might well have first crack at acquiring such properties or at least some influence over their resolution. Intimacy with the estates and business dealings of former commercial rivals and their heirs, and the investment opportunities they afforded, was no doubt a tremendous advantage as well.

Aycinena controlled other income-related offices also. In 1762 he was appointed receiver of funds collected from the government's newly established rum monopoly.[16] More important, Aycinena controlled alcabala collections for the Kingdom at least as early as 1769. In August of that year, he arranged to loan out the alcabala revenues of 18,000 pesos for the period of one year, to be repaid at 5 percent interest, to the peninsular merchant Andrés Ortíz de Manzaneda.[17] A similar transaction took place four years later. On June 21, 1773, Aycinena acknowledged that 6,000 pesos of the alcabala had been loaned out to Fernando Palomo and Felipe Manrique of Santiago.[18] A subsequent agreement concerning the rest of the alcabala collections (some 12,000 pesos) identified Aycinena as the "depositario del ramo y sobrante de alcavalas [sic]" (trustee of alcabala revenues, including surplus).[19] Juan Fermín's control of alcabala revenues has strong overtones of the private use of public monies. At the very least, Aycinena had extraordinary access to the purse strings of colonial government in the Kingdom of Guatemala.

And finally, as mentioned earlier, Aycinena controlled tax revenues for the entire Kingdom for a ten-year period following the decision in the mid-1770s to transfer the Central American capital to a new site some thirty miles to the east. According to Wortman, Aycinena was responsible for provisioning the city and directing its construction, allocating labor, and arbitrating land use. To carry out his task, he was granted control of the isthmian alcabala for ten years (some 1.5 million pesos).[20] It was in this context that Wortman stated that "Juan Fermín de Aycinena held more power than any one man in the history of Central America."[21]

Aycinena made the *traslado* (transfer) a family affair. In August 1776 Juan Fermín and his brother-in-law Ventura Nájera provided the fianza for Manuel de Llano (father-in-law of Pedro de Beltranena), who was appointed administrator of the traslado fund and the Tribunal de Cuentas.[22] The traslado also involved Aycinena's commercial contacts outside the Kingdom. In 1776 two intimate business associates of Aycinena in Mexico City, his brother, Pedro de Aycinena, and Francisco Yraeta, were named by Mexican Viceroy Antonio María Bucareli as Mexican depositors for construction funds.[23] Public and private monies, it seems, flowed through the same channels, through the same hands, and perhaps into the same pockets.

Aycinena's immediate kin also acquired positions of status and power. We have already noted in this and earlier chapters the prevalence of Aycinena family members throughout the colonial bureaucracy. Offices held by his peninsular nephews and his children might be considered to be almost directly under his control. His nephew Pedro de Aycinena y Larraín served as alcalde ordinario of Guatemala City in 1785 and 1807. He was elected biennial regidor in 1783–84, 1788–89, and 1792–93. And in 1794 he became a permanent councilman as well as depositor general, the post held formerly by his uncle and which Pedro held until 1799. Pedro remained a councilman until 1806, when he renounced his seat supposedly because of advanced age.[24] Juan Fermín's other nephew, Pedro de Beltranena, was regidor and alcalde ordinario of Guatemala City as of 1783.

Aycinena's oldest children, Vicente and José Alejandro, also held useful offices near the end of their father's life. Vicente held the posts of *síndico* (counsel), *alférez mayor* (standard-bearer, 1793), and *fiel ejecutor* (inspector of weights and measures, 1798). He served as a regidor perpetuo of the ayuntamiento until at least 1806. José Alejandro was an attorney who also served as a colonel in the colonial militia, rector of the University of San Carlos (1797), consul of the merchant guild (1798), alcalde ordinario of the Guatemalan cabildo (1803), director of the Economic Society (1810), and interim intendant of El Salvador (1811), before moving to Spain in 1812, where he became a councillor of state and later a member of the Council of the Indies.[25] Obviously, these posts brought not only prestige but considerable opportunities to assert power as well.

TIES WITH THE BUREAUCRACY

Still, direct office holding by Juan Fermín de Aycinena and his immediate family members was not the only, and probably not the most important, source of their access to political power in late colonial Central America. Aycinena maintained close relations, mostly of a financial nature, with a variety of colonial officials spread throughout the isthmus.[26] Imperial officers in the Kingdom of Guatemala included the captain general, judges of the audiencia, treasury officials, regional governors (alcaldes mayores, corregidores, and gobernadores), their tenientes, and military officers. The captain general post and the seats on the audiencia were almost universally excluded from native sons or *radicados* (peninsulars "rooted" in the colony by family ties). Still, even the highest officials were not completely immune to the influence of local notables, regardless of Crown efforts to insulate them. Particularly in an area as remote and as relatively unimportant for Spain as Central America, with its small European population amid a "sea of Indians," illicit business dealings and other occasions for extralegal cooperation were practically unavoidable and unpreventable. And, besides, even if the highest colonial officials managed somehow to remain pure, the positions immediately below them were usually held by individuals native to or rooted in the Kingdom of Guatemala.

We should be careful not to presume too much from Juan Fermín's financial ties with colonial officials. Some ties may have reflected only a onetime loan from a leading colonial banker. Specific cases in which Aycinena benefited from a friendly or financially beholden judge's decision are difficult to establish. At a minimum, the connections with officials were potential sources of valuable assistance. If, as the anthropologist Richard N. Adams argues, wealth for colonial elites represented "stored power," so too did the connections with colonial officials.[27]

CAPTAINS GENERAL AND OIDORES

We know relatively little about Juan Fermín de Aycinena's relations with Central America's highest officers. Nine individuals served as captain general during Juan Fermín's time in Guatemala (see table 17). The evidence we do have is at best suggestive rather than conclusive. For example, Martín de Mayorga (1773–79)

TABLE 17
Guatemalan Captains General in the Time of Juan Fermín de Aycinena, 1750–1800

José Vásquez Priego[a]	1752–53
Juan Velarde y Cienfuegos[b]	1753–54
Alonso de Arcos y Moreno	1754–60
Juan Velarde y Cienfuegos[b]	1760–61
Alonso Fernández de Heredia	1765–66
Pedro de Salazar y Herrera[a]	1765–71
Juan Gonzáles Bustillo y Villaseñor[b]	1771–73
Martín de Mayorga	1773–79
Matías de Gálvez	1779–83
José de Estachería	1783–89
Bernardo Troncoso Martínez	1789–94
José Domás y Valle	1794–1801

Notes: [a] died in office
[b] interim, assumed office as senior oidor.
Source: Juarros, *Compendio*, 147–49.

counted on Aycinena's support in the divisive traslado decision. Matías de Gálvez (1779–83) was supportive of Juan Fermín's application for a noble title, probably in gratitude for his support during the war with Great Britain. José de Estachería (1783–89) was reputedly a supporter of capital merchant interests against those of the provinces.

Juan Fermín had explicit connections with at least three captains general: Pedro Salazar, José de Estachería, and Bernardo Troncoso Martínez. As of 1771 Aycinena owed the estate of the late Pedro Salazar some 19,000 pesos. This debt most likely resulted from litigation involving the deceased captain general's estate, which presumably fell to Aycinena to administer in his capacity as depositor general. If this is the full extent of Aycinena's connection with Salazar, it does not tell us a great deal about Aycinena's dealings with Salazar during the latter's term.

The other two cases are perhaps more intriguing. At the end of their respective terms, both José de Estachería and Bernardo Troncoso Martínez appointed Aycinena their representative in their residencias. They did so to allow themselves to retire from their positions without remaining at their posts for the duration of their judicial reviews, as they were legally obligated to do. Moreover, in identical transactions of 1789 and 1794, Aycinena's family members and subordinates undertook to cover all expenses and financial judgments coming out of the judicial proceedings.[28] As the Kingdom's most distinguished subject, with unquestioned resources at his command, the Marqués de Aycinena might simply have been the only individual whose prestigious backing would overcome objections from Madrid or elsewhere to Estachería and Troncoso leaving their posts prematurely. But these proceedings might just as well represent a favor returned, if not for specific actions (or inactions), then perhaps for a generalized pattern of friendship between the region's highest officer and its wealthiest inhabitant.

Aycinena had significant financial relations with at least two audiencia judges. As of 1777 Joaquín de Plaza, an oidor from 1773 to 1781, owed Aycinena some 4,570 pesos. Even more notable, perhaps, was the case of Eusebio Beleña. Beleña served in Guatemala from 1773 to 1777, before moving on to the audiencia of Mexico City. On leaving Guatemala, he had a debt to Aycinena of 6,000 pesos.[29] In Mexico, Beleña had ties with two of Aycinena's important Mexico City associates, the consulado merchants Francisco Yraeta and Pedro de Aycinena, who were Mexican depositors of the goods and monies destined for the construction of a new Guatemalan capital. Connections of money and power, of trade and politics, were not severed by imperial borders. Needless to say, Aycinena's financial leverage against one or more oidores, members of the highest court in the land, gave him a tremendous advantage in cases that came before it involving himself or his friends and family. Certainly they increased the chances of receiving a favorable judgment.

In an excellent example of the benefits accruing from close ties or preferential access to the audiencia, in 1791 Pedro de Aycinena y Larraín "designated Manuel Riviero of Vera Paz to represent him in receiving from the alcalde mayor of Vera Paz, 12,000 pesos belonging to the community fund [*cajas de comunidad*], conceded to him for personal use (to be repaid with interest) by the Supreme Tribunal of the Real Audiencia."[30] Once again, public revenues were destined for the private use of the well-to-do and the well connected.

Aycinena's power over high officials was by no means absolute. He was simply the most powerful of numerous claimants of royal patronage. He did not always prevail. In 1767, for example, the cabildo of Tecpan convinced the captain general to nullify their "forced contract" with Aycinena to furnish Indians to lead a dozen indigo-laden mules in the dangerous trek to the coast.[31]

LESSER OFFICIALS

Lesser royal officials were on the payroll as well, including new Bourbon appointees whose jobs had been created for the explicit purpose of guarding the imperial treasury from the clutches of local notables. This included officials in Guatemala City. As *contador de cuentas reales* (royal accountant), Salvador Domínguez was a watchdog of the imperial revenues flowing into Guatemala City. As of 1777 he owed Aycinena 2,795 pesos. At the same time, Miguel Arnais, another treasury official, owed Aycinena 400 pesos. Their impartiality was at least compromised by such encumbrances. And Juan Fermín's brother-in-law Francisco Nájera, another treasury official in Guatemala City, compounded his family ties with financial obligations to Juan Fermín of 698 pesos.[32]

Officials in strategic posts on the Caribbean and Pacific coasts were also on the lengthy roster of Aycinena debtors. These included Francisco Arroyo (154 pesos) and Antonio Verganza (1,008 pesos) in Omoa, both of whose debts were written off by 1771. In

September 1779 Omoa commandant Antonio Fernandín made arrangements to obtain a 2,000-peso loan from Aycinena.[33] Similarly, in Sonsonate, the royal official Manuel de Larreta owed 1,105 pesos in 1777. For officials whose primary tasks involved shutting off illicit trade, being financially beholden to the leading long-distance trader in Central America was an obvious threat to their desired impartiality.

GOBERNADORES, CORREGIDORES, ALCALDES MAYORES

The best-documented ties between Juan Fermín de Aycinena and colonial officials are those he maintained with regional or provincial magistrates—alcaldes mayores, corregidores, and gobernadores. This is no great surprise. Illicit relations between merchants and provincial officials were an expected and almost accepted part of colonial life. The expenses of entering office and the relatively meager salaries those offices provided practically encouraged illegal ties between officials and their merchant sponsors. The provincial official's favorable or dominant position with respect to forced trade, the control of labor, the provisioning of miners and planters, and the access to exportable commodities made him a desirable, even a crucial, connection for wholesalers. Their assignment to remote areas minimized the possibilities of supervision. Fines levied during a term-ending *juicio de residencia* (judicial review) were factored in as part of the risks of illicit trade. For merchants, these costs were simply part of the price of doing business in colonial Central America.

Aycinena maintained financial connections with a variety of strategically placed regional officials.

Tegucigalpa, heart of the Honduran silver-mining district, was one crucial locale. As Floyd has shown, the alcalde mayor there was usually the leading aviador of Honduran miners, financing operations, provisioning mine owners with mercury and salt, and controlling the labor drafts essential to mining success.[34] The former alcalde mayor, Francisco Nicolás Busto y Bustamante, owed Aycinena 6,500 pesos as of 1768. Considered doubtful of repayment even then, the debt was written off completely by 1771. The Tegucigalpa alcalde mayor, Gerónimo Lacayo, owed Aycinena over 2,000 pesos in 1768. And Ignacio Domezaín, appointed expressly as part of an official housecleaning, owed Aycinena 381 pesos in 1777.[35]

Aycinena had helpful ties in other regions as well. In 1768 Sebastián Labayru, the corregidor at Realejo, Nicaragua, owed Aycinena 11,724 pesos. Realejo was a principal port of entry and departure in the isthmus's vital Pacific trade. In June 1769 Aycinena delegated powers to represent him in commercial matters to Domingo Cavello, governor of Nicaragua from 1766 to 1776. Aycinena maintained additional links to the Nicaraguan province of Costa Rica. In April 1765 Pablo Montiel y Coronado, the *adelantado* (literally, "advancer," or frontier ruler) of Costa Rica, stated that he had an account with Captain Juan Fermín de Aycinena.[36] Two years later Pablo's relative and successor, Diego Montiel y Coronado, delegated his *poder especial* to Juan Fermín de Aycinena.[37] In 1773 Aycinena underwrote the *media annata* (officeholder's bond, equal to half a year's salary) of Juan Fernández Bobadilla, *gobernador provisto* (acting governor) of Costa Rica.[38] Finally, the Costa Rican area of Nicoya seems to have been of especially lasting interest to

Aycinena. Corregidor Manuel de Mella owed Aycinena substantial sums throughout the 1760s and 1770s. Mella had debts exceeding 10,000 pesos in 1768, 8,000 pesos in 1771, and 1,480 pesos in 1777.[39] In 1772 Mella's successor, Juan Antonio de la Peña, who would marry Juan Fermín's first wife's cousin, obtained from Aycinena 4,334 pesos in goods and cash to develop his office. As of 1777 de la Peña had a debt with Aycinena of 2,475 pesos.[40] Closer to home, in the Indian textile manufacturing center of Totonicapán, the corregidor Matías de Manzanares owed Aycinena over 11,000 pesos in 1777.[41] In July 1773 Aycinena furnished Rafael Pérez, justicia mayor of Escuintla and Guazacapán, 2,021 pesos worth of mercantile goods.[42] Turning the tables, in Guazacapán, Juan Fermín owed the alcalde mayor Juan de Rivera some 2,717 pesos in 1768; and in Chiquimula, as of 1771, he owed the alcalde mayor José González Rancaño some 1,078 pesos.

As the discussion of Aycinena's business endeavors demonstrated, his most vital area was El Salvador. Close ties with crucial officials were an important part of his effort to dominate the indigo trade. A typical case perhaps is that of the Salvadoran merchant and minor official, Francisco Becerril. Becerril served on occasion as a teniente, or subordinate, to the alcalde mayor of El Salvador. He maintained a lengthy if troubled relationship with Aycinena and other merchants of Santiago. Becerril's ties with Aycinena commenced before 1760. A merchant and resident of San Miguel, Becerril stated in October 1760 that his debts new and old to Capt. Juan Fermín de Aycinena amounted to 3,900 pesos.[43] Over the years, Becerril had a great deal of difficulty remaining solvent. In October 1767 the unfortunate Becerril had fled to the Convent of San Juan de Dios, in

Santiago, to seek refuge from his many creditors. Becerril owed Aycinena and other capital city merchants more than 18,000 pesos. Aycinena, together with Juan Tomás de Micheo and Pedro de Echandía, fellow Santiago merchants and Navarran natives, agreed to take Becerril off the hook. They renegotiated his debt, bringing his total obligation to them to 20,826 pesos, to be repaid in indigo within two years.[44] Three years later, however, Aycinena was again obliged to cover debts of Becerril, this time totaling 7,770 pesos.[45] Becerril's vulnerability to Aycinena over so many years suggests at the very least a rich opportunity for the use of a local colonial official for his commercial interests.

Bernabé de la Torre Trassiera, Alcalde Mayor

The most fascinating chapter in Juan Fermín de Aycinena's relations with Salvadoran officials, however, involves Bernabé de la Torre Trassiera, alcalde mayor of El Salvador.[46] Almost immediately after he assumed office in 1757, de la Torre became embroiled in controversy. In August 1757 he was formally charged with improper conduct by the cabildos of San Salvador, San Miguel, and San Vicente, and he was removed by order of the audiencia of Guatemala shortly thereafter. The ensuing litigation, in Guatemala and in Spain, consumed almost fourteen years. Amazingly, de la Torre was restored to office in October 1771. The story opens a fascinating window into the politics of Bourbon Central America and raises interesting questions about Aycinena's connection with the state and with the dominant family network he had joined in 1755.

De la Torre was a native of Burgos, connected through marriage to the prominent Tagle y Bracho family of Peru.[47] Prior to arriving in Central America, he was apparently active in South American commerce, and, in fact, he stationed his family in Buenos Aires while he took office in San Salvador. He was probably not prepared for the harsh reception he received in the isthmus. De la Torre took office at a time of rising tension, spurred by the expansion of indigo. In 1755 Spanish merchants and Salvadoran planters had come to blows over the former's efforts to acquire property and offices in the province. This set the scene for what happened next.

In 1757 the cabildos of San Salvador, San Vicente, and San Miguel issued a joint denunciation of the new alcalde mayor. They charged him with excessive demands on Indians and with assigning them to "a few of the most powerful families" and asked that he be removed.[48] The complaints against de la Torre prompted the audiencia of Guatemala to dispatch the oidor Juan Antonio Velarde y Cienfuegos to San Salvador as *visitador* (royal investigator). Quickly completing his investigation, Velarde removed the alleged offender from his post. De la Torre's replacement (as interim alcalde mayor) was none other than Cristóbal de Gálvez Corral, uncle of Aycinena's wife, Ana María Carrillo y Gálvez. The plot thickens: one of those instigating the suit against de la Torre was Gálvez's first cousin and brother-in-law, Agustín Cilieza. Agustín Cilieza Velasco y Varón (1711–86) was an hacendado and regidor in San Salvador.[49] With de la Torre's removal, the Gálvez-Cilieza axis gained an almost proprietary control of the alcalde mayor post for more than a dozen years. The prompt intervention of the audiencia suggests that the Gálvez Corral network enjoyed an unusually close relationship with the high court, which in turn seemed unusually solicitous and responsive to its needs.

There is no doubt that de la Torre was commercially active in El Salvador. He owned several properties in the province.[50] De la Torre's commercial background and property holdings indicate that he sought to take full advantage of the commercial opportunities traditionally attached to his position.[51] But in so doing, he ran up against an entrenched oligarchy. Perhaps, as he was charged, de la Torre appropriated the Salvadoran labor supply for his own haciendas, or those of his associates. De la Torre defended himself before the Crown by stating that his efforts to enforce royal legislation protecting the Indians of El Salvador from excessive labor in the indigo haciendas and factories and from the notorious repartimientos of labor and goods conflicted with the interests of the local oligarchy. He portrayed himself as a victim of the greedy Gálvez Corral and his kinsmen.[52] That his arguments ultimately succeeded illustrates both de la Torre's powers of persuasion and, perhaps more notably, the power of his allies at the Spanish court. In a sense, the de la Torre case represents a victory for the Bourbon attack on local establishments in Central America.

At that point, however, a curious series of transactions took place. With de la Torre's restoration, his financier was none other than Juan Fermín de Aycinena, with his nephews Pedro Aycinena y Larraín and Pedro de Beltranena acting as guarantors. On June 5, 1771, de la Torre conferred his *poder generalissimo* (broadest powers) on Aycinena.[53] On the same day, the Guatemalan merchant Mateo de Irungaray, acting on de la Torre's behalf, contracted a debt with Aycinena of 51,932 pesos.[54] The huge loan was added to an existing balance of 65,057 pesos (15,684 in cash and 49,373 in goods). De la Torre had pledged to repay the cash loan in indigo at the prices determined by the indigo fair of Apastepeque. The 49,373 pesos worth of merchandise would be repaid in dyes at the prices set at the Santiago fair in 1773.[55] But even this was not all. On January 13, 1773, de la Torre contracted a last obligation to Aycinena of 26,134 pesos. His total debt, built up in the furnishing of his office, amounted to the staggering sum of 143,124 pesos.[56] It is the largest single debt to Juan Fermín de Aycinena that appears anywhere in available documentation. Aycinena's ties with Bernabé de la Torre represented a major effort to dominate trade and production in El Salvador.

Alas, de la Torre, perhaps worn out by his long legal struggle, died in 1773. This ended what had the makings of a beautiful friendship. The disposition of de la Torre's debts to Aycinena is not clear. Aycinena's patent of nobility hints that Aycinena wrote many of them off.[57] We do know that de la Torre's son, Bernabé Santiago de la Torre y Tagle, became a close associate of Aycinena in the 1770s. In fact, the younger de la Torre supervised the construction of Aycinena's magnificent residence in the new capital city, completed in the 1780s at a cost of over 90,000 pesos.[58] This may have represented an effort to repay the monumental debts of his father. Ironically, the Salvadoran alcalde mayor post, so bitterly contested for more than a dozen years beginning in the late 1750s, returned once again to the hands of family members of Aycinena shortly after de la Torre's demise. Melchor de Mencos Varón de Berrieza, cousin of Ana María Carrillo y Gálvez, assumed the post in 1774.[59] He was succeeded by Manuel Fadrique y Goyena in 1777. The colonial establishment held.

One of the most interesting aspects of the entire episode is the fact that the very people confronting de la Torre were Aycinena's own family members by marriage. By supporting de la Torre, it might appear that Aycinena was going against the interests of his own family network. True, it might be significant that with the death of Ana María Carrillo y Gálvez in 1768 Aycinena's connections with the Gálvez Corral extended family network had diminished somewhat. In 1771, at the time he undertook to support the office-holding of de la Torre, Aycinena was on the verge of establishing intimate family relations with the powerful Nájera family. But the Nájera family too was closely tied by blood and marriage to the Gálvez Corrals. So the change probably means little if anything. Obviously, the timing of Aycinena's alliance with de la Torre is critical. In fact, the crucial connection appears to have been established *after* de la Torre's restoration in 1771. Aycinena had indirect dealings with de la Torre as early as April 1769, if not before, when de la Torre signed on as fiador for Tomás Escamilla, who refinanced an earlier loan from Aycinena.[60] Escamilla managed de la Torre's estates during the course of his legal battles. Certainly Aycinena and de la Torre knew of each other from the time of de la Torre's removal (if not before). But the establishment of a major partnership between official and merchant came afterward.

A likely explanation is that with de la Torre's legal victory, Aycinena decided to make the most of his family's misfortune, which after all seemed irreversible.

One might keep in mind, moreover, that the reversal of family fortunes occurred after more than a dozen years of its possession of the alcalde mayor post. Regardless, in 1771, Aycinena joined the winner. Siding with de la Torre, he stood to gain substantial control of Salvadoran indigo production and, at the same time, the regional market for imported goods through de la Torre's control of the repartimiento of goods. In so doing, Aycinena maneuvered to assert himself as the supreme power broker in Guatemala. The de la Torre affair might well have announced, in effect, Juan Fermín's supplanting of the aging Cristóbal de Gálvez as head of the Santiago oligarchy. If that endeavor was cut short by de la Torre's death, Aycinena reasserted the claim in the course of the traslado of the capital. His acquisition of a noble title placed Aycinena's position beyond all doubt.

CONCLUSION

Juan Fermín de Aycinena established financial connections with strategic colonial officials in a wide array of positions and locations. He exercised personally a variety of colonial offices that not only attested to his power and position but were instrumental to those very attainments. He was particularly active in the ayuntamiento of Santiago/Guatemala City. When that body failed to protect adequately the interests of the Guatemalan merchant community, Aycinena led the fight for a merchant guild in Guatemala. The merchants were frustrated by their inability to dominate provincial courts. Many recalled bitterly the unsuccessful legal battle over Asian cinnamon. The struggle bore fruit in 1793, when the Council of the Indies conceded rights to establish a merchant guild.

As noted, Aycinena became the first president of the new body. Although this was only one of several new guilds, and thus reflective of a wider Bourbon strategy to limit the power of Cádiz, Lima, and Mexico City, it also illustrated the Guatemalan merchants' powers of persuasion.

A curious item unearthed in the Yraeta papers may have something to do with that persuasiveness. In his summary of Juan Fermín de Aycinena's account in 1795, Mexico City merchant Francisco Ignacio de Yraeta made an intriguing entry. It reads,

> On 14 April, [1795], I charged 10,000 pesos [to Aycinena's account] that I have sent in cash to Sor. D. Juan José Villalengua, Counselor of His Majesty (for the Indies) in virtue of his letter [orn.] that he sent me dated 23 of October [1794] according to the receipt that I signed.[61]

Why would Yraeta be sending 10,000 pesos to a member of the Council of the Indies on Aycinena's behalf? Was the offering a not-too-subtle inducement? And for what services? We do not know. Regardless of the meaning of this intriguing transaction, there is no doubt that Aycinena exploited the institutions of the state to advance his private interests. At the same time, Aycinena became an important Central American institution himself, a purveyor of wealth and patronage. As such, he became the object of other individuals' efforts to advance their needs. Thus Bernabé de la Torre and other officials sought to take advantage of their relationship with Aycinena as much as the reverse was true.

The commingling of state and private interests, inherent in the private use of public office, was the essence of the "colonial establishments" that the Spanish Bourbons tried so hard to eliminate from their distant realms. They faced an almost impossible task. Colonial elite families in the eighteenth century maintained a foothold in every conceivable area of strategic or bureaucratic importance.[62] Office holding, and influence over officeholders, helped to make them elites in the first place. Colonial Central America, it seems, exhibited an attitude similar to that of Porfirian Mexico, where, Alan Knight tells us, "politics was less a high-minded Gladstonian striving in the public interest, than a source of power, security and patronage."[63] We now turn to look at Aycinena's relations with the church establishment in colonial Central America. Were they similarly "high-minded"?

Chapter 7

Aycinena and the Church

The Catholic Church occupied a central place in colonial Central America. Apart from its obvious religious functions, the church supervised education, maintained hospitals, asylums, and orphanages, and oversaw numerous other essential and charitable enterprises. In the absence of banking institutions, the church served as a leading supplier of credit. In a volatile economy, church agencies were a reasonably secure field of investment. The network of churchmen throughout the isthmus provided essential unity. Indeed, in the view of the late Adriaan Van Oss, the Kingdom of Guatemala was held together not so much by its military or civil bureaucracy as by its churchmen.[1]

The church pervaded nearly all aspects of isthmian life. And much like the state to which it was so often and so closely linked, it could be manipulated for the private benefit of individuals and families. As was the case with the state bureaucracy, use of the isthmian church apparatus was often vital to the success, or not, of ambitious colonials. As was the state, the church was a crucial source of wealth and patronage and, therefore, a key to power.

As with the state, Juan Fermín de Aycinena both served and was served by the church establishment in Central America. His noble title, awarded in 1783, specifically commended him for his service to the church during his nearly two-decade residence in Central America to that point. Aycinena was a patron of the Colegio de Misioneros Franciscos de Cristo Crucificado as well as the Reverendas Madres de Capuchinas, "devoting his wealth and person and counsel to both communities."[2] Through his patronage of the Colegio de Cristo Crucificado, moreover, Aycinena furthered missionary activities in Costa Rica. Almost certainly, Aycinena was active in one of the cofradías of Santiago and Guatemala City.[3] Ultimately, he contributed two of his children (from his third marriage) to the church as well.[4] Aycinena's contemporary Father Domingo Juarros praised him in the highest terms not only for his title but also for his efforts on behalf of the less fortunate.[5]

If the saintly Navarran cared for the needy and graciously endowed the church, he reaped substantial benefits as well. If they were not unique to him, or the main foundation of his success, the benefits he derived from his use of the church apparatus nevertheless proved extremely helpful. The church was one more institutional support of the Aycinena enterprise. In this regard, his ties with the church establishment assumed

Cathedral of La Merced, Antigua, Guatemala. (The Sidney David Markman Collection, Latin American Library, Tulane University.)

a character similar to those he maintained with the state and its agents—mutually beneficial relations serving multifarious ends.

As we have noted, the responsibilities of the Central American church were divided between the secular hierarchy and the mendicant orders. The secular hierarchy in the Kingdom descended from the archbishop of Guatemala (a post created in 1744) through the various members of the *cabildo eclesiástico* (cathedral chapter)—dean, *maestreescuela* (supervisor of schools), chantry, and *canónigo* (canon)—down to the level of the parish priest and his auxiliaries. These were the most prestigious and desired posts in the Central American church. Secular parishes were administered by beneficed clergy (the *cura beneficios, proprietarios,* or *propios*). The secular parish priest was to reside in his assigned district and was responsible for administering the sacraments to his parishioners. For these duties, he derived an income directly from his congregation.[6] The extreme shortage of secular posts made for intense competition for those that came open. The "best families" enjoyed preferential access to them.[7]

Once acquired, beneficed clergy resisted subdividing their parishes, even when they grew too large for one priest to serve adequately. To do so would diminish their revenues. Instead, to help them carry out their duties, the *beneficios* made wide use of unbeneficed auxiliaries, whom they paid a salary out of general parish funds. In the 1770s, Archbishop Pedro Cortés y Larraz called the auxiliaries "most pure mercenaries whose only objective . . . is to gain money."[8] In fairness, the unbeneficed clergy had little choice given the nature of the system. On occasion, the competitive ethic fostered by the scarcity of benefices encouraged exemplary behavior among secular clergy who looked to gain promotions by impressing superiors through their good works. But it just as often encouraged extracurricular activities, including illicit commerce, that deepened the abuses the system inflicted on those it was meant to serve.

The aggressive individualism demanded of the secular clergy stood in contrast to the more egalitarian ethic of the friars, who lived communally and rotated among the various doctrinas maintained by their orders. For most of the colonial period, the countryside was dominated by the mendicants, principally Franciscans, Dominicans, and Mercederians. Despite the Crown goal of "secularizing" rural parishes (i.e., transferring them from the orders to hierarchical control) as soon as feasible, religious orders remained responsible for extending and maintaining the faith in frontier areas well into the late colonial era. Friars used and even encouraged Indian ignorance of Spanish, and bureaucratic ignorance of Indian languages, to maintain their indispensability.[9]

Nevertheless, in the eighteenth century the state continued to secularize rural parishes. Secularization reflected the centralizing tendencies that were at the heart of the Bourbon reforms. One by-product of this policy was to accelerate the integration of the provinces into the economic web fanning out from the capital city. In this respect, secularization offered obvious benefits to the merchants of the capital.[10]

Through its varied agencies, the church and churchmen in Central America came to control extensive wealth. Indeed, Van Oss calls the church "in the most prosaic sense . . . the greatest business of the colonial period."[11] The church establishment received part of its considerable wealth from the state. In accordance with its responsibilities of royal patronage, the state was to collect the tithe, or diezmo, on the "fruits of the earth," roughly a tenth of a parish's agricultural produce. In 1769 church tributes approached 200,000 pesos.[12] The Crown was to keep one-ninth of the revenues to cover the costs of collection, which probably fell well short of the expenses involved. The revenues raised theoretically were to be devoted to the diverse church functions and agents. In practice, the bishops and cathedral chapter (cabildo eclesiástico) absorbed all diezmo revenues. Individuals and families with close ties to the chapter stood to benefit from its control of revenues.[13]

In Hispanicized parishes, pious works (obras pías) and chaplaincies, or capellanías, provided additional sources of revenue for secular priests. In 1769 cofradía collections furnished some 265,000 pesos.[14] With their activities free from taxation, cofradías served as tax shelters. Church agencies often made their funds available for colonial businessmen.[15] The Santa Cruzada was another lucrative endeavor. In Central America, it had figured prominently in the fortunes of Aycinena's relatives. Receipts from the sale of church bulls (most sold illegally to Indians) were sent to the metropolitan church in Mexico, where they were either used or sent to Spain—the only church monies that were formally sent out of the colony. "Investments" in the Santa Cruzada allowed merchants to evade the alcabala. They provided a cover for the purchase of indigo and other commodities.[16]

In addition to the institutional support the church gave isthmian businessmen, individual clergy played an important commercial role. The church apparatus abetted the activities of colonial entrepreneurs by placing presumably trustworthy Hispanicized persons in remote and otherwise inaccessible areas. Through necessity, ambition, or avarice, they were disposed to participate in commerce. Although clerical business activities worried the colonial authorities from the beginning of the colony, there was little that could be done. Effective supervision of rural clerics proved as difficult to enforce as oversight of officials of the state.[17]

By the eighteenth century, nearly all isthmian clergy, except for the archbishop and the various provincials, were likely to be creoles and therefore rooted in the colony. Many conducted business, individually or with their families. Some priests gained assignments in areas where they or their families were economically active.[18]

Despite the diversion of official revenues to the cathedral chapter, the incomes of parish priests were still impressive. Devices such as the *ración* and the *servicio*, fees for sacraments, and the income generated by cofradía activities more than made up for the loss of the tithe.[19] Van Oss estimated that in 1802 the average salary of twenty sample parish priests was 2,265 pesos. This compared favorably with an audiencia judge's salary of 2,757 pesos. At the same time, parish expenditures were subject mostly to the discretion of the cura propio. On average, 93 percent of revenues went to clergy themselves, divided roughly 70 percent to 30 percent between the beneficiado and his auxiliaries. In fact, there was little investment in the parishes. For instance, no parish hospitals were ever established.

So, if the clergy did not spend the church monies on their parishioners, what did they do with it? Many, it turns out, invested in commerce, either in their own enterprises or in the ventures of isthmian entrepreneurs. They rarely distinguished between church business and their own.[20] And if a colonial merchant were to operate in any remote areas at all, he had to deal with the local priest. The strategic position of clergy in the countryside made them a "select rural elite."[21]

Individually and collectively, clergymen were some of the wealthiest, best-connected, and best-placed people in the Kingdom of Guatemala. Churchmen became part of the isthmian distribution and collection network for goods and capital, an integral part of the colonial economy. At the same time, they furnished a vast intelligence network, providing essential information about political and market conditions in distant areas. In short, the importance of the Catholic Church in Central America rested not only on its spiritual mission, or its role as an agency of social control, or even its educational and charitable functions; it was important also for its commercial contributions. As he did with the state, Juan Fermín de Aycinena exploited these opportunities.

FRIENDS IN HIGH PLACES

Aycinena enjoyed close ties with many of the isthmian high clergy. Of course, this had as much to do with the church officers protecting themselves by lining up with the wealthy and powerful as the reverse. Once Aycinena had reached the apex of Central American society, such ties naturally came his way. The most obvious connections were family ties. Aycinena was related to numerous churchmen by blood or marriage. Although we should be careful not to fall prey to a simplistic familial determinism, such ties provided real or potential allies in strategic positions. We have already noted the considerable wealth controlled by the church. But also, having relatives directly involved in, or even in control of, decisions determining the admittance of students to universities, the occupants of university chairs, the allocation of benefices or other church posts, and the collection and distribution of church monies helps to explain why such a narrow social group monopolized power in colonial Central America. Having high church officials as relatives might even provide a means of evading inconvenient Crown and papal strictures (e.g., on the marriages of first cousins).

Probably the most important Aycinena relative in the cathedral chapter was Dr. Miguel de Cilieza y Velasco (1707–68). The uncle of Aycinena's first wife, Father Miguel became *provisor* (ecclesiastical deputy) and vicar general of León, Nicaragua, in 1738. In Guatemala he became a *presbítero domiciliario* (beneficed clergyman), *sinodal examinador* (supervisor of salaries), canónigo (1743), maestreescuela (1761), and afterward provisor and vicar general of Santiago. Cilieza held degrees from the University of San Carlos in both civil and canon law. He served as rector of his alma mater in 1743, 1752, 1755, and 1758. In 1766 he was named bishop of Adramittio and ended his career as the bishop of Chiapas, where he died in 1768.[22] Cilieza attained such prominence at the very time that his first cousins Cristóbal and Manuel de Gálvez Corral had consolidated their grip on local politics and provincial administration in El Salvador.[23]

Another powerful family connection was Juan José González Batres. If Cilieza was well established at the time Juan Fermín arrived in Santiago, González Batres's career paralleled in ecclesiastical circles Aycinena's rise in commercial and civic prominence. González Batres was the brother-in law of Melchor de Mencos y Varón (alcalde mayor of El Salvador and a cousin of Ana María Carrillo y Gálvez). González Batres was a canónigo in 1761, maestreescuela in 1767, chantry in 1773, archdeacon in 1777, and dean in 1779.[24]

Aycinena maintained ties of a financial nature with other prestigious church officers. Santiago native Tomás Alvarado y Guzmán became canónigo of the cabildo eclesiástico in 1730. In that same year he served as rector of the University of San Carlos. He was chantry in 1758 and archdeacon by 1761. On July 4, 1765, Alvarado y Guzmán, "being gravely ill," named Juan Fermín de Aycinena *albacea* (estate executor).[25] As of 1771, Aycinena controlled 6,593 pesos of the Guzmán estate. Juan Fermín founded a capellanía of 2,650 pesos in Alvarado's name in December 1785. In the twenty years between the original empowerment and the time he implemented its provisions, Aycinena enjoyed rights to manage the Alvarado estate. Aycinena named as patron of the capellanía and *capellán*, Pedro de Guzmán y Alvarado, a *clérigo diácono* (secular priest).[26] In the process of transferring the proceeds of Alvarado's estate to the late cleric's kinsman and colleague, Aycinena's ties with influential clergy passed on to a new generation.

Another intriguing contact among high church officials was Father Juan José de Ganuza. A native of Mirafuentes, Navarre, Ganuza was also a merchant heavily involved in the importation of European and Oriental goods.[27] His cousin Pedro de Ganuza was an extremely prominent merchant in Mexico City and up to his death in 1769, a commercial associate of

Aycinena. In December 1769 (perhaps on learning of his cousin's death) Ganuza named his fellow Navarrans Juan Fermín de Aycinena, Pedro de Aycinena, and Pedro de Beltranena his executors.[28] In this capacity, Juan Fermín established an obra pía in his name in December 1787.[29] Juan Fermín and Father Juan José occasionally shared common commercial interests.[30] As of 1771 Aycinena owed Ganuza a total of 9,896 pesos. The correspondence from the Mexican merchant and Ganuza's family member Francisco Ignacio de Yraeta suggests that Aycinena's links with Juan José Ganuza were almost of a familial nature.[31]

Estate records document other ties. As of 1768 Canónigo Antonio Marcos de Soto owed Aycinena some 229 pesos. Soto became canónigo in 1735 and was the chapter's treasurer in 1752. The former canónigo José de la Guardia owed Aycinena 2,847 pesos. As of 1768 Juan Fermín had already written off 90 pesos owed by the canónigo Miguel Cabrejo. Although these sums are relatively meager, they do reflect clear financial ties between Aycinena and high church officials. These connections, like those with royal officials, presented significant opportunities to influence the church hierarchy.

PATRON OF MONASTICS

Aycinena also maintained ties with prominent monastics in the Kingdom of Guatemala. As of 1771, for example, he owed 448 pesos to Father Buenaventura Lem, provincial of the Convent Nuestra Señora de la Merced in Santiago. Aycinena served as principal lay spokesman for the Colegio de Cristo Crucificado and for the Capuchin Mothers, both of Santiago and later

Guatemala City.³² Patronage of the Colegio de Cristo Crucificado was a role Aycinena apparently had inherited from his uncle, Cristóbal de Gálvez Corral.³³ As *síndico apostólico* (lay agent) of the Colegio de Cristo Crucificado, Aycinena enjoyed some measure of control over the destination of its revenues.³⁴ As of 1768, for example, he had at his disposal some 1,353 pesos belonging to the Colegio, money that "exists in his power as síndico." But on the whole, his patronage of monastics was probably a losing venture, at least from a financial standpoint. As of 1771 the fathers owed their patron some 196 pesos. As of 1777 their debt to him was 2,125. Similarly, in 1777 the Capuchin Mothers owed him some 1,588 pesos. In either case, the sums involved were minuscule. But then money was not the only consideration.

As noted, the Colegio de Cristo Crucificado spearheaded the pacification of Costa Rica. Aycinena had a stake in the southern frontier of the Kingdom of Guatemala as early as 1765.³⁵ In the conquest of Talamanca, he was owed some 304 pesos on its account in 1771. On January 22, 1776, don Antonio de la Fuente, a vecino of Cartago, stated that he owed Aycinena (then residing in Villanueva de Petapa) 4,407 pesos, the value of goods Aycinena provided on credit. De la Fuente agreed to repay the advance within the year in cash.³⁶ These too were minor sums. Still, it must be stressed, they were a small price to pay for the new commercial possibilities the enterprise could bring to Aycinena. To be sure, Talamanca was a marginal area. But someone had to provision the region and its merchants and officials. The conquest might open up lands for the cattle or cacao trades, or at least end military pressures on producers in the region by "pacifying" its native inhabitants.

ACCESS TO CHURCH REVENUES

Like his fellow colonials, Aycinena viewed the church as an important source of credit. On January 26, 1762, Aycinena and fellow merchants Basilio Vicente Roma and Juan Sebastián de Barrutia empowered the Mexico City merchant Juan Bautista Aldasoro to represent them before the Ecclesiastical Court of Mexico City. Aldasoro was to solicit a loan of 30,000 pesos for six years to be repaid at the conventional interest rate (*a usura pupilar*) of 5 percent.[37] Closer to home, in a similar action, on April 30, 1774, Aycinena, along with Bartolomé Equizabal, pledged himself as fiador to his relative and fellow merchant, Matías de Manzanares, then alcalde mayor of Totonicapán, who sought to borrow some 12,050 pesos from the Real Junta de Temporalidades de los Regulares Expatriados.[38] While we are unaware of the outcome of either application, both instances reveal the expectations of colonial merchant/officials that the revenues of church agencies were available for private ends.

On a smaller scale, individual churchmen were also an important source of capital for colonial entrepreneurs. Thus, on February 3, 1770, Pedro de Aycinena y Larraín and Pedro José de Beltranena, as principals, with Juan Fermín as their fiador, arranged to borrow a substantial sum from Father Juan Antonio Gallardo y Varona.[39] "Needing money for our use and convenience," and knowing "that the Illustrious don Juan Antonio Gallardo y Varona, Cura of Esquipulas, had 6,000 pesos," the two Pedros agreed to borrow the money for six years, at which time the money was to be repaid, along with interest computed annually at 5 percent.[40] Two years later, on February 28, 1772, Juan Fermín's

Navarran nephews borrowed an additional 2,000 pesos from Father Gallardo, again with their uncle as fiador.[41] In all, 8,000 pesos were placed in their hands, with the only obligation being to pay the modest annual interest. Churchmen had money to lend; merchant endeavors were worthy investments.[42]

CHURCH FINANCIER

More often, however, the roles were reversed, with Juan Fermín playing the part of creditor rather than debtor. The religious acquired their debts in a variety of ways. In March 1774 Aycinena loaned the bishop of Comayagua, Dr. Francisco José de Palencia, 2,000 pesos to cover pontifical expenses, ornaments, and other items required for him to take office. This was not charity, for Palencia pledged to repay the money, mortgaging his personal and church-related wealth.[43] Thus Aycinena financed the activities of strategically placed but financially strapped clergy in much the same way he did those of royal officials.

Most often, however, the ties were commercial. That probably says more about the participation of churchmen in the economy than it does about Aycinena's use of the church. Likewise, Aycinena's ties with clergymen were mostly in the context of his commercial enterprise, the simple conduct of business wherever and with whomever it was possible to do so. The essential fact was not that many of his partners were clergy but that they were commercially active, that they desired the goods and credit he could provide, and that they were in a solid position to make good their debts. In short, they were sound investments. That they were clergy added an important additional sanction to their activities, at times giving them exclusive access to (or a reason to locate in) certain parts of the isthmus. To wit, if they were not clergy, they would not have been where they were, doing what they were doing. As agents of the church, they enjoyed the support of perhaps the strongest institution on the isthmus. In this limited respect alone, the isthmian church network was an important support for the commercial activities of Aycinena and his fellow merchants.

The church network, in addition to furnishing business relationships (financing, buying, and selling), also served as a distribution and collection agency, dispensing goods and credit while collecting export items and pursuing debts for the wholesaler. In June 1766, for example, Juan de Cáceres, a vecino of San Miguel, reported that he had received from Aycinena 3,623 pesos worth of merchandise, with Father Blas de Bargas acting as his intermediary.[44] In effect, Bargas was a vehicle for commercial transactions. On occasion Aycinena made far-flung priests his commercial agents. Thus, for example, on March 14, 1768, Aycinena conferred his poder general on Joachín Luceno, the cura beneficiado of Gotera.[45] On April 25, 1768, he conferred his poder cumplido on don Ignacio de Villa Aliva, *presbítero* (priest) and vecino of San Vicente.[46] These "complete" or "full" grants of power established permanent commercial relationships between Aycinena and rural clergy.

From the beginning, Aycinena conducted business with economically active clerics. On November 7, 1755, Father Ramón Suria, the cura of Mita, contracted a debt with Aycinena of 4,000 pesos: 2,000 pesos in cash and 2,000 pesos worth of mercantile goods. Suria pledged to repay the cash loan within one year, at 5 percent interest. The obligation resulting from the provision of trade goods would be made good within two years. To secure the debt, Suria mortgaged his sugar hacienda and mill worth some 6,000 pesos.[47]

Similarly, on December 13, 1757, Aycinena signed on as a fiador of the merchant Gregorio de Villamagan, who had borrowed some 3,000 pesos from Father Miguel de Almeida, *presbítero domiciliario* (beneficed clergyman). Aycinena was joined in the guarantee by Manuel Salmerón, who had previously managed the estate inherited by his wife, Ana María Carrillo y Gálvez.[48] As of 1768 Aycinena owed Almeida, then of Santiago, 2,000 pesos. The debt likely originated in Aycinena's duties as fiador.

And on May 26, 1775, Bernardo Perdomo, cura of Santiago Jocotán de Chiquimula, contracted a debt with Juan Fermín along with his mother-in-law, Manuela de Gálvez. The obligation had to do with an *ingenio* (mill) named Guaraquiche, which Perdomo had inherited from Antonio Yriarte. Yriarte in turn was indebted to both Aycinena and his mother-in-law for 8,768 pesos (6,778 of which belonged to Aycinena). Perdomo agreed to repay the debts by March 1778. Thus Perdomo pledged to continue the relationship Yriarte had maintained with Aycinena, a tie that in effect came with the ingenio.[49]

Isthmian clergy who engaged in long-distance trade unavoidably crossed paths with Aycinena. On May 29, 1767, Aycinena filed suit in Ecclesiastical Court (Juzgado Eclesiástico) against Matías de Larrave, cura of Escuintla. The suit originated in Larrave's role as *fiador de mancomun* (cosigner, bondsman) of Domingo Velázquez de las Reyes, of Lima. The suit was for 2,000 pesos Aycinena had furnished Larrave as shipping insurance (*riesgo de mar*).⁵⁰

Yet another contact was Father Manuel Lorenzo García, of Realejo (and later of Lima). As of 1768 García owed Aycinena some 11,066 pesos. As owner of the merchant vessel *La Fama* García was active in the Pacific trade, involving Mexico and Peru. Apparently Father García was unable to make good the debts, for by the early 1770s he had forfeited his vessel to Aycinena.

One of Aycinena's most important relationships with isthmian clergy was with Father Francisco Nicolás Zeage (1726–93), the cura of San Agustín Sumpango. Zeage was the son of Ana Micaela de Gálvez y Varón and General Francisco Zeage, of Galicia. An uncle of Ana María Carrillo y Gálvez, Father Francisco Nicolás was an aggressive businessman who owned several haciendas and other commercial properties.⁵¹ In fact, he came in for particularly harsh criticism in the famous *visita* (royal investigation) of Archbishop Pedro Cortés y Larraz. The archbishop was scandalized by the poor state of the church in Sumpango, which contrasted dramatically with the opulence of Zeage.⁵² Aycinena and Zeage were for many years commercial associates: in July 1767 Zeage gave Aycinena his complete power of attorney.⁵³ Aycinena's ties with Zeage represent interlocking connections of church, business, and family.

PLANTER PRIESTS

It was Aycinena's ties to Salvadoran priests who doubled as indigo producers that were most important, however. On April 4, 1766, for example, Diego José López, *presbítero abogado* (church lawyer) of the Real Audiencia and a vecino de San Vicente, announced that he owed Juan Fermín de Aycinena 11,629 pesos: 10,120 had been provided in cash, the remaining 1,509 in goods. Typically, López agreed to repay the debt within one year, in indigo discounted one-half real from the prices determined in the Apastapeque fair of November 1766.[54]

Similarly, Aycinena financed the operations of Father Ambrosio Andino y Arce, the cura of Nanualco. On March 29, 1769, Manuel de Andino, a vecino of Santiago Nanualco acting on behalf of his brother, Ambrosio, solicited from Juan Fermín funds and goods needed for the development of their indigo hacienda. Aycinena furnished the Andinos 3,557 pesos—2,340 pesos in silver and 1,216 in goods. They agreed to repay Aycinena in indigo by March 1770.[55] In April 1770, however, the brothers Andino were forced to take out an additional loan. On top of the debt of the previous year, which they were unable to pay off completely (some 1,218 remained), they arranged another loan of 5,692 pesos—4,447 pesos in cash and 1,245 in goods. Their debt now totaled 6,911 pesos. Again, they pledged to repay the debts in indigo, as follows: 5,665 pesos in dyes at the prices set at the Apastepeque fair, but delivered to the Aycinena house in Santiago free of all encumbrances except the alcabala (which Aycinena would cover). The remaining 1,245 pesos were to be paid in dye set at the general prices of the Santiago fair. All debts would be repaid by January 1771. To secure the debts, the brothers obligated their persons and goods, including the hacienda Miraflores situated near the Pueblo San Pedro Mártir, San Salvador.[56] By 1777 the Andino brothers' debt had reached 36,151 pesos. And by 1780 Aycinena had acquired their hacienda. Priests proved no more immune than laymen from the vicissitudes of colonial commerce.

Aycinena not only treated with planter priests in El Salvador, he also had an interest in church revenues from the region. At the same time Aycinena and his underlings had undertaken to finance the officeholding of Bernabé de la Torre, newly reinstated as alcalde mayor of El Salvador in 1771, Aycinena involved himself in tithe collections in the same regions. On July 9, 1771, Aycinena agreed to serve as fiador of one Licenciado Jáuregui, who had pledged to cover the diezmo of Chalatenango and Texutla, amounting to 1,850 pesos annually (1771–72).[57]

Similarly, on February 3, 1770, Father Blas de Bargas acquired in public auction the diezmo farm covering the province of San Miguel for three years (1770–72), amounting to 2,250 pesos per year. Aycinena had conducted business with Bargas at least as early as 1766, and probably before then.[58] As of 1768 Bargas owed Aycinena some 13,680 pesos. By 1771 Bargas's tab had reached 21,360 pesos. His were among the largest debts to Aycinena on record. In the 1771 transaction, Bargas agreed to pay as follows: the first year's collections would be paid in the second year, the second's in the third, and so forth. The appropriate amounts of indigo would be deposited in Santiago without penalty. Aycinena would receive the dyes. In effect, Aycinena financed a commercial venture that took the guise of church collections while guaranteeing himself access to a significant supply of the valuable dye. When that grant expired, Blas renewed his tax farm for an additional two years (1773 and 1774).[59]

Father Bargas was also subjected to the wrath of Archbishop Pedro Cortés y Larraz. Cortés y Larraz noted that Bargas had been implicated in the management of two indigo and cattle haciendas and had admitted to fathering children. It especially outraged Cortés y Larraz that even though Bargas had been convicted of such wrongdoing in ecclesiastical courts, he had not been punished.[60] This is both a damning indictment of the state of the church in late colonial Central America and a sad comment on the behavior of certain men of the cloth. His moral shortcomings, however, did not seem to make Bargas any less useful as a business associate.

CONCLUSION

There is no evidence that the behavior of priests like Bargas or Zeage much troubled Juan Fermín de Aycinena. He exploited the isthmian church and churchmen to enhance his commercial opportunities, much as he used the officials and patronage power of the state. Although we need not doubt Aycinena's genuine religious feeling or his sincere commitment to sustaining the church, we should make note of the fact that clerical connections contributed, in at least a supporting if not central role, to his success. It was a reciprocal tie, involving mutual obligations and multiple benefits. Aycinena could be a powerful ally and friend of those within the church, who in turn could be valuable assets in his acquisition of wealth, status, and power.

Chapter 8

Prestige, Profits, and Persistence

By 1780 Juan Fermín de Aycinena had become the wealthiest man in the Kingdom of Guatemala. He made his fortune through marriage, wise business practices, and the astute use of the apparatuses of church and state. His fortune secure, he now undertook a series of actions that signaled something of a departure from his previous endeavors. Beginning in the late 1770s, Aycinena the merchant had also become Aycinena the planter. In 1780 he retired from active participation on the Guatemala City ayuntamiento (although he did serve as alcalde ordinario in 1784). In 1780 Aycinena applied for and in 1783 acquired a noble title, Marqués de Aycinena, thereby becoming the only nobleman in the Kingdom of Guatemala. Shortly thereafter, he took steps to join a prestigious Spanish military order, the

Knights of Santiago. About the same time, he asked for and in 1781 was granted the right to establish his home on the central plaza of Guatemala City. Thus around 1789 he and his large retinue took up residence in the finest home in the Kingdom. And in 1796, the year of his death, he established a costly entailed estate to be passed down to his eldest son.

Several important studies have placed beyond doubt the economic rationality of colonial merchants.[1] Yet a number of Aycinena's actions seem to be curiously out of character for a businessman. What prompted Aycinena, a uniquely successful colonial entrepreneur and a man who knew well the value of productive investment, to seek such gaudy status symbols as a title and knightship? We might just as well ask, Why did he work so hard? Why did he go to such great lengths (including moving halfway around the world) to create such a fortune in the first place? What drove Juan Fermín de Aycinena and other colonial entrepreneurs? To what ends would his wealth be put?

A promising resolution of the apparent contradictions of Aycinena's behavior comes from the notion of mixed investments offered by the historian Doris Ladd. Those who prevailed in the colonial economy had to adopt a "modern" entrepreneurial mentality and wise business tactics if they wished to succeed. But they also operated within a traditional Hispanic system of social prestige in which "investment to gain social status was considered as integral a part of finance as investment calculated to gain economic profit."[2]

In 1780 Aycinena was fifty years old. He had buried two wives and was responsible for five children and a former mother-in-law. Perhaps intimations of his mortality gave him pause as he contemplated the future.

But other factors were at work as well. We have mentioned the conditions of commerce and the government reforms that spurred Juan Fermín's move into landholding. The other steps he took at roughly the same time seem to be part of a change in outlook, or at least the realization on Juan Fermín's part that he had reached a new stage in his life. Aycinena began to acquire the appropriate accoutrements of his hard-earned economic success and social preeminence: a noble title, membership in a military order, and a prestigious plot on which to build his home. Together these acts announced that Aycinena had arrived, that he was now beyond the "mere" accumulation of wealth and now into the enjoyment of its fruits—not that he had denied himself previously and not that he abandoned his profit-making interests thereafter. We might add, as well, that he was surely impressed with the way that Navarran emigrés (especially those from the Baztán Valley) in Spain and the Indies had commemorated their success.[3]

In retrospect, we can see that Aycinena's aim was to acquire not only great wealth but also exalted status for himself and his family and the assurance that they would endure. What is striking, perhaps, is the degree to which entrepreneurial means were adapted for the pursuit of "traditional" ends. Aycinena went to great lengths in reconciling prestige and profit motives. In doing so, he acted in comfortable accord with the values of his time and place.

Part of the explanation for the shift in Aycinena's behavior around 1780 is provided in his correspondence with the Spanish apoderados he charged with pursuing a noble title and other imperial emoluments. The designees were Manuel de Llano, Tomás de Arzú, and his nephew Juan Miguel Aguerrevere. In October 1779 he prefaced his requests with the lament, "I am tired of work on the cabildo of this capital for the benefit of the public," especially the labors associated with the transfer of the capital.

> I have resolved to solicit my relief from the office of councilman, and enter into positions [*pretensiones*] of pure honor, in which I may pass comfortably the last stage [*tercio*] of my life.... Above all I await the... retirement of my regimiento [council seat], because I desire with impatience to leave the ayuntamiento to retire to quiet and rest, because neither my age nor my weariness may tolerate any longer the hardships and agitations in which I spent my vigorous youth.[4]

THE MARQUESADO AND THE ORDER OF SANTIAGO

These efforts bore fruit. In 1783, Aycinena became the first Marqués de Aycinena, the only nobleman in late colonial Central America. Despite his unique status within the isthmus, we must not assume that pursuing a noble title was an unusual act, even in the late eighteenth century. In fact, more titles were issued in Spanish America than at any other time in the colonial era. Charles III might well be called the great title giver.[5] Successful wholesale merchants were often the recipients of such recognition. What Juan Fermín's uniqueness indicates, rather, is that he alone in the Kingdom of Guatemala had the means to acquire such a title. He was perhaps the only man, or certainly one of the very few, in late colonial Central America who enjoyed a personal worth in excess of one million pesos—the figure that for Kicza distinguishes the truly wealthy of New Spain.[6]

Titles were costly investments. Apart from the prestige of lineage, the demonstrable wealth, and the prodigious services one had to render to the Crown to be considered for a title, one also had to pay significant amounts in taxes for the title itself. To accompany his application, Aycinena sent a "voluntary donation" of some 4,000 pesos, most likely to ease the process along.[7] The two main taxes, however, were the *lanza* and the media annata. Technically, the lanza "was a feudal obligation of military service owed to a liege."[8] But such service most often took the form of cash payments. As of May 3, 1783, Aycinena had sent to the Royal Treasury some 160,000 reales de vellón (about 8,000 pesos) in payment of the lanza—the figure set in 1773 as the amount required of those in the Indies applying for a title of Castile.

The title itself, signed on June 19, 1783, and proclaimed in Guatemala City on January 10, 1784, declared, however, that the act of *gracia* (grace) would be nullified if the media annata was not paid within two months of the title's proclamation. The exact amount of the media annata Aycinena paid is unknown, but Ladd tells us that "originally, the tax represented half of the income produced by the property ceded to the noble by the King and collected the year the noble died."[9] The title of Castile makes repeated references to the fact that Aycinena's "superabundant" wealth allowed him to provide the 6,000 ducats of annual income necessary to maintain the title and its holder in requisite dignity. The properties offered in the capacity of providing income to support the title were Aycinena's

Salvadoran hacienda Yaguatique and the two homes he possessed in the Barrio de la Hermita. It is not clear what Aycinena's media annata totaled; perhaps it was half of the income generated by the properties put up to support the title. Regardless, it was a substantial sum, part of the price of assuming the noble lifestyle.

Given the prohibitive costs, why would a businessman such as Aycinena commit himself to such expenses in the pursuit of a title? Ladd explains that titles reflected on the worth, purity, and piety of the entire family—forebears and descendants—"in a society that viewed individual achievement with some skepticism."[10] Mexican nobles "sought prestige and respectability by ostentatious conformity to the most cherished values of colonial society," to remove all doubt as to their commitment to "God, king and family."[11] What better way, then, for an enormously successful merchant to allay any skepticism that might greet his endeavors than to acquire a title of nobility?

Although their economic success has been called "revolutionary," the eighteenth-century merchants of Guatemala made uncomfortable revolutionaries. Once established among the colonial elite, they wrapped themselves tightly in the comfortable robes of the ancién regime. They became part of the status quo, inextricably bound to the prevailing order.

Membership in colonial militias or even military orders had similar appeal. In New Spain, the Prussian scientist Alexander von Humboldt observed that the Mexican elite made tremendous financial sacrifices to satisfy "their rage for titles."[12] Military participation brought power and privilege, and proved a "mixed investment" popular among the Mexican nobility. Ladd tells us further that "military orders, which conferred the rank of knight, dispensed honors that were highly prized.... Uniforms were splendid, the investiture ceremonies imposing. Membership gave a *fuero* and an important tax exemption, freedom from the obligation to tithe the church."[13]

Of course, Aycinena acquired many, if not all, of these same privileges by virtue of his noble title. The decision to pursue a knightship perhaps derived from motives personal and imponderable. We recall the propensity of successful Navarrans to seek such honors.[14] Aycinena perhaps had some fondness for the perquisites of military rank: as a younger man he had served in the colonial militia. At any rate, such honors were as rare as they were cherished. Between 1726 and 1800 only nine Guatemalans (or Spaniards in Guatemala) became Knights of Santiago. And only eighteen Guatemalans were received in any military order during that same period.[15]

THE MANSION

Once attained, nobility demanded conspicuous consumption. A man of Juan Fermín's wealth and stature had little choice but to fulfill his expected role. Gamely defending the indigo merchants of Guatemala City, Floyd declared, "There is no evidence ... that these Basque, Navarrese, and Catalan merchants flaunted their wealth." Ironically, Floyd made this remark immediately after noting that Aycinena had built a house worth 80,000 pesos.[16] Floyd also announced that the capital city battalion of the colonial militia was the "showiest military unit of the Kingdom."[17] As Ladd declares, "The show of luxury that characterized the Mexican nobility was more than a simple reflection of their vanity and delusions of grandeur." Rather, "it was behavior demanded of them as a requisite of their position."[18]

The requisite displays required a suitable arena. As a reward for his prodigious efforts on behalf of the Crown and his fellow subjects in the move of the Central American capital and, no doubt, in recognition of his preeminent place in colonial society, in 1781 Aycinena received rights to establish his residence, a customs office, and a marketplace on the south side of the central plaza of Guatemala City. There he built the most imposing residence in the capital. The mansion contained "fifteen rooms, seven patios, and twenty-four stores."[19] Slated initially to cost 75,000 pesos, final construction costs exceeded 97,000 pesos. The house was built under the supervision of Bernabé de la Torre (the younger) and was a fitting tribute to the first subject of the Kingdom. It enjoyed the use of some 16 *pajas* of water.[20] It stretched some 91½ varas from east to west and some 100 varas from north to south, or in the estimation of the American traveler John Lloyd Stephens, "a square of 200 feet."[21] Stephens actually underestimates its size.

Such a home, and its inhabitants as well, must be properly furnished. As Ladd notes for Mexican nobility, "conspicuous consumption glittered in dress, jewels, furniture and trappings."[22] We have few descriptions of the furnishings of Aycinena's late eighteenth-century mansion. But we may get some idea from earlier inventories.

The 1771 inventory of the Aycinena estate provided a separate detailed list of silver and jewelry belonging to the Aycinena household. As of 1771 the household contained some 7,600 pesos worth of silver furnishings (*alhajas de plata*). Many of these might well have been provided as part of the dowry of his late wife Ana María. At the same time, Aycinena and his mother-in-law, Manuela de Gálvez, also boasted an impressive array of jewelry, with a preference for fine pearls. The value of the jewelry counted in the household inventory of 1771 amounted to nearly 19,000 pesos. The most impressive piece was a string of thirty-three pearls with the centerpiece a pearl in the shape of an avocado, appraised at 4,830 pesos. Two other pieces exceeded 2,200 pesos in value, and a third was worth more than 1,500 pesos. Aycinena's earnings did not always go toward conventionally "productive" enterprises, even in his first decades in the isthmus. Still, this is not surprising; it would be more surprising that such luxuries were not part of his lifestyle. Glittering jewelry draped around the Marquesa was yet another testament to the great wealth (i.e., stored power) of Aycinena.

We have few contemporary descriptions of the lifestyle of Juan Fermín de Aycinena. But observations of travelers in subsequent generations perhaps give us a taste. The English traveler George Thompson recalled his reaction in 1825 to the opulence of the Aycinena family.

> I was invited into the house of the Marquis of Ayzinena: the large rooms looking into the street were full of company; the windows were all open and the ladies were disposed in groups on the windowseats; and their mothers, many of whom were indisposed by colds, which they were thus increasing, were seated in chairs behind them. As the Host passed, the whole company knelt down, and after a minute's silence and recollection, the buzz of mirth and business again filled the

apartment. On one of the pier tables, was a representation in wax work of the shepherds coming to adore our Saviour; the rooms of all the houses, from the first to the lowest class, are so filled with these images and representations, that I should not have mentioned this circumstance, in particular, had not some beads on the neck of one of the shepherds, which looked like pearls, but which I thought of course they could not be so from their extraordinary size. I found however that I was mistaken. I had hardly supposed it possible that such enormous pearls existed and wishing to ascertain their value, I guessed them at 10,000 pesos sterling. The Marquis, I understand, had given more for them: the necklace consisted of 21 pearls, the centre one being in the shape of, and as large as, a pigeon's egg, and the others large in proportion but round and decreasing in size, gradually, towards one end.[23]

John Lloyd Stephens was similarly impressed with the Aycinenas in the late 1830s. Stephens spent a memorable day at an Aycinena hacienda, El Naranjo.

[The hacienda was] about seven miles from the city. Beyond the walls all was beautiful, and in the palmy days of Guatimala the Aycinenas rolled to the Naranjo in an enormous carriage, covered with carving and gilding, in the style of the grandees of Spain, which now stands in the courtyard of the family house as a reminder of better days.... We entered by a spacious gate into a road upon their land, undulating and ornamented by trees, and by a huge artificial lake, made by damming up several streams. We rode around the borders of the lake, and entered a cattle yard of considerable extent, in the centre of which, on the side of a declivity, stood the house, a strong stone structure, with a broad piazza in front, and commanding a beautiful view of the volcanoes of Antigua.[24]

PHILANTHROPY

If conspicuous display was one of the requisites for noblemen, so too was conspicuous giving. Juan Fermín de Aycinena, as did nobles in Mexico and elsewhere, took seriously the responsibilities incumbent on his social position. We have noted already Aycinena's bountiful gifts to the church (and state) and the didactic ends of such generosity. The *cédula real* (royal decree) conceding his noble title commended him especially for his great sacrifices on behalf of the residents of Santiago during the terrible aftermath of the 1773 earthquake. The portrait that introduces this study depicts a scene of Aycinena the nobleman dispensing comfort and alms to the women and children of his "realm." The colonial chronicler, Father Domingo Juarros, placed Aycinena among those "illustrious in saintliness who have flourished in this city."

> Lastly, we might mention the memorable Sr. Marqués D. Juan Fermín de Ayzinena: not only for having founded the Marquesado, the only title of Castile in this city; but also because, despite his grandeur, he maintained a humble heart and treated everyone affably; and because, far from becoming a slave to his wealth, he spent profusely on behalf of the needy.[25]

To be sure, Juarros was a member of Aycinena's circle and writing in part to celebrate his class. But this fact does not negate the importance of Aycinena's image (which may or may not have approximated the reality): Marqués de Aycinena, noble in stature, noble in spirit, humble of heart, patron of the poor, faithful servant of God, King, and his adopted homeland. The fact that

Juarros commends such virtues, no matter how self-serving his intent, reinforces our portrait of late colonial Central America and the values it held dear. Again, we need not cast doubts on the sincerity of Aycinena's charitable impulses. The most important thing was that his philanthropy played a functional role in the maintenance of society by providing justification for the social hierarchy of the colonial order and his place within it.

In his study of late colonial Mexico, Tutino views elite charity with ardent skepticism. He admits that "the great families were . . . viewed as likely sources of charity by persons fallen on hard times. . . . The large number of requests . . . suggest that charitable gifts from elites to the urban poor were not unknown."[26] Such personal relations, Tutino notes, touched only a few. More important was the elite response to general crises afflicting urban dwellers in Mexico City. In times of crisis the elite would often intervene with charitable giving. But, as Tutino asserts, oligarchic giving was more rhetoric than reality. And indeed, the hoarding by the Mexico City elite of agricultural stores in the great food crisis of the 1780s is a less than noble chapter in the history of New Spain. Rather than some humanitarian impulse or sense of Catholic duty, Tutino argues, elites in Mexico City intervened primarily to keep the urban population at a level necessary to ensure the success of their provisioning businesses. In other words, the dead made poor customers! "In an economy that supported elite families through their control of subsistence resources, it was very much in the interests of that elite to maintain the consuming population at undiminished levels."[27]

Tutino's view is probably extreme, and focuses too exclusively on economic concerns. Edith Couturier's view is more charitable. In her pioneering study of the philanthropy of the Conde de Regla, Couturier discerned that the Mexican plutocrat patronized institutions that emphasized his Christian charity, supported the Franciscan cause, and enhanced his family's social and economic position by providing employment or opportunities for patronage.[28] Couturier estimates that the Conde de Regla dispensed in charity between 900,000 and 1.12 million pesos, or about 20 percent of his estate. Despite his generosity, however, Couturier stresses in nearly all his giving "the mixing of private interests and public benefits."[29] Philanthropy too was a mixed investment.

Aycinena's giving, while certainly not on the scale of the Conde de Regla, more closely approximated Couturier's view than Tutino's. The hierarchical conception of society implicit in the Spanish colonial order (and one who acquired a noble title almost certainly bought into this conception) was justified in part by the responsibilities the more fortunate had toward the less fortunate.

In an organically conceived society, cross-class connections of *compadrazgo* (godparenthood) and charitable giving muted class and ethnic conflict. Nobles played a role inextricably bound up with those of the church and Crown. This vision of the proper organization of society stood in stark contrast to the atomistic liberalism of early nineteenth-century Central America. Whatever its virtues, the attack on monarchy, nobility, and the Catholic monopoly that came with independence was a challenge to an internally coherent way of life many held dear.[30] Parenthetically, both the persistence and the obvious shortcomings of this worldview were revealed in the words of Archbishop Mariano Rossell Arellano, an adamant opponent of the Guatemalan Revolution of 1944-54. According to the archbishop, the inequality that persisted in Guatemala was "divine permission for the wealthy to be masters and fathers of the less fortunate."[31]

THE MAYORAZGO

Ladd also reflected on the problems nobles faced in both displaying and preserving their position. The financial demands of their station threatened the position itself. "Prestige, in short, imposed a great drain on property."[32] Another drain on colonial wealth was the inheritance practices of Spanish America. Inheritance laws called for the equal division of all property among all legitimate heirs. In Aycinena's case, as of 1796 such a division would mean that his empire would be carved into some twelve parts (for his wife and his eleven living children). Apart from the practical difficulties of coming up with a dozen equitable shares of nonliquid wealth, such a division would gravely threaten the stature Aycinena had acquired for himself and his lineage. The primary means of preventing the rapid dissipation of colonial fortunes was to establish a mayorazgo, or entailed estate, which consolidated a major part of the estate into an indivisible and inalienable legacy to be passed down whole to a single heir.[33]

In February 1796 Aycinena was "moved by fatherly love" to establish a mayorazgo to be passed down, along with the family title, to his firstborn son, Vicente de Aycinena y Carrillo. The entail's purpose was "to perpetuate the splendor of my house and lineage, and to better serve God and King," to keep Vicente and his successors from material want and, ideally, from any loss of stature.

> I, Juan Fermín de Aycinena e Yrigoyen, Marqués de Aycinena, Knight of the Order of Santiago, regidor, retired depositor general of the very noble and loyal municipal council [ayuntamiento] of this capital, first and current Prior of the Royal Tribunal of the Consulado of this kingdom, ... in order to maintain my family in the grace and privileges which in his royal munificence and kindness the King, Our Lord, has seen fit to bestow, conceding the title of Marqués de Aycinena and to me and my primogenitor and successors perpetually and for always, and to ensure that for the lack of adequate funds the title does not decline in luster ... in order to obviate the damages that the indigence of my successors would occasion ... upon sound and mature reflection I have resolved to entail the necessary properties, prohibiting their separation and alienation and erect them in mayorazgo forever.[34]

Along with his title, Aycinena arranged to pass down whole to Vicente his principal residence in the capital and its contents, along with the stores and shops adjacent to it. In addition to the house, Aycinena also entailed his hacienda Miraflores in El Salvador, acquired in a legal cession in 1784 and now worth 57,991 pesos. The properties earlier put up for the title, the two homes in the Barrio de Hermita and the hacienda Yaguatique, were now liberated from that obligation.

Aycinena minutely prescribed the order of succession. If Vicente were unable to assume the entail, it was to pass down to the survivors of the male line, in order of birth. If no male children survived, the estate would make its way down the female line. From there it would proceed to closest legitimate relatives. Restrictions did apply. Priests could assume the entail if they were legitimate descendants, but nuns, or novices, or the illegitimate offspring of priests could not. Other conditions could also prevent an individual from assuming the entail: those born mad (*loco*), demented (*mentecato*), or deaf and mute were so forbidden. Potential heirs who succumbed to these maladies were also enjoined from assuming command of the estate. The successor was required to ensure that they lived in some decency.

If there were no legitimate successors, the last holder was to name his successor, subject to the following restrictions: no priests and only one holder at a time. The holder of the entail was not obligated to provide sustenance for his successors with the exception of his minor children or his legitimate descendants. He was obligated to provide for his own siblings "with as much decency as possible." However, once his or her siblings married, joined the church, or reached majority, the holder was free of the obligation. The holder was also expected to provide for the poor widows of previous holders, unless or until they were to remarry. Possessors should not hold vile offices and should only marry those of noble lineage and pure blood (no Jews, Moors, or Indians allowed). Holders should be of good moral character: any holder convicted of the crimes of heresy, sodomy, or bestiality or who violated other laws of God and man was to be deprived of the estate and to incur "infamy." It was Aycinena's "will that all its possessors should be Catholic, Christian, obedient to the Divine and ecclesiastical precepts, and faithful vassals of the Kings of these dominions."[35]

Successors were obligated to assume the title and be addressed as Marqués de Aycinena. Rightful successors had to present their claim within a year of the death of the previous holder or else pay a penalty of 3,000 pesos per year, to be added to the value of the estate, until the obligation was met. And holders (with the exception of Vicente) had to inventory their holdings within six months, under penalty of an annual payment of 4,000 pesos to the hospital San Juan de Dios until the obligation was carried out. Apart from the charitable donations called for in preceding clauses (ironically as penalties for noncompliance), clause 22 obliged the holder to "venerate and preserve as patron María Santísima de los Dolores."

Perhaps most interesting were Aycinena's dictates for the future management of the estate. These were included in clauses 12, 18, and 20. Clause 12 decreed that "all possessors of the mayorazgo have the indispensable obligation to separate annually the fifth part of the liquid proceeds of the stores and shops, and the hacienda Miraflores . . . and to enhance its value, by employing the fifth either in long-term loans [*a censo*] or toward the purchase of new lands or additional fincas or houses or their construction." The fifth was to be invested solely at the discretion of the estate holder. A fifth of the proceeds from any new purchases was also to be so employed in the future. It was Juan Fermín's earnest wish that the mayorazgo not stand idle but constantly grow. If for some reason the holder were to go two years without meeting this obligation, 2,000 pesos were to be paid to the "Hospital Real de San Juan de Dios, for the relief of the sick and destitute." Clause 18 established further restrictions. The holdings of the mayorazgo were not to be "divided, sold, ceded, renounced, bequeathed, bartered, taxed, pawned, nor encumbered by liens (partially or completely)." No part of the mayorazgo was to be alienated as part of a dowry or *arras* (groom's gift to the bride, which becomes part of the bride's personal estate), obra pía or public works, or other religious offering. Only in the most extraordinary circumstances were the proceeds of the mayorazgo to be so diverted, and only by government decree. Clause 20 held the occupant responsible for maintaining the mayorazgo's value and keeping its properties in good repair.

Vicente assented to all conditions, and the mayorazgo was signed in Guatemala City on February 29, 1796. For Juan Fermín de Aycinena, the establishment of an entailed estate served several purposes. It represented an effort to direct family behavior from beyond the grave. It was intended to maintain family honor (something he had taken great pains and expense to establish in the first place). It was an effort to promote sound economic behavior on the part of his descendants. In this regard, he discouraged encumbrances on the family patrimony and dictated that the holder make constant improvements. It obliged the holders to contribute to charity. More broadly, the entail demanded moral rectitude as well as fealty to church and king. Entail was a remarkably flexible device. To the extent that it contributed to the maintenance of the Aycinena family stature, it was a remarkably successful one as well.

The establishment of an entailed estate displayed tremendous prescience. Juan Fermín de Aycinena, Marqués de Aycinena, died on Sunday, April 3, 1796. He was sixty-six years old. He left behind twelve heirs, including his third wife. Aycinena died just as Spain and Great Britain were once again at war, a war that brought British blockades of Spanish ports, wreaked havoc on Spanish American trade, and ended the "brief golden age" of colonial commerce that began with imperial free trade in 1778. But his place, and the place of his progeny, was secure beyond doubt and almost beyond challenge.

Chapter 9

Epilogue

The death of the Marqués de Aycinena in early April 1796 gave rise to an unseemly spectacle. The newly established consulado de comercio asked that it be allowed to take part in the funeral procession of its late prior. It offered to compromise with the ayuntamiento of Guatemala City, proposing that two representatives of each body escort the Marqués to the sepulcher. The ayuntamiento, however, insisted that it alone merited this distinction. In Solomonic fashion, the captain general reasoned that it was not an issue suited to lengthy deliberation and resolved the matter in favor of the consulado.[1]

Whatever the dispute says about the politics of late colonial Central America, privately at least affairs were handled more tastefully. On May 31, 1796, by agreement of the widow and heirs of Juan Fermín de Aycinena, Vicente—soon to be confirmed as the second holder of the title of Marqués—and his brother, José Alejandro de Aycinena, assumed the management of the Casa de Aycinena. They had long experience conducting the commercial affairs of the house. José contributed valuable legal expertise as well. The decision was a conscious effort to maintain and continue the family business intact. Juan Fermín had trained his sons well. Among their first decisions was to grant representative powers to Francisco Ignacio de Yraeta in Mexico City, their father's old correspondent and business associate.

It is beyond the scope of this study to detail the history of the Aycinena family in the nineteenth and twentieth centuries. No doubt, their history bears directly on the history of Central America itself. As late colonial Central America's wealthiest family, with the only noble title in the region at independence, the Aycinenas entered the national period holding extraordinary wealth and power. Their position, in fact, became a central issue of independence era politics. Pedro Molina, in a famous passage from his independence era newspaper, raged about the isthmian ruling class.

> The nobility of Guatemala, more tyrannical than the kings of Spain, used the lower classes as beings sprung from nature only to serve them; they had all the positions in Administration which the European Spaniards did not hold; they alone had the privilege of cultivating their natural talents and to receive a good and decent education. Even in the line of the Church they made it their exclusive patrimony; they sold justice and those from the provinces, never, never, won a suit against them. They purchased the fruits of the country at the

lowest possible price; being the only buyers they purchased at their whim, because as trade was not free it was not licit to sell to others. The same occurred with the herds of cattle that were brought to be sold. The monopolists of Guatemala City paid the prices they desired.[2]

The Aycinena family was at the core of the nobility that so angered Molina. Juan Fermín's first wife, Ana María Carrillo y Gálvez, bore three children before her death in June 1768.[3] The two children who survived infancy, Vicente (1766–1814) and José Alejandro (1767–1826), went on to become extremely prominent figures in late colonial Central America. Vicente inherited the family title and became the second Marqués de Aycinena in 1796. He held a number of municipal offices in Guatemala City, including a permanent seat on the cabildo from 1794 until at least 1806.[4] He reached the height of his power in 1813, when the Guatemala City cabildo elected him *jefe político superior* (political chief) of Central America. This election amounted to a *coup d'état* meant to depose Captain General José de Bustamante (1811–18). In the imperial crisis occasioned by the Napoleonic invasion of the Iberian peninsula and the subsequent Hidalgo and Morelos revolts in neighboring New Spain, Bustamante had cracked down on the first families of Guatemala City for their supposed independence leanings and contraband trading.[5] The restoration of Ferdinand VII in 1814 preserved Bustamante's place and Vicente never assumed the post. Vicente died on December 21, 1814, at the age of forty-eight.[6] After his death, the family title descended on Juan José de Aycinena, third and last Marqués de Aycinena and an eminent priest, statesman, and conservative intellectual in nineteenth-century Guatemala.[7] Vicente's numerous offspring dominated Guatemalan history for much of the nineteenth century.

José Alejandro had an exceptionally remarkable career. He received a doctor of laws degree from the University of San Carlos in 1792.[8] In his distinguished public life, he served as a colonel in the colonial militia, rector of the University of San Carlos (1797), a consul of the consulado de comercio (1798), alcalde ordinario of the Guatemalan cabildo (1803), director of the Economic Society (1810), and as interim intendant of El Salvador (1811) (having pacified provincial unrest in an area crucial to the family's economic interests). In 1813 his career took an unlikely turn: he moved to Spain to serve as a councillor of state, and later joined the Council of the Indies. From his lofty perch, José maneuvered to have the hated José de Bustamante removed from office, the Jesuit order restored to Central America, and his kinsmen inducted into the Knights of the Order of Isabela la Católica. Caught up in the swirl of post-Napoleonic Spanish politics, José died in Spain in 1826.[9] What an extraordinary scenario: two brothers, the elder sons of Juan Fermín de Aycinena, operating on either side of the Atlantic to guide Central America's transition to independence.[10]

If Juan Fermín's first marriage had supplied him with suitable male heirs, his second marriage produced three daughters whose own marriages established valuable linkages with other notable families or with up-and-coming peninsulars. The three children of Juan Fermín's marriage to María Micaela Josefa Brigada de Nájera y Mencos who survived infancy were María Bernarda, María Josefa Sebastiana, and María Micaela

Josefa Margarita. María Bernarda wed Tadeo Francisco Piñol y Muñoz. He was a native of Santiago, the son of José Piñol y Sala, who had already given two daughters to the Aycinena family, the wife of Vicente and the third wife of Juan Fermín de Aycinena. In 1796 María Micaela married Manuel José Pavón y Muñoz. He was the son of Cayetano Pavón y Gil of Extremadura and creole María Teresa Muñoz y Barba. The Pavón family was perhaps one of the few that could rival the wealth and influence of the Aycinenas. Where her sisters María Bernarda and María Micaela wed prominent and powerful creoles, María Josefa Sebastiana renewed links with the peninsula in her marriage to the extraordinarily successful Navarran trader, Juan Bautista Marticorena, in 1794.[11]

Finally, the children of Aycinena's third marriage became some of the most notable figures of nineteenth-century Central America. Perhaps most intriguing of all was his youngest daughter, María Teresa, who in 1816 reputedly had several visitations from the Virgin Mary. María Teresa later became the subject of an extensive but unsuccessful campaign for canonization. A less controversial but still important religious figure was María Teresa's brother, Miguel Aycinena y Piñol. Juan Fermín de Aycinena y Piñol and Mariano de Aycinena y Piñol became extremely important political leaders during the independence era. In fact, Mariano, Juan Fermín's youngest son, became chief of state of Guatemala in 1826 and led the losing side of the Central American civil war of 1826–29.[12]

The civil war struck a mighty but far from fatal blow at the La Familia's dominance in Guatemala. Despite their defeat, the confiscation of their Salvadoran properties, and the exile of family patriarchs (including Mariano, Antonio, and Juan José), they displayed a remarkable tenacity. Through the convulsions of the nineteenth century, they managed to persevere. They returned to power in the conservative era dominated by Rafael Carrera (1840–65), which aimed to restore much of the comfortable colonial past. Manuel Francisco Pavón y Aycinena was a leading Carrera minister until his death in 1854. His cousin, Father Juan José Aycinena y Piñol, son of Vicente and briefly recognized as the third Marqués de Aycinena, became the Carrera regime's dominant intellectual figure. Juan José's brother Pedro de Aycinena y Piñol served as foreign minister from 1851 until 1871 and interim president in 1865. Another brother, José Ignacio, was corregidor of Guatemala City from 1851 to 1871. The Aycinena family was again cast out of power with the liberal revolution of 1871. Still, even in political defeat, the Aycinenas eventually regained much of their former preeminence. Deprived of their political hegemony in the late nineteenth century, the Aycinena family today remains among Guatemala's social and commercial elite. Doctors, scholars, diplomats, bankers, and architects,[13] they are part of a ruling class that lives in fear of communism, of the Indian majority, and even of their protectors in the Guatemalan military.

Conclusion

The story of Juan Fermín de Aycinena is the stuff of legend. Leaving Navarre perhaps before he turned twenty, he became the wealthiest and most powerful man in late colonial Central America. This study has attempted to penetrate the mythic veil that shrouds this remarkable figure, to render him in reasonably accurate scale.

As an emigrant, Aycinena took part in a well-established Iberian pattern of younger or "nonelected" children seeking greener pastures far away. Emigration improved their prospects as individuals, lessened pressures on family resources, and extended their family's network of useful contacts. Aycinena passed his first years in the Indies in Mexico. He used his Mexican interlude to make contact with powerful relatives and to acquire valuable commercial experience and lasting business connections.

Aycinena moved to Santiago de Guatemala by 1754. Perhaps the single most important event of his whole story was his marriage to Ana María Carrillo y Gálvez in 1755. She was surely the most sought after bride in the Kingdom of Guatemala. Ana María's dowry alone made Juan Fermín a wealthy man. Her powerful family network, along with her wealth, placed Aycinena immediately among the Santiago elite. His wife was the niece of some of the most powerful figures in the Kingdom of Guatemala—Cristóbal de Gálvez, Manuel de Gálvez, and Father Miguel de Cilieza. In joining such wealth and power, Aycinena continued another historic pattern—that of the isthmian elite renovating itself with peninsular blood. Juan Fermín perpetuated the pattern himself by importing peninsular nephews to reinforce his isthmian kinship network. Through their marriages Pedro de Aycinena y Larraín and Pedro de Beltranena provided loyal business associates as well as opportunities to widen family connections.

But Aycinena's story does not end with a fortunate marriage or useful family ties. Aycinena's remarkable rise was also due to his skill in business. He did not sit on his newfound wealth but multiplied it many times over. Obviously, his fortunate marriage gave him unique advantages in his business endeavors. The infusion of "start-up capital" and the established commercial relationships he obtained through his exchange of vows permitted him to invest more readily, more widely, and more aggressively than his Guatemalan merchant peers. His great bounty gave him a longer reach and a surer supply of import and export goods than his fellow merchants could ever hope to enjoy. Because he could

CONCLUSION

assume greater risks, he reaped greater rewards. Aycinena's business career is distinguished by a seemingly relentless movement to expand, diversify, and vertically integrate his holdings. Aycinena could, if he chose, supply his haciendas with goods from his own stores, produce indigo in his own fields with workers "recruited" by colonial officials under his influence (or even in his employ), transport it across the isthmus on his own mules, and ship it to distant ports across the seas in his own ships, where it might be handled by his own kin.

Although vertical integration of the family enterprise was a desired end, and though it is beyond doubt that Aycinena became a major planter, the enthusiasm with which he did so may be questioned. It is sometimes argued that entrepreneurs in Bourbon Spanish America looked to move into landholding as soon as possible. Aycinena's career at least partially modifies this picture. The timing of his land acquisitions, nearly all of which took place between 1780 and 1785, strongly suggests that his move to the land was not foreordained, that it was certainly not a priority. The gap between his arrival in Guatemala and his emergence as a planter is about twenty-five years. Aycinena's landed wealth resulted from a convergence of factors: the dangerously mounting debts of several planters, the overextension of his banking operations, wartime disruptions of commerce, and a series of governmental reforms aimed at protecting producers from merchants. Other, more personal, considerations came into play as well. But this much is clear: for Aycinena there was no rush, certainly no mad rush, into landholding. When his move to the land came, however, it was swift and massive. As much as anything else, Aycinena's ultimately extensive landed wealth reflects the scale of his commercial activities, his prominence as a lender, the volatility of colonial business, and producers' resulting vulnerability to merchants.

One of the more striking findings of this study of a fabulously successful, late colonial merchant is the great extension of Aycinena's family-based trading network throughout the Indies. He was armed with strategic contacts, primarily of a family nature, in practically every significant center of colonial trade: Mexico City, Lima, Santiago de Chile, Guayaquil, Havana, and, above all, Cádiz. The family enterprise, with its access to goods, markets, and transportation, gave him an extraordinary reach, once again distinguishing him from his isthmian merchant peers.

Aycinena promoted his interests by asserting his influence on (and through) the institutional apparatus of colonial Central America. He controlled crucial offices in colonial government and exercised extraordinary leverage over officeholders. He was able to influence government policy and practice on matters of greatest concern to himself. In turn, the power generated from his ties to the state and church expanded and reinforced his opportunities to create wealth.

Aycinena's seat on the cabildo gave him a voice in matters of vital concern—land, labor, taxes, and monopolies. It provided him with an institutional vehicle for defending his interests against an encroaching bureaucracy or the occasional hostile captain general. His subsequent leadership of the merchant guild founded in 1794 brought similar advantages. Aycinena's positions as depositor general and supervisor of alcabala collections (before and during the transfer of the capital city) gave him extraordinary control over "public" resources.

Influence over the destination of certain ecclesiastical revenues had similar benefits.

As chapters 6 and 7 make clear, Aycinena maintained substantial financial connections with officials of the state and church. The isthmian institutional apparatus reinforced (and sometimes reproduced) Aycinena's commercial network. Financially beholden officials, such as the alcaldes mayores Bernabé de la Torre and Manuel Fadrique y Goyena in El Salvador or Governor Domingo Cavello in Nicaragua, were tremendous assets for Aycinena the entrepreneur. In their "recruitment" of labor, dispensing of goods and money, collection of debts, and pursuit of legal actions, they performed roles that marked the intersection of public office and private interests. We see much the same thing with rural clerics such as Father Blas de Bargas of El Salvador, who acted as an intermediary not only between his flock and their Lord but also between buyers and sellers, workers and owners.

All this is not to say that Aycinena was not a good and faithful servant of the Spanish Empire or the Roman Catholic Church. His contributions to both entities were many, prodigious, and conspicuous. Aycinena realized that his own interests, and those of his family, were inextricably linked with the fortunes of church and empire. His social position and wealth-making opportunities could but suffer in the face of dramatic challenges to the status quo—from foreign invasions or indigenous uprisings. It was as much for his own benefit that he endowed the church and state in Central America. Aycinena did not seek to challenge the existing order in the Kingdom of Guatemala. He sought rather to join or perhaps supplant existing power holders. But he dared not challenge the bases of their power.

No doubt it was Aycinena's appreciation of the role of the state and the church, as well as genuine gratitude for their assistance, that prompted him to invest his wealth so conspicuously in traditional status symbols. Aycinena secured his position in the Kingdom of Guatemala with the finest trappings the Spanish colonial world had to offer: a noble title, a knightship, an entailed estate, and a magnificent home in Guatemala City. Yet, it must be borne in mind, prestige and profits cohabited in his motives and in his actions. A mayorazgo served not only to symbolize exalted stature but also to protect the name and honor of the founder's family by ensuring that at least one descendant would retain the economic means to preserve its wealth and position, in theory at least, for eternity. As the subsequent history of Central America and especially Guatemala makes clear, he was remarkably successful.

Notes

INTRODUCTION

1. Ralph Lee Woodward, Jr., "The Historiography of Modern Central America Since 1960," *Hispanic American Historical Review* 67, no. 3 (August 1987): 461–96. This is not to suggest that all recently published works are fashionable responses to the intense popular demand for information about Central America.

2. Jim Handy, *Gift of the Devil: A History of Guatemala* (Boston: South End Press, 1984), 9.

3. Carol A. Smith, "Preface," in *Guatemalan Indians and the State, 1540–1988*, ed. Carol A. Smith (Austin: University of Texas Press, 1990), viii.

4. See, for example, Samuel Z. Stone, *The Heritage of the Conquistadors: Ruling Classes in Central America from Conquest to the Sandinistas* (Lincoln: University of Nebraska Press, 1992).

5. David McCreery, "Guatemala," in *Research Guide to Central America and the Caribbean*, ed. Kenneth J. Grieb (Madison: University of Wisconsin Press, 1985), 29.

6. Donald E. Schulz, "El Salvador: Revolution and Counterrevolution in the Living Museum," in *Revolution and Counterrevolution in Central America and the Caribbean*, ed. Donald E. Schulz and Douglas H. Graham (Boulder: Westview Press, 1984), 189.

7. Richard Graham, "Political Power and Landownership in Nineteenth-Century Latin America," in *New Approaches to Latin American History*, ed. Richard Graham and Peter H. Smith (Austin: University of Texas Press, 1973), 113. See also the comments of James Lockhart regarding what he calls the "Law of Preservation of the Energy of Historians" in his groundbreaking article, "The Social History of Colonial Spanish America: Its Evolution and Potential," *Latin American Research Review* 7, no. 1 (Spring 1972): 8.

8. Emilia Viotti da Costa, *The Brazilian Empire: Myths and Histories* (Chicago: Dorsey Press, 1988), xvii. Fellow Brazilianists Joseph L. Love and Bert J. Barickman point out that "elite studies, even in an age of 'little people's history,' require no apology to the degree that they reveal patterns of social stratification and the dynamics of power, both economic and political." "Rulers and Owners: A Brazilian Case Study in Comparative Perspective," *Hispanic American Historical Review* 66, no. 4 (November 1986): 743.

9. John E. Kicza, "The Great Families of Mexico: Elite Maintenance and Business Practices in Late Colonial Mexico City," *Hispanic American Historical Review* 62, no. 3 (August 1982): 429.

10. Miles Wortman writes, "The clan's commercial policies created the economic pattern for the colony, controlling trade in most regions of the colony as well as capital, serving as the banker for government and private citizen alike. With the decline in Spanish power the Aycinenas switched their trade to Britain, becoming a leading force in the move for independence. Once freedom from Spain

was achieved, the Aycinenas were the single most powerful family during the federal period. The Aycinena name is still prominent in commercial and political affairs in Guatemala." *Government and Society in Colonial Central America, 1680–1840* (New York: Columbia University Press, 1982), 123.

11. Ralph Lee Woodward, Jr., *Rafael Carrera and the Emergence of the Republic of Guatemala, 1821–1871.* (Athens: University of Georgia Press, 1993), 9.

12. David Tobis and Susanne Jonas, *Guatemala* (Berkeley: NACLA, 1974), 216–51.

13. Diana Balmori, Stuart F. Voss, and Miles Wortman, *Notable Family Networks in Latin America* (Chicago: University of Chicago Press, 1984), 65.

14. Mario Rodríguez, "Research Topics for Bourbon Central America, 1700–1821," in *Research Guide to Central America and the Caribbean*, ed. Kenneth J. Grieb (Madison: University of Wisconsin Press, 1985), 22.

15. Floyd continues: "He was the leading indigo exporter, probably the only ship owner of the resident merchants in Guatemala, owned perhaps half a dozen plantations, was the leading contributor to the war effort (1779–1783), purchased a marquisate in 1783 to become the only titled noble in the Kingdom of Guatemala, was regidor jubilado in the ayuntamiento in the 1790s, and was named first prior of the consulado of Guatemala in 1795. His sons were to become prominent members of the conservative centralists after independence." Troy S. Floyd, "The Guatemalan Merchants, the Government, and the *Provincianos*, 1750–1800," *Hispanic American Historical Review* 41, no. 1 (February 1961): 98 n. 24.

16. Given the ambiguous nature of the colonial economy, Louisa Schell Hoberman calls for "a theoretical framework more appropriate to colonial society, one acknowledging the coexistence of different modes of production," a framework "which recognizes the colonial merchant as a distinct type. He applied traditional techniques to enterprises with modern elements, and he cannot be dismissed as

a parasite on the peripheral economies." *Mexico's Merchant Elite, 1590–1660: Silver, State, and Society* (Durham: Duke University Press, 1991), 275. Steve J. Stern offers a masterful review of the issues and literature in "Feudalism, Capitalism, and the World-System in the Perspective of Latin America and the Caribbean," *American Historical Review* 93, no. 4 (October 1988): 829–72. On late colonial merchants, see especially John Kicza, *Colonial Entrepreneurs: Families and Business in Bourbon Mexico City* (Albuquerque: University of New Mexico Press, 1983), and Susan M. Socolow, *The Merchants of Buenos Aires, 1778–1810: Family and Commerce* (Cambridge: Cambridge University Press, 1978).

17. Enrique del Cid F., *Origen histórico de la Casa y Marquesado de Ayzinena* (Guatemala City: published privately, 1969). A four-volume, bound copy of this work is available in the Academia de Historia y Geografía of Guatemala City.

CHAPTER 1

1. Brief accounts of the Aycinena story are found in Balmori, Voss, and Wortman, *Notable Family Networks in Latin America*, 60–69; Wortman, *Government and Society*, 122–23; and Ralph Lee Woodward, Jr., *Central America: A Nation Divided*, 2d ed. (New York: Oxford University Press, 1985), 74–75.

2. "Libro de Reales Cédulas, 1782–1785," 232–243, Archivo General de Centroamérica (hereafter cited as AGCA), Guatemala City, A1.23, Leg. 4633.

3. Protocolo de Manuel Francisco de Rueda, Antequera, Oaxaca, February 17, 1753, 49–51, Archivo General de Notarias del Estado de Oaxaca (hereafter cited as AGNEO).

4. AGCA, A1.20, Leg. 881, Exp. 9374, Protocolo de Antonio González, July 1754.

5. AGCA, A1.20, Leg. 893, Protocolo de Sebastián González, Testament of Ana María de Gálvez y Carrillo, July 25, 1768. This was almost the same amount that Juan Fermín's cousin in Oaxaca, Pedro Bernardo de Yrigoyen,

claimed to have invested in Juan Fermín, his business associate in Guatemala. AGNEO, Protocolo de Francisco Rueda, November 22, 1754, 170.

6. Aycinena Family Papers, "Resumé del Caudal de Juan Fermín de Aycinena, 1796."

7. D. A. Brading, "Bourbon Spain and Its American Empire," in *Colonial Spanish America*, ed. Leslie Bethell (Cambridge: Cambridge University Press, 1987), 136.

8. Balmori, Voss, and Wortman, *Notable Family Networks in Latin America*, 69.

9. It was also known as the Audiencia of Guatemala and the Captaincy General of Guatemala.

10. Wortman, *Government and Society*, 290.

11. Oakah L. Jones, Jr., *Guatemala in the Spanish Colonial Period* (Norman: University of Oklahoma Press, 1994), 164.

12. Castas included mestizos, mulattos, Indians acculturated into the European lifestyle, and free blacks.

13. W. George Lovell and Christopher H. Lutz, *Demography and Empire: A Guide to the Population History of Spanish Central America, 1500–1821* (Boulder: Westview Press, 1995), 14.

14. On "core" and "periphery," see Christopher H. Lutz and W. George Lovell, "Core and Periphery in Colonial Guatemala," in *Guatemalan Indians and the State, 1540–1988*, ed. Carol A. Smith (Austin: University of Texas Press, 1990), 35–51. Also see Lovell's *Conquest and Survival in Colonial Guatemala: A Historical Geography of the Cuchamatán Highlands, 1523–1821* (Montreal: McGill-Queens University Press, 1992); David McCreery, *Rural Guatemala, 1760–1940* (Stanford: Stanford University Press, 1994), esp. 33–110; Christopher H. Lutz, *Santiago de Guatemala, 1541–1773: City, Caste, and the Colonial Experience* (Norman: University of Oklahoma Press, 1994); Adriaan C. Van Oss, *Catholic Colonialism: A Parish History of Guatemala, 1524–1821* (Cambridge: Cambridge University Press, 1986), esp. 130–31; and José Antonio Fernández Molina,

"Colouring the World in Blue: The Indigo Boom and the Central American Market, 1750–1810" (Ph.D. dissertation, University of Texas at Austin, 1992), 70–225. On the "Mosquito Coast," see Troy S. Floyd, *The Anglo-Spanish Struggle for Mosquitia* (Albuquerque: University of New Mexico Press, 1967); Robert A. Naylor, *Penny-Ante Imperialism: The Mosquito Shore and the Bay of Honduras, 1600–1914: A Case Study in British Informal Empire* (Cranbury, N.J.: Fairleigh Dickinson University Press, 1989); and Craig L. Dozier, *Nicaragua's Mosquito Shore: The Years of British and American Presence* (Tuscaloosa: University of Alabama Press, 1985).

15. Severo Martínez-Peláez, *La patria del criollo: Ensayo de interpretación de la realidad colonial guatemalteca* (Guatemala City: EDUCA, 1985). See also Christopher H. Lutz, *História sociodemográfica de Santiago de Guatemala, 1541–1773* (Antigua: CIRMA, 1982). For the notion of a creole-dominated society, see John Tutino, "Creole Mexico: Spanish Elites, Haciendas, and Indian Towns, 1750–1810" (Ph.D. dissertation, University of Texas at Austin, 1976).

16. On colonial establishments, see, among others, the following works: Leon G. Campbell, "A Colonial Establishment: Creole Domination of the Audiencia of Lima During the Late Eighteenth Century," *Hispanic American Historical Review* 52 (February 1972): 1–25; Mark A. Burkholder, "From Creole to *Peninsular*: The Transformation of the Audiencia of Lima," *Hispanic American Historical Review* 52 (August 1972): 395–415; Stanley Stein, "Bureaucracy and Business in the Spanish Empire, 1759–1804: Failure of a Bourbon Reform in Mexico and Peru," *Hispanic American Historical Review* 61 (February 1981): 2–28; Jacques Barbier, *Reform and Politics in Bourbon Chile, 1755–1796* (Ottawa: University of Ottawa Press, 1980); and D. A. Brading, *Miners and Merchants in Bourbon Mexico, 1763–1810* (Cambridge: Cambridge University Press, 1971).

17. Stephen Webre, "The Social and Economic Bases of Cabildo Membership in Seventeenth-Century Santiago de

Guatemala" (Ph.D. dissertation, Tulane University, 1980), 132–33. For Webre, "the assimilation of peninsular Spaniards . . . into the local elite" was a constant rather than "occasional occurrence suggested by some historians."

18. Lutz, *Santiago de Guatemala*, 167.

19. Sidney D. Markman, *Colonial Architecture of Antigua Guatemala* (Philadelphia: American Philosophical Society, 1966), 15–18. On the university, see John Tate Lanning, *The Eighteenth-Century Enlightenment in the University of San Carlos de Guatemala* (Ithaca: Cornell University Press, 1956).

20. See Adriaan C. Van Oss, "Central America's Autarkic Colonial Cities (1600–1800)," in *Colonial Cities*, ed. Robert J. Ross and Gerald Telkamp (Boston: Leiden University Press, 1985), 33–49; and Fernández Molina, "Colouring the World in Blue," 343–403.

21. See Domingo Juarros, *Compendio de la historia del reino de Guatemala, 1500–1800* (Guatemala City: Editorial Piedra Santa, 1981).

22. See Floyd, *Anglo-Spanish Struggle for Mosquitia*.

23. For example, until 1740, Nicaraguan cattlemen looked south to the Portobello fair; afterward they relied on Santiago/Guatemala City. Floyd, "Guatemalan Merchants," 91.

24. Fernández Molina, "Colouring the World in Blue," v–vi, 404.

25. The foregoing comes from Murdo J. MacLeod, *Spanish Central America: A Socioeconomic History, 1520–1720* (Berkeley: University of California Press, 1973).

26. See Héctor Lindo-Fuentes, *Weak Foundations: The Economy of El Salvador in the Nineteenth Century* (Berkeley: University of California Press, 1990), 9, 17, 23. In contrast, Fernández Molina, in "Colouring the World," 79–105, holds that the population of the Salvadoran indigo centers had become acculturated to indigo production over some two centuries, so that far from being disruptive, the majority of the population benefited from its spread.

27. William L. Sherman, *Forced Native Labor in Sixteenth-Century Central America* (Lincoln: University of Nebraska Press, 1979). Also see the pioneering works of Robert S. Smith: "Forced Labor in Guatemalan Indigo Works," *Hispanic American Historical Review* 36, no. 3 (August 1956): 318-28; and "Indigo Production and Trade in Colonial Guatemala," *Hispanic American Historical Review* 39, no. 2 (May 1959): 181-211.

28. See McCreery, *Rural Guatemala*, 9, 17-21.

29. Jones, *Guatemala*, 45, 54.

30. Ibid., 31-57.

31. Wortman, *Government and Society*, 311 n. 19.

32. Jones, *Guatemala*, 54-55.

33. Floyd explains that "provinces became known for the income from commerce a provincial office might expect in five years. El Salvador was the best mercantile venture in the kingdom, yielding about 30,000 pesos annually. An official in Nicoya, on the other hand, would count himself as fortunate to realize 1,000 pesos a year." Troy S. Floyd, "The Indigo Merchant: Promoter of Central American Economic Development, 1750-1808," *Business History Review* 39 (1965): 472.

34. "More than any other institution, the *parishes* of Guatemala constituted the base upon which Spanish rule depended." Van Oss, *Catholic Colonialism*, 183. In 1769-71, Pedro Cortés y Larraz counted a total of 289 parish priests— 123 beneficed, 166 auxiliaries. Of these, only 34 were *regular* clergy. The overwhelming majority were creoles. Cited in Jones, *Guatemala*, 71.

35. Lovell, *Conquest and Survival in Colonial Guatemala*, 75-94; Van Oss, *Catholic Colonialism*, 9-49.

36. Van Oss, *Catholic Colonialism*, 126-52. For example, cofradías in Indian communities functioned as both municipal governments and lay organizations. See, for example, Nancy Farriss, *Maya Society under Colonial Rule: The Collective Enterprise of Survival* (Princeton: Princeton

University Press, 1984); and MacLeod, *Spanish Central America*.

37. The Holy Inquisition operated out of Mexico City. Jones, *Guatemala*, 65–66.

38. Jones, *Guatemala*, 74–75.

39. Wortman, *Government and Society*, 91–111.

40. Ibid., 129–57.

41. Wortman, *Government and Society*, 41; also see Van Oss, *Catholic Colonialism*, 131.

42. Wortman, *Government and Society*, 103.

43. By the eighteenth century, if not even earlier, encomiendas had assumed the form of governmental pensions that hardly resembled the conquest era grants. See Lovell, *Conquest and Survival*, 95–101.

44. Wortman, *Government and Society* 104–5. The commercial deputation was a predecessor of the consulado de comercio that was established in 1794. On the consulado, see Ralph Lee Woodward, Jr., *Class Privilege and Economic Development: The Consulado de Comercio of Guatemala, 1793–1871* (Chapel Hill: University of North Carolina Press, 1966).

45. Troy S. Floyd, "Salvadoran Indigo and the Guatemalan Merchants: A Study in Central American Socio-Economic History, 1750–1800" (Ph.D. dissertation, University of California, Berkeley, 1958), 27.

46. Victor H. Acuña Ortega, "La reglamentación del comercio exterior en América Central durante el siglo XVIII," *Mesoamérica* 1, no. 1 (January 1980): 7–55.

47. Wortman, *Government and Society*, 166–71.

48. Buffeted by wars, plagued by locusts, and besieged by rising foreign competition, the Salvadoran indigo industry declined at the end of the eighteenth century and collapsed into full-scale depression after 1800. Wortman, *Government and Society*, 184–94.

49. Fernández Molina, "Colouring the World in Blue," 371–93.

50. See Woodward, *Class Privilege and Economic Development*. The Guatemalan merchant guild was one of seven new guilds the Spanish Bourbons recognized in the Indies. The establishment of regional merchant guilds was part of the broader attempt to break the power of the Cádiz-Mexico City-Lima axis that had dominated colonial trade since the sixteenth century. In effect, in trying to dilute the power of Mexico City merchants, the Bourbons actually strengthened merchant power in peripheral areas like Guatemala.

CHAPTER 2

1. In the words of Viotti da Costa, "the historian's task is neither to elevate nor to denigrate, but to analyze the relationships between a real historical individual and the larger structures that shape him and are in turn shaped by him. One of the tasks of historians is to reduce myths and heroes to their actual proportions." *The Brazilian Empire*, 25.

2. See the special issues of the *Journal of Family History* 3, no. 4 (Winter 1978) and 10, no. 3 (Fall 1985), devoted exclusively to Latin America, and the review essay of Elizabeth Anne Kuznesof, "The History of the Family in Latin America: A Critique of Recent Work," *Latin American Research Review* 24 (February 1989): 168–86. An especially valuable work is Balmori, Voss, and Wortman, *Notable Family Networks in Latin America*. The general thrust of the historical literature on the Latin American family is that, rather than being a passive reactor to events and processes largely beyond its control, the family acted to shape its world. Kuznesof and the late Robert Oppenheimer go so far as to say, "For Latin America we would propose that the family is that central complex of relationships through which political, entrepreneurial, and agrarian history may be viewed to make societal sense out of seemingly impersonal phenomena." Elizabeth Anne Kuznesof and Robert Oppenheimer, "The Family and Society in Nineteenth-Century Latin America:

An Historiographical Introduction," *Journal of Family History* 10, no. 3 (Fall 1985): 220.

3. Mark A. Burkholder and Lyman L. Johnson, *Colonial Latin America* (Oxford: Oxford University Press, 1990), 200.

4. Diana Balmori, "Family and Politics: Three Generations (1790–1890)," *Journal of Family History* 10, no. 3 (Fall 1985): 248.

5. Three additional Basque territories are found in southwestern France: Labourd, Basse Navarre, and Soule.

6. Rachel Bard, *Navarra: The Durable Kingdom* (Reno: University of Nevada Press, 1982), xi–xiii, 41–58, 104–22, 138–48.

7. AGCA, A1.40, Leg. 4797, fol. 451. Without archival work in Spain itself, we are somewhat limited in our ability to probe Juan Fermín de Aycinena's peninsular background. Our information comes primarily from testimony provided by Aycinena in the pursuit of hidalgo status for his offspring.

8. Bard, *Navarra*, 132.

9. James Lockhart and Stuart B. Schwartz, *Early Latin America: A History of Colonial Spanish America and Brazil* (Cambridge: Cambridge University Press, 1983), 20.

10. Bard, *Navarra*, 129, 146.

11. AGCA, A1.40, Leg. 4797, fol. 451. They owned the Aldecoa ancestral home in the center of the village. Juan Fermín's paternal grandparents had previously owned the same home. Juan Miguel de Aycinena's parents (and Juan Fermín's paternal grandparents) were also natives of Ciga.

12. Ibid. Ana Antonia's parents were don Fermín de Yrigoyen e Echandía and doña María de Yturralde y Perurena. At the time of Juan Fermín's birth, they owned the ancestral home of the Echandia family in Ciga.

13. AGCA, A3.10, Leg. 204, Exp. 3696.

14. Paloma Fernández-Pérez explains, "Among other reasons, Basques and Navarrese went away from their regions

because of the traditional systems of transmission of property. In general, the donor had the right to name a single heir regardless of sex or age of his or her choice, and because no new family houses, or *casas solariegas* could be created the non-elected offspring often decided to seek their fortune away from their valleys." "Family and Marriage Around Colonial Trade: Cádiz, 1700–1812" (Ph.D. dissertation, University of California, Berkeley, 1994), 81 fn. 40.

15. AGCA, A1.40, Leg. 4797.

16. Fernández-Pérez, "Family and Marriage," 81. Ida Altman demonstrates that even in areas where property was divided equally, family strategies encouraged migration to further the extended family's interests, giving rise to a paradox of stability and mobility. See Ida Altman, "Emigrants and Society: An Approach to the Background of Colonial Spanish America," *Comparative Studies of Society and History* 30, no. 1 (January 1988): 179. For a sense of the scale of migration to the Indies, see Magnus Mörner, "Spanish Migration to the New World Prior to 1810: A Report on the State of Research," in *First Images of America: The Impact of the New World on the Old*, ed. Fredi Chiappelli (Berkeley: University of California Press, 1976), 2:766.

17. Julio Caro Baroja, *La hora navarra del XVIII (Personas, Familias, negocios e ideas)* (Pamplona: Diputación Foral de Navarra, Institución Principe de Viana, 1969), 38.

18. Ibid., 24.

19. Ibid., 81–170.

20. Ibid., 120. He was a patron of Father Benito Feijoo and translated a work on the commerce of Holland, which he saw as a role model for Spain.

21. Ibid., 185. Juan Francisco's fellow Arizcun native and business associate Juan Bautista Iturralde (1674–1741) acquired the tax concession for the Kingdom of Granada and later served as minister of hacienda in the 1730s.

22. Peggy K. Liss, *Atlantic Empires: The Network of Trade and Revolution, 1713–1826* (Baltimore: Johns Hopkins University Press, 1983), 50–51.

23. Caro Baroja, *La hora navarra*, 289–339. On the Casa de Uztáriz, see Brian Hamnett, *Trade and Politics in Southern Mexico, 1750–1821* (Cambridge: Cambridge University Press, 1971), 29–31.

24. Fernández-Pérez, "Family and Marriage," 11.

25. Ibid., 14, 81, 231–34.

26. Archivo General de Notarias del Departamento de Distrito Federal (Mexico City) (hereafter cited as AGNDDF), Protocolo de Juan Antonio de la Serna, April 16, 1751.

27. Fernández-Pérez, "Family and Marriage," 17–18.

28. AGNDDF, Protocolo de Juan Antonio de la Serna, Mexico City, April 16, 1751.

29. AGNEO, Protocolo de Manuel Francisco Rueda, Antequera, Oaxaca, February 17, 1753.

30. AGNDDF, Protocolo de Diego Jacinto de León, September 1783.

31. Brading, *Miners and Merchants*, 107.

32. Caro Baroja noted the tendency of Spanish emigrants to gather according to place of origin. As he puts it, "Fuera, lejos, los Navarros se agruparán con los navarros y de modo mas amplío con los vascongadas en general." *La hora navarra*, 25.

33. AGNDDF, Protocolo de Antonio de la Serna, Mexico City, August 11, 1751. In this transaction, Juan Joseph acknowledged the receipt of 1,000 pesos of goods and cash from his family in Spain (including his mother, María de Yrigoyen, in Ciga, Navarra) via a Spanish merchant in Mexico, Juan Joseph Fagoaga.

34. On December 15, 1750, Joseph Matos y Rivera of Mexico City gave his power of representation to Pedro Bernardo de Yrigoyen, "alcalde que fue de . . . Jicayan, y proximo a pasar a la ciudad de Oaxaca." AGNDDF, Protocolo de Antonio de la Serna, Mexico City.

35. AGNEO, Protocolo de Francisco Rueda, January 8, 1752.

36. AGNDDF, Protocolo de Juan Antonio Arroyo, Mexico City, 1752, 727–49. On Juan Fermín's presence in

Oaxaca, see AGNEO, Protocolo de Francisco Rueda, Antequera, February 1753.

37. John K. Chance, *Race and Class in Colonial Oaxaca* (Stanford: Stanford University Press, 1978), xi, 32.

38. Ibid., 146.

39. Ibid., 144.

40. "In 1767 the [Villa Alta] post was still ranked administratively at the top of the 'first class' alcaldías mayores of New Spain, with neighboring Nejapa as number two. A Mexico City official observed in 1779, 'Only a few alcadías mayores were profitable and most of these were in Oaxaca. Villa Alta was the best of all, because of the diversity of its trades, which offered a profit in both peace and war. Jicayan, Miahuatlán, and Nejapa also rendered profits in peacetime, but their dye-trade suffered in war time.'" John K. Chance, *Conquest of the Sierra: Spaniards and Indians in Colonial Oaxaca* (Norman: University of Oklahoma Press, 1989), 101.

41. AGNEO, Protocolo de Francisco Rueda, October 15, 1740. The Oaxacan official was Yrigoyen's fellow Navarran, Miguel de Ibarra (of Irurita). The Veracruz merchant was Juan Bautista de Belaunzaran.

42. Ibid.

43. Ibid., February 14, 1742.

44. Ibid., December 15, 1745.

45. Ibid.

46. See Chance, *Conquest of the Sierra*, 187.

47. He was "Prior de Velate Dignidad de la Santa Iglesia Cathedral de la Ciudad de Pamplona, Reino de Navarra." AGNDDF, Protocolo de Arroyo, Mexico City, 1751, 1297. Pedro Angel de Yrigoyen married María Margarita de Larraínzar of Puebla in June 1734. She brought a dowry of 7,114 pesos. AGNDDF, Protocolo de Juan Antonio Arroyo, April 2, 1752 (Esc. 19, vol. 149), 309v, 727–49; and 1753 (Esc. 19, vol. 150), 190–200. María Margarita was a native of Veracruz, the daughter of Martín Fermín de Larraínzar and

Sebastiana Rosa Sabeli. Typically, Martín was a native of Estela, Navarra, while Sebastiana was from Veracruz. AGNDDF, Protocolo de Andres Delgado Camargo, Mexico City, 1758.

48. AGNEO, Protocolo de Francisco Rueda, February 9, 1750, and April 22, 1751.

49. AGNDDF, Protocolo de Juan Antonio Arroyo, Mexico City, 1752, 742.

50. His other daughters married Mexico City merchant José Echeverría and Martín de Azpiros, "oficial mayor de la secretaria del Exmo. Senor Virrey de este Reyno." AGNDFF, Protocolo de Diego Jacinto de León, Mexico City, March 1762.

51. AGNEO, Protocolo de Francisco Rueda, December 16, 1743.

52. Ibid., October 1, 1744.

53. After 1677, these posts were directly appointed by the Crown, demanding connections at the Spanish court. Thereafter, magistrates tended to be peninsular noblemen, mostly military men, and Knights of the Order of Santiago. Chance, *Conquest of the Sierra*, 37.

54. Rueda, 1742. On the death of Juan Francisco de Goyeneche in August 1744, Yrigoyen y Echenique conceded his powers of representation to Gregorio Fernández de Perline of Madrid. Rueda, 1744. Fernández de Perline was described in Goyeneche's testament (in which he was named an albacea) as "un simple vecino de la corte." Caro Baroja, *La hora navarra*, 208.

55. Caro Baroja, *La hora navarra*, 196.

56. AGNEO, Protocolo de Francisco Rueda, November 23, 1747.

57. "Obligación por 70,000," in AGNEO, Protocolo de Francisco Rueda, Antequera, December 24, 1744.

58. AGNDDF, Protocolo de Juan Antonio Arroyo, Mexico City, March 11, 1751. On the deaths of Miguel and María Luisa, see AGNEO, Protocolo de Francisco Rueda, August 1745.

59. AGNEO, Protocolo de Agustín Tomás Cañas Ximenez, February 11, 1757, which identifies Pedro Bernardo as a "vecino de esta ciudad y del comercio de Guathemala."

60. AGNEO, Francisco Rueda, February 17, 1753. The statement opens as follows: "yo don Juan Fermín de Aysinena, e Yrigoyen, residente en esta ciudad, y proximo a hasen biaje a el Puerto de Acapulco, y Reyno de Guatemala, ... otorgo que doy todo mi poder cumplido y bastante, el que se requiere, y nesesario fuere a dn. Pedro Bernardo de Yrigoyen, vesino de esta ciudad, a dn. Pedro de Aysinena e Yrigoyen, mi hermano, de el comersio de España, residente en la ciudad de Veracruz, y a dn. Ant[oni]o Salgado, vesino y de el comersio de la ciudad de Guatemala."

61. ACGA, A1.20, Leg. 881, Protocolo de Antonio González, July 27, 1754.

62. AGCA, A1.20, Leg. 893, Protocolo de Sebastián González, July 25, 1768. That Ana María's wealthy father had died when she was a young child left her with rights to inherit her part of his estate on entering marriage; this largely accounts for the size of the dowry she furnished. To appreciate the enormous size of the dowry, one might compare Ana María's contribution with the dowries listed by John Kicza in his study of Bourbon Mexico, *Colonial Entrepreneurs*, 163. Only one of the dowries (180,244 pesos) exceeds that received by Juan Fermín. No other dowry exceeds 64,400 pesos. Similarly, Ladd's figures on noble marriages and noble dowries shows only one dowry (323,107) greater than that of Juan Fermín and only three others that exceeded 100,000 pesos. Doris Ladd, *The Mexican Nobility at Independence 1780–1826* (Austin: University of Texas Press, 1976), 23.

63. See Fernández-Pérez's comments on the Navarran propensity toward endogamy and on what she dubs "yernocracia"—the power of sons-in-law, whom merchant families anointed to lead the family business in the succeeding generation. "Family and Marriage," 81, 234, 237–54.

64. AGNEO, Protocolo de Francisco Rueda, November 22, 1754. In his estate inventory, Pedro asserts that

he has "en la ciudad de Santiago la [suma] de 20,702p 5 1/4 rr. en la misma linea que el antecedente en don Juan Fermin Aizinena e Yrigoyen comerciante en ella hasta de [Octubre]."

65. See AGNEO, Protocolo de Francisco Rueda, June 20, 1740, which delegates his powers in Oaxaca as Pavón departed for Guatemala; and December 16, 1750, in which a Oaxacan merchant extends powers to Pavón to represent him in Guatemala.

66. According to Wortman, "Simón Larrazábal came [to Guatemala] in 1725 as a ship captain and merchant working for Pedro Carrillo of Cádiz." *Government and Society*, 122.

67. Hamnett, *Politics and Trade*, 18.

68. Archivo General del Estado de Oaxaca (hereafter cited as AGEO), Alcaldías Mayores, Leg. 17, Exp. 6, Antequera, February 4, 1737. Shortly before his death, Larrazábal transferred his alcabala concession to his cousin, Juan Crisotomo de Barroeta. Barroeta went to Mexico City shortly thereafter; he was regent of the Real Tribunal de Cuentas at least as early as 1744. See AGNEO, Protocolo de Francisco Rueda, July 10, 1744. Barroeta in turn ceded the concession to Felisiano Larrazábal in 1737. As of 1759, Felisiano was still (or again) "Juez Administrador de Reales Alcabalas" in Oaxaca. He was also the treasurer of the Santa Cruzada and alcalde ordinario de primer voto of the Antequera ayuntamiento. No doubt, he was well known to Pedro Bernardo de Yrigoyen (and his young cousin Juan Fermín de Aycinena). AGNEO, Protocolo de Francisco de Lara, May 29, 1759.

69. AGNEO, Protocolo de Francisco Rueda, April 1, 1751.

70. Ramiro Ordóñez Jonomá, "La Familia Varón de Berrieza," *Revista de la Academia Guatemalteca de Estudios Genealógicos, Heráldicos e Históricos* 9 (1987): 561.

71. AGCA, A1.20, Leg. 972, Exp. 9465, Protocolo de Miguel Vicente Guzmán, 1759. Those children, especially Simón de Larrazábal the younger and Nicolas de Obregón,

themselves became Santiago notables and integral parts of Juan Fermín's isthmian network of family and friends.

CHAPTER 3

1. Wortman, *Government and Society*, 122–23.

2. There is a somewhat greater emphasis on the antiquity of the immigrant pattern in Balmori, Voss, and Wortman, *Notable Family Networks in Latin America*, 58–59.

3. Webre, "Social and Economic Bases of Cabildo Membership," 142. Webre cautions that it is "possible to overestimate the importance of these families and the connections that existed among them as well as between them and others, both old and new. For one thing, to borrow an observation, when one reaches the point at which everyone of importance is related to everyone else, 'the very generality of the fact [of kinship] makes it a less useful tool for tracking down alignments and groupings'" (p. 146).

4. Ordóñez Jonomá, "La Familia Varón de Berrieza," 603.

5. Kuznesof and Oppenheimer, "Family and Society in Nineteenth-Century Latin America," 219. Defying the law, colonial elite families intermarried at a furious pace. Marriages between first cousins, uncles and nieces, even between widowed aunts and much younger nephews, occurred with startling frequency. Endogamous unions often aimed at preventing the dispersion of family property. Because all legitimate children, regardless of sex or birth order, could claim equal inheritances, many families preferred to intermarry rather than fragment the family estate. The state tolerated illegal marriages because they strengthened the existing social order, or because the powerful had the means to evade the law with impunity. Nor were the marriage practices of the socially exalted the most pressing concern of the Catholic Church. Ecclesiastical objections that might arise could be overcome with the aid of well-placed kinsmen in the clerical hierarchy.

6. Ordóñez Jonomá, "La Familia Varón de Berrieza," 531–35.

7. Webre, "Social and Economic Bases of Cabildo Membership," 77.

8. Wortman, *Government and Society*, 62.

9. MacLeod, *Spanish Central America*, 359 n. 27.

10. Webre describes the abortive 1698 cabildo as "an attempt to establish control of the municipal corporation by a powerful familial alliance centered upon the commercial house of don Bartolomé de Gálvez y Corral." "Social and Economic Bases of Cabildo Membership," 140.

11. For the full extent of the interconnections yielded by the marriages of the offspring of José Varón de Berrieza, the reader should consult the massive work of Ordóñez Jonomá, "La Familia Varón de Berrieza." Due to limitations of space and the desire to spare the reader, I have tried to refrain from reproducing, in the style of Genesis, all the "begats" issuing from Varón de Berrieza. The fecundity of the Santiago elite and their shameless propensity to intermarry render a complete discussion overwhelming in its detail and damaging to the purpose of illustrating the importance of the family connections Aycinena established so soon after his arrival. Instead, I have tried to focus on the most immediate and most important connections for Juan Fermín de Aycinena. Other connections will be noted as they arise. Gustavo Palma Murga makes a valiant effort to disentangle the Guatemalan interconnections in the period from 1776 to 1821, in "Nucleos de poder local y relaciones familiares en la ciudad de Guatemala a finales del siglo XVIII," *Mesoamérica* 12 (December 1986): 241–308.

12. From 1693 to 1700, María Manuela was married to the Logroño native Captain and Maestre de Campo don Francisco Navarro. He was alcalde mayor of San Antonio Suchitepequez, a post previously held by his father-in-law, José Varón de Berrieza. María Manuela's second husband, don Pedro Carrillo y Mencos, was the son of Pedro Carrillo y Eguia and Isabel de Mencos y Medrano, who in turn was the sister

of another family ally, General Melchor de Mencos. Ordóñez Jonomá, "La Familia Varón de Berrieza," 602.

13. AGCA, A1.23, Leg. 4592, fol. 161; A1.24, Leg. 1570, Exp. 10214, fol. 280; and A1.23, Leg. 4594, fol. 335.

14. AGCA, A1.24, Leg. 1576, Exp. 10220. Curiously, he sued his relative, Bernardo de Mencos, for a "cierta suma" in 1700. AGCA, A1.15, Leg. 2453, Exp. 18946.

15. Webre, "Social and Economic Bases of Cabildo Membership," 255. For the transfer of the concession, made July 19, 1729, see AGCA, A1.40, Leg. 5790, fol. 37. This concession from the Council of the Indies is substantially the same one acquired by Carrillo's associate Simón de Larrazábal in Oaxaca.

16. AGCA, A1.43, Leg. 5043, Exp. 42677, "Mortuales de Pedro Carrillo de Mencos." In drawing up his testament, he named as executors his son Pedro de Carrillo y Varón and his nephew Cristóbal de Gálvez Corral.

17. Ibid. Pedro's mother, María Manuela, died sometime between 1725 and 1729. Thus, because the younger Pedro's half-siblings had either died or renounced their inheritances in joining the church, he inherited the whole of his parents' estate, including the estate of his mother's first husband, don Francisco Navarro.

18. She entrusted the estate to the management of Manuel Salmerón y Gallo. That Pedro died when Ana María de Carrillo y Gálvez was a young child, gave her, the only child, the right to inherit the whole of her share of the estate at the time she married Juan Fermín de Aycinena in 1755. Ordóñez Jonomá, "La Familia Varón de Berrieza," 604. Also see Juarros, *Compendio de la história del reino de Guatemala*, 197. Of Pedro Carrillo y Varón's brothers, José Bernardo Navarro y Varón (b. 1695) became a Jesuit and died before 1725. Francisco Navarro y Varón was also a Jesuit priest and was still living as of 1742. Rodrigo Manuel Navarro y Varón was born November 9, 1698. Don Rodrigo was a maestre de campo, still living as of 1727, and traveled constantly to the province of San Salvador. He died sometime before 1743.

Conveniently for us, therefore, Ana María exhausts her father's lineage.

19. AGCA, A1.39, Leg. 256, Exp. 5672.

20. Manuel Rubio Sánchez, *Alcaldes mayores* (San Salvador: Ministerio de Educación, 1979), 1:319–30; see also AGCA, A1.23, Leg. 4586, fol. 119.

21. Webre, "Social and Economic Bases of Cabildo Membership," 76. Also see AGCA, A1.23, Leg. 4593, fol. 63v.

22. AGCA, A1.43, Leg. 5017, Exp. 42621. Also see Ordóñez Jonomá, "La Familia Varón de Berrieza," 557.

23. José Tomás de Gálvez y Varón (1696–1769) inherited the family mayorazgo in Málaga on his father's death in 1715. In 1719 he was admitted to the Order of Santiago, and a year later he served as alcalde ordinario of Santiago de Guatemala (along with his uncle, Pedro Carrillo y Mencos). Chronically ill, he was dependent on his younger brother Cristóbal, who became the true heir to his father's power. Ordóñez Jonomá, "La Familia Varón de Berrieza," 557–58. His brother Bartolomé Nicolas (1698–1748) was granted the commission to collect the alcabala in the pueblos of El Salvador in 1725; AGCA A3.5, Leg. 2732, Exp. 39276. In 1727, however, "the Crown rejected [his] offer of 26,000 pesos for the treasury office (contaduría of the Santa Cruzada)," so that for a time at least, the lucrative post passed out of family hands; Webre, "Social and Economic Bases of Cabildo Membership," 77. By 1729 Bartolomé had repatriated to Málaga, Spain, where he too became a Knight of Santiago. Ordóñez Jonomá, "La Familia Varón de Berrieza," 558.

24. Ordóñez Jonomá, "La Familia Varón de Berrieza," 577. Also see AGCA, A1.39, Leg. 1754, fol. 276.

25. Luisa's brothers provided additional family connections. Tomás José (1691–1755) was a mine owner and priest in Metapán. Miguel Cilieza Velasco y Varón (1707–68) became an especially eminent priest (see chap. 7). Luisa's youngest brother was Agustín Cilieza Velasco y Varón (1711–86). A regidor in San Salvador, Agustín owned the hacienda San José de la Bermuda. He became involved in the

Bernabé de la Torre affair of 1757. Ordóñez Jonomá, "La Familia Varón de Berrieza," 546–51.

26. Ordóñez Jonomá, "La Familia Varón de Berrieza," 577. He also became *sargento mayor* in the colonial militia as well as the *contador mayor* of the Colegio de Cristo Crucificado, an order later patronized by Juan Fermín de Aycinena. AGCA, A1.23, Leg. 2830, Exp. 25186; and A1.2, Leg. 5551, Exp. 48052.

27. AGCA, A3.5, Leg. 2737, Exp. 393370; and A3.8, Leg. 2885, Exp. 42098.

28. See Rubio Sánchez, *Alcaldes mayores*, 1:443–61, 2:21–36. The importance the Gálvez Corral family placed on possessing the office is indicated in the testament of Cristóbal's mother, Francisca Rosa Varón de Berrieza de Gálvez Corral, in which she stated, "con caudal mío se pagó el Donativo que mi hijo don Cristoval dio por la Alcaldía Mayor de San Salvador, y sirbió el suso dho tres años y continuó mi hijo Don Manuel, que uno, y otro la serbieron en veneficio de mi caudal pues todo los aprovechamientos y emolumentos me han pagado, por lo que no se les ha de pedir cuenta ni de esta Administración, ni de otran que hayan tenido con mi caudal, lo que quiero se guarde ymbiolablemente." Ordóñez Jonomá, "La Familia Varón de Berrieza," 577.

29. AGCA, A3.1, Leg. 8, Exp. 131, fol. 5. See also A1.2, Leg. 8, Exp. 76, June 1761, in which Gálvez Corral was "nombrado contador de las rentas de la catedral y de los propios de la ciudad de Guatemala es nombrado alcalde mayor de San Salvador y San Miguel, por el tiempo de 10 años y con el sueldo de 1200 pesos anuales, pidiendo nombre por su teniente a su hermano don Manuel, siempre y cuando otorgue finquito de 26,000 pesos y de otras sumas, valor del remate del oficio de contador que había servicio y que fuera suprimido." A3.1, Leg. 8, Exp. 131, reveals that in 1763 Gálvez Corral "quien había obtenido en su basta el oficio de Contador Mayor del Tribunal de la Bula de Santa Cruzada, oficio

mandado suprimir con 3% anual sobre el valor del remate que había sido de 26,000 pesos, cobrada dicho asignación anual."

30. Fadrique y Goyena was a native of Arguedas, Navarre, colonel in the Royal Army, and Knight of the Order of Charles III. In 1766, he married Gálvez Corral's daughter, María Gertrudis de Gálvez y Cilieza (1743–1807). Fadrique y Goyena was alcalde mayor of El Salvador from 1761 to 1763, 1765 to 1767, and 1777 to 1785. Ordóñez Jonomá, "La Familia Varón de Berrieza," 579–80; and Rubio Sánchez, Alcaldes mayores, 2:7–13, 35–44, 100–51. Also see AGCA, A3.5, Leg. 2884, Exp. 42011; A1.39, Leg. 1752, fol. 447; and A1.39, Leg. 2337, fol. 17535.

31. Shortly after de la Torre's death in 1773, kinsmen of Gálvez Corral (and thus Juan Fermín de Aycinena) recovered the alcalde mayor post: Bernardo de Mencos y Varón (1774–77) and Manuel Fadrique y Goyena (1777–85). Rubio Sánchez, Alcaldes mayores, 2:83–151.

32. AGCA, A3.1, Leg. 175, Exp. 3326; A3.1, Leg. 176, Exp. 3335, fol. 70; A1.23, Leg. 4612, fol. 277v; A1.23, Leg. 4614, fol. 100. Also see Ordóñez Jonomá, "La Familia Varón de Berrieza," 575.

33. Ordóñez Jonomá, "La Familia Varón de Berrieza," 575–76. Also see AGCA, A1.43, Leg. 2671, Exp. 22563; A1.57, Leg. 6004, Exp. 52865; and A1.20, Leg. 1096, fol. 46.

34. Del Cid F., Origen histórico, 94.

35. Ordóñez Jonomá notes that shortly before her death in 1787, Josefa declared that the "cuantioso caudal heredado por su hija, que por fin se logró en su primer matrimonio, ha sufrido grave deterioro y decadencia, originados en los gastos de la casa y varios contratiempos; y aclara que en la administración de los bienes unicamente han intervenido su padre, don Cristobal, y ella, y que su segundo esposo, don Nicolás, ha sido totalmente ajeno a sus negocios." "La Familia Varón de Berrieza," 578.

36. Balmori, Voss, and Wortman, Notable Family Networks in Latin America, 61.

37. Ventura served as alcalde ordinario of Santiago in 1767 and 1772 and of Nueva Guatemala in 1776 and 1793. He was married to María Manuela Batres (1769–1836), daughter of another notable Santiago family. Francisco was "tesorero juez oficial real de las cajas de Guatemala." This was one of the new posts established to ensure the integrity of royal tax collections. That it was held by a prominent creole testifies to the difficulty the Bourbons faced in rooting out "colonial establishments" from strategic offices. Francisco was married to the daughter of yet another Santiago merchant and cabildo fixture, Francisco Barrutia. Francisco's marriage to the daughter of Barrutia made him the brother-in-law of Pedro de Aycinena y Larraín. Another of Juan Fermín's Navarran nephews, Pedro de Beltranena, was also married to a Nájera, María Josefa Ana Llano y Nájera. On Ventura, María Micaela, and their seventeen other siblings, see Ordóñez Jonomá, "La Familia Varón de Berrieza," 671–708.

38. Fortuitously, Juan Fermín's merchant associate in Mexico City, Francisco Ignacio de Yraeta, congratulated Aycinena on his surprisingly quick marriage to the youthful Micaela and was thoughtful enough (of historians) to specify the date on which the event took place: July 7, 1781. Yraeta Papers, 2.1.8, July 11, 1781.

39. José Piñol y Sala served as alcalde ordinario of Santiago de Guatemala in 1774. Wortman, *Government and Society*, 123; and Balmori, Voss, and Wortman, *Notable Family Networks in Latin America*, 60–61.

40. Brading, *Miners and Merchants*, 103.

41. In 1808, Pedro de Aycinena reflected, "desde mis primeros años vine de la Reyno de España a esta ciudad a la casa de mi tío el difunto Sor Marquéz de Ayzinena donde me casé; despues me casé con Da Francisca Xaviera Barrutia y Echeverría de familia bien conocida." AGCA, A1.29, Leg. 2331, Exp. 17425.

42. Wortman confuses the lineage of Pedro de Beltranena, calling Martín de Beltranena his paternal uncle (rather than his father) and Manuel Eugenio de Llano his

"maternal uncle" (rather than his father-in-law). This causes Wortman to misstate the true relationship of Beltranena to Juan Fermín de Aycinena. Balmori, Voss, and Wortman, *Notable Family Networks in Latin America*, 62.

43. For example, the inventory of 1768 shows Beltranena to be a cajero of Juan Fermín's firm. Ana María Carrillo's testament of that year also names him as an heir and seems to hint at a lengthy acquaintance. Aycinena Family Papers.

44. Ordóñez Jonomá, "La Familia Varón de Berrieza," 678–83. Not to be too seriously outdone by the Nájera Mencos family, Beltranena and Llano produced fifteen children, including the first vice president of the Central American Federation, Manuel de Beltranena y Llano.

45. Martínez-Peláez, *La patria del criollo*, 110–14.

CHAPTER 4

1. Floyd, "Guatemalan Merchants," 99. Also see Victor H. Acuña Ortega, "Capital comercial y comercio exterior en Centroamérica durante el siglo XVIII," *Mesoamérica* 4 (December 1982): 302–31.

2. Juan Fermín received "dinero, efectos de mercancía, alhajas de oro y plata, y dependencias, segun consta de el formal recibo que por ante testigos di a Dn Manuel Salmerón y Gallo que me hizo la entrega como administrador que era entonces de este caudal, a él que agregue. Yo aporto la cantidad de 21,000 pesos que mití por parte al matrimonio lo que así declaro para que conste." AGCA, A1.20, Leg. 893, Protocolo de Sebastián González, Testament of Ana María Carrillo y Gálvez, July 25, 1768.

3. Burkholder and Johnson, *Colonial Latin America*, 202–3.

4. Socolow, *Merchants of Buenos Aires*, 40–41.

5. See AGCA, A1.43, Leg. 4167, Exp. 33029. This document established Ana María's rights to the estate of her father, Pedro Carrillo y Varón, which included the holdings and dependencies of his father, Pedro Carrillo y Mencos, and

María Manuela Varón de Berrieza, as well as those of her maternal grandmother's first husband, Francisco Navarro.

6. AGCA, A.35, Leg. 1105, Exp. 20007.

7. Aycinena Family Papers, Inventory of 1768.

8. AGCA, A1.20, Leg. 882, Exp. 9375, Protocolo de Antonio González, 1755.

9. As Kicza discovered for Mexico City, "a major part of the total value of commercial establishments of every size and character in the city consisted of 'dependencias activas,' the collective debts of the many customers compelled to buy on credit." *Colonial Entrepreneurs*, 55.

10. Aycinena's active accounts exceeded his total wealth because the latter was adjusted not only for lost and doubtful dependencies but also for his own debts, which amounted to 281,160 pesos.

11. Fernández Molina, "Colouring the World in Blue," 45, explains that its quality was the principal advantage of Central American indigo.

12. Floyd, "Salvadoran Indigo and the Guatemalan Merchants," 237.

13. Wortman, *Government and Society*, 188.

14. Floyd, "Salvadoran Indigo and the Guatemalan Merchants," 230. Also see the table in Floyd, "The Indigo Merchant," 486.

15. In 1768, Archbishop Pedro Cortés y Larraz described the conditions suffered by cutters and carriers as being "of the most painful and rigorous [work] that could be imagined, for the labor went on day and night in great heat, among a flood of insects.... [T]he workers, dead tired and bathed in sweat, [for relief], would throw themselves into the river, clothes and all." Cited in Floyd, "Salvadoran Indigo and the Guatemalan Merchants," 39. Excellent discussions of the harsh labor conditions associated with indigo and the difficulties the Spanish Crown faced in reconciling the humane treatment of Indian subjects and the need to ensure an adequate labor supply to indigo producers appear in Smith,

"Indigo Production and Trade in Colonial Guatemala," 186–93; and Sherman, *Forced Native Labor*, 251–55.

16. Floyd, "Salvadoran Indigo and the Guatemalan Merchants," 145.

17. Floyd, "Guatemalan Merchants," 94.

18. Ibid., 100.

19. AGCA, A1.20, Leg. 1000, Exp. 9193, Protocolo de José Matías Guzmán, 1760.

20. AGCA, A1.20, Leg. 1120, Exp. 9613, Protocolo de Francisco Márquez Rendón, 1771.

21. AGCA, A1.20, Leg. 974, Exp. 9467, Protocolo de M. V. Guzmán, 1768.

22. AGCA, A1.20, Leg. 1119, Exp. 9612, Protocolo de Francisco Márquez Rendón, 1769. On April 4, 1770, Rodríguez conferred his poder cumplido on Juan Fermín de Aycinena. AGCA, A1.20, Leg. 1120, Exp. 9613, Protocolo de Francisco Márquez Rendón.

23. Fernández Molina, "Colouring the World in Blue," 154–55, discusses Aycinena's relationship with Antonio Molina, which was that of patron and client and involved Aycinena sponsoring one of Molina's children in the capital. Antonio Molina was not bound to a single financier, however.

24. Kicza, *Colonial Entrepreneurs*, 56.

25. Troy S. Floyd, "Bourbon Palliatives and the Central American Mining Industry, 1765–1800," *The Americas* 18 (1961): 108.

26. Ibid., 107.

27. AGCA, A3.1, Leg. 20, Exp. 5270.

28. AGCA, A1.20, Leg. 1046, Exp. 9539, Protocolo de Lucas Martínez García, 1766.

29. AGCA, A1.20, Leg. 1046, Exp. 9539, Protocolo de Lucas Martínez García, 1767.

30. "para trabajar las fundan en ellas hacienda fabricar ingenios le pedimos ambos el fomento necesario al Capitán Juan Fermín de Ayzinena." AGCA, A1.20, Leg. 892, Exp. 9385, Protocolo de Sebastián González, 1767.

31. Floyd, in "Bourbon Palliatives," 108, states that "the mining district of Yuscarán, southeast of Tegucigalpa, was by far the largest region, with five mines employing about 200 workers. Yuscarán, in fact, seems to have been the only district in Central America where mining was carried on continuously and extensively enough that empirical knowledge of techniques was passed on from one generation to another. Here were the most prominent miners, and mines whose depth and tunneling showed some foresight and technical knowledge. Worked to a depth of 300 feet, the Yuscarán mines were an exception to the shallow exploitation which characterized most of the mining areas."

Unfortunately, Floyd gives no explanation for why Yuscarán was different. Although it remains speculation at this point, it may be the case that Aycinena's substantial investment helped to resolve at least some of the basic problems afflicting the industry. Or it may simply be that Juan Fermín invested in the most promising area.

32. For example, see the transactions reported in AGCA, A1.20, Leg. 1120, Exp. 9613, Protocolo de Francisco Márquez Rendón, January 9, 1771; and A1.20, Leg. 1341, Exp. 9832, Protocolo de Antonio Santa Cruz, December 2, 1776.

33. Floyd, "Salvadoran Indigo and the Guatemalan Merchants," 124.

34. AGCA, Protocolo de Antonio Santa Cruz, December 27, 1788.

35. Wortman, *Government and Society*, 127–28.

36. Ibid., 310.

37. ACCA, A1.20, Leg. 1025, Exp. 9518, Protocolo de Manuel Laparte, 1796.

38. The changing perceptions are reflected in Enrique Florescano, "The Hacienda in New Spain," in *Colonial Spanish America*, ed. Leslie Bethell (Cambridge: Cambridge University Press, 1987), 250–85. See also Florescano's bibliographical essay in the same volume, pp. 427–33, especially p. 432.

39. Brading, *Miners and Merchants*, 100.
40. Ibid., 100.
41. Kicza, *Colonial Entrepreneurs*, 19.
42. John Tutino, "Power, Class, and Family: Men and Women in the Mexican Elite, 1750–1810," *The Americas* 39 (January 1983): 363. He adds, "If landed investment conferred status in colonial Mexico, it was not because of an uneconomic, hispanic preference for the soil, but because landed investment was the best available means to preserve wealth, and thus elite status."
43. Fernández Molina comes to this same conclusion in "Colouring the World in Blue," 364–65.
44. AGCA, A1.23, Leg. 4633, "Libro de Reales Cédulas, 1782–1785," 232–43.
45. Fernández Molina, "Colouring the World in Blue," 363, attributes Aycinena's unique acquisition of land to his noble aspirations. Yet this does not explain the scale of Aycinena's holdings.
46. Kicza, *Colonial Entrepreneurs*, 61.

CHAPTER 5

1. Fernández-Pérez, "Family and Marriage," 34.
2. See, for example, Colin MacLachlan and Jaime Rodriguez O., *The Forging of the Cosmic Race*, 2d ed. (Berkeley: University of California Press, 1990), 146–47; and Kicza, *Colonial Entrepreneurs*, 30. In his study of the indigo merchants of Guatemala, Floyd states, "The characteristic mode of operation was that of the individual merchant." Floyd's main point is that there existed no "monopoly" or collusion in any formal sense on the part of the merchants of Santiago. "The Indigo Merchant," 469.
3. Kicza, *Colonial Entrepreneurs*, 59.
4. Aycinena Family Papers, Estate Inventories, 1768, 1771, 1777. At this point, we know little of Manuel Maldonado, Tomás Beteta, or Juan de Beteta.
5. Aycinena Family Papers, Estate Inventories, 1768, 1771, 1777.

6. Aycinena Family Papers, Inventory of 1768. For additional commercial activities of the two Pedros, see the following: AGCA, A1.20, Leg. 1119, Exp. 9612, Protocolo de Francisco Márquez Rendón, November 8, 1769; A1.20, Leg. 1121, Exp. 9614, Protocolo de Francisco Márquez Rendón, January 13, 1773; A1.20, Leg. 1024, Exp. 9517, Protocolo de Manuel Laparte, March 27, 1775; A1.20 Leg. 1341, Exp. 9832, Protocolo de Antonio Santa Cruz, February 14, 1777.

7. AGCA, A1.20, Leg. 1345, Exp. 9836, Protocolo de Antonio Santa Cruz, September 30, 1789.

8. Floyd, "The Indigo Merchant," 486.

9. For example, Yraeta Papers, 2.1.4, March 4, 1778, and February 24, 1779; 2.1.7, March 8, 1780.

10. AGCA, A1.20, Leg. 973, Protocolo de M. V. Guzmán, 1765. Aycinena Family Papers, Inventories of 1768 and 1771.

11. AGCA, A1.20, Leg. 973, Protocolo de Miguel Vicente Guzmán, 1765. In his testament of 1765, Gortari named Juan Fermín as both heir and albacea. He was the son of Martín de Gortari and Agustina de Echandía. Juan Fermín's grandparents were owners of the casa solar de Echandía in Ciga. AGCA, A1.40, Leg. 4797, fol. 451.

12. Aycinena owed Gortari some 6,097 pesos in 1771 in this capacity. In 1777 the amount was 6,617 pesos. Aycinena Family Papers, Inventories of 1771 and 1777.

13. María Cristina Torales Pacheco et al., *La compañía de comercio de Francisco Ignacio de Yraeta (1767–1797): Cinco ensayos* (Mexico City: Instituto Mexicano de Comercio Exterior, 1985), 2:198. *La Fama* was acquired sometime after 1768 from Manuel Lorenzo García of Realejo, who in 1768 owed Juan Fermín 11,066 pesos. Aycinena Family Papers, Inventory of 1768.

14. AGCA, A1.20, Leg. 1345, Exp. 9836, Protocolo de Antonio Santa Cruz, November 27, 1789. Not long thereafter, Pedro de Lara was named Juan Fermín's agent in San Miguel. Another important figure was attorney Francisco Ortíz, who

represented the Casa in a variety of legal matters. On Ortíz, see, for example, AGCA, A1.15, Leg. 4193, Exp. 33281.

15. AGCA, A1.43, Leg. 5169, Exp. 43579, reveals him to be a debtor to the estate of Father Martín Ruíz Calatayud in 1778. Also see A1.15, Leg. 5907, Exp. 50284.

16. AGCA, A1.23, Leg. 4640, fol. 205v. Also see A3.1, Leg. 266, Exp. 5802.

17. The partnership, sealed March 4, 1778, involved a cash investment of 70,000 pesos by Mariano Nájera, with José García Goyena providing his expertise, and was slated to last ten years. A few months later, however, they agreed to dissolve the company. AGCA, A1.20, Leg. 1342, Exp. 9833, Protocolo de Antonio Santa Cruz, August 27, 1778.

18. Yraeta Papers, 2.1.11, March 14, 1787.

19. These had been granted in 1781 to Luis Pérez and Pedro Juan de Lara. AGCA, A1.20, Leg. 1345, Exp. 9836, Protocolo de Antonio Santa Cruz, November 27, 1789.

20. Aycinena Family Papers, March 31, 1791, "Instrucción y carta a Manuel Rodrigo López sobre la distribución y gobierno de las haziendas del Señor Marquéz y preveenciones a dn Ambrosio Marín, todo comunicado con fecha de 31 Marzo 1791." García Goyena died at the age of fifty-three in early October 1796, a few months after the death of his patron, the Marqués de Aycinena. AGCA, Libro de defunciones, 1773–1816, fol. 35v. He named as his principal heirs and albaceas the family Aycinena. Also see the earlier testament in A1.20, Leg. 1346, Exp. 9837, Protocolo de Antonio Santa Cruz, August 10, 1791. The abundant García Goyena commercial records found among the Aycinena family papers further substantiate García Goyena's intimacy with the Casa.

21. Yraeta Papers, 2.1.16, February 23, 1791.

22. Aycinena Family Papers, March 31, 1791, "Instrucción y carta a Manuel Rodrigo López sobre la distribución y gobierno de las haziendas del Señor Marquéz y preveenciones a dn Ambrosio Marín, todo comunicado con fecha de 31 Marzo 1791."

23. See chapter 4.
24. AGCA, A1.20, Leg. 890, Exp. 9383, Protocolo de Sebastián González, 1765.
25. Ibid.
26. AGCA, A1.20, Leg. 1120, Exp. 9613, Protocolo de Francisco Márquez Rendón, 1770.
27. Derived from the examination of protocolos from 1750 to 1800, AGCA, A1.20.
28. Brading, *Miners and Merchants*, 100. Brading adds, "By 1807, [Abad y Quiepo] stated that two-thirds of all commercial transactions were paid in bills rather than cash. The notes drawn by silver miners upon their Mexico City correspondents were especially acceptable, and changed hands ten or twelve times before their final payment three or four months after their issue."
29. Ibid., 101–2. "In part, the libranza filled the vacuum left by the export of silver specie. But its widespread employment sprang from the peculiarly centralised nature of New Spain's commercial and financial system. From Mexico City flowed merchandise issued on credit and to it flowed all silver to be minted, most taxes, and libranzas for the payment of goods."
30. Fernández Molina, "Colouring the World in Blue," 153.
31. In 1985 the Instituto Mexicano de Comercio Exterior, with the collaboration of the Universidad Iberoamericana, published a lengthy collaborative study of the colonial era commercial firm of Francisco Yraeta, covering the years 1767 to 1797: Torales Pacheco et al., *Compañía de comercio*. That study and Yraeta's career cover roughly the same period as the career of Juan Fermín de Aycinena. The work features separate studies by María Cristina Torales Pacheco, Tarsicio García Diaz, and Carmen Yuste exploiting the sizable Yraeta commercial archive. The work includes a biographical sketch and chapters treating the organization of his business, his various partnerships, his involvement in trade within New Spain and overseas, including Europe and

the Philippines. An especially valuable section of the work is the series of appendixes, which include a glossary, a chronology, personal documents (e.g., an inventory of his estate on his death in 1797), and correspondence.

32. On the deaths in rapid succession of his father-in-law and his own wife in 1769, Yraeta entered into a commercial partnership with his mother-in-law, Ana Gómez de Valencia. Torales Pacheco et al., *Compañía de comercio*, 1:116.

33. Christiana R. Borchart de Moreno, *Los mercaderes y el capitalismo en la ciudad de Mexico: 1759–1778*, trans. Alejandro Zenker (Mexico City: Fondo de Cultura Económica, 1984), 255.

34. Aycinena Papers, Inventories of 1768, 1771, 1777.

35. See, for example, Yraeta Papers, 2.1.23, January 22, 1794.

36. AGCA, A1.20, Leg. 1344, Exp. 9835, Protocolo de Antonio Santa Cruz, 1787. Earlier that month, Juan Fermín had acted as albacea to Yraeta's uncle, Juan José de Ganuza, in establishing an obra pía. Ibid., December 5, 1787.

37. Torales Pacheco et al., *Compañía de comercio*, 1:74–78, 83.

38. Ibid., 55. He received the commission in company with fellow Mexico City merchant Pedro de Aycinena.

39. AGCA, A1.20, Leg. 1025, Exp. 9518, Protocolo de Manuel Laparte, 1797. When they learned of Yraeta's death, they named in his stead his son-in-law, Gabriel de Yturbe. In 1803 the brothers Aycinena, along with their cousin Pedro de Aycinena Larraín, appealed to Yturbe to help secure a loan of some 20,000 pesos. A1.20., Leg. 953, Exp. 9446, Protocolo de José Díaz González.

40. Yraeta Papers, 2.1.3, February 5, 1777; 2.2.5, 8, 9, 90; 2.2.6, 66, 110–12.

41. Yraeta Papers, 2.1.4, February 11, 1778.

42. Pérez de Elizalde owed Juan Fermín de Aycinena 3,157 pesos in 1771. Aycinena Family Papers, Inventory of 1771.

43. Torales Pacheco et al., *Compañía de comercio*, 1:280.

44. Ironically, Francisco Yraeta's rivalry with Gabriel Pérez de Elizalde involved Francisco's cousin and former protégé, José Yraeta. Set up by his cousin to handle the Acapulco trade, José married a daughter of Gabriel Pérez de Elizalde in 1776. At this point José ended his partnership with his cousin Francisco. Francisco Yraeta then turned to his nephew, Gabriel Yturbe e Yraeta. Like his uncle, Gabriel was a native of Anzuloa, Guipuzcoa. In 1785 Yturbe married Francisco's second daughter (and his first cousin), María Margarita. "In particular, Yraeta confided to his nephew the *abastecimiento* [provisioning license] of oriental products for the Kingdom of Guatemala." Yturbe ultimately inherited control of Francisco's company on his father-in-law's death in 1797. Torales Pacheco et al., *Compañía de comercio*, 1:286.

45. Archivo General de la Nación (hereafter cited as AGN), Mexico City, Consulado, vol. 142, Exp. 3, 112–275.

46. Aycinena Family Papers, Inventories of 1768, 1771, and 1777.

47. Borchart de Moreno, *Los mercaderes*, 128 n. 4.

48. Ibid., 34.

49. AGNDDF, Protocolo de Diego Jacinto de León, November 10, 1767, which refers to a document notarized by Veracruz escribano Francisco Joseph Guiraldes on April 25, 1764.

50. Borchart de Moreno, *Los mercaderes*, 38, 103.

51. Ibid., 113. Also see Christiana R. Borchart de Moreno, "Los miembros del consulado de la ciudad de México en la época de Carlos III," *Jahrbuch für Geschichte von Staat, Wirtschaft und Gesellschaft Lateinamerikas* 14 (1977): 142.

52. Borchart de Moreno, *Los mercaderes*, appendix 8, 251. Also see Borchart de Moreno, "Los miembros," 142.

53. AGNDDF, Protocolo de Diego Jacinto de León, September 12, 1783.

54. Antonio García-Baquero González, *Cádiz y El Atlántico (1717–1778): El comercio colonial español bajo el*

monopolio gaditano (Seville: Escuela de Estudios Hispano-Americanos, CSIC, Excelentísima Diputación Provincial de Cádiz, 1976), 1:511–13.

55. AGNDDF, Protocolo de Diego Jacinto de León, December 1782. He was the son of Domingo de Elizalde and Ana María de Aycinena e Yrigoyen.

56. AGNDDF, Protocolo de Diego Jacinto de León, Mexico City, February 27, 1775. Juan Angel was the son of Juan de Aguerrevere (deceased) and Ana María de Ayzinena (still living). Conceivably, given the same name of their mothers, he could have been the half-brother of Fermín de Elizalde.

57. Borchart de Moreno, *Los mercaderes*, 246.

58. Aycinena Family Papers, Inventories of 1768, 1771, and 1777.

59. Borchart de Moreno, *Los mercaderes*, 250.

60. AGCA, A1.20, Leg. 1166, Protocolo de Francisco José Palacios, January 26, 1762.

61. In 1771, Aycinena owed Aldasoro 242 pesos. Aycinena Family Papers, Inventories of 1768, 1771, and 1777.

62. Father Juan José de Ganuza was involved in the importation of European and Oriental goods, especially through his ties to his cousin and later his nephew, Francisco Ignacio de Yraeta. Torales Pacheco et al., *Compañía de comercio*, 1:27.

63. Floyd, "The Indigo Merchant," 470 n. 17. Also see his "Salvadoran Indigo and the Guatemalan Merchants," 123. As of 1768, Pedro de Ganuza owed Juan Fermín 3,280 pesos while also having received 24 zurrones of indigo from him. Aycinena Family Papers, Inventory of 1768.

64. AGCA, A1.20, Leg. 881, Exp. 9374, Protocolo de Antonio González, 1754.

65. Feliciano Larrazábal owed him 970 pesos in 1777. The debt appears to have been acquired in the course of Feliciano's service as a subordinate to his father, Simón de Larrazábal, who became the Kingdom of Guatemala's *correo mayor* (postmaster general) in 1770. On his role in Oaxaca, see Hamnett, *Politics and Trade*, 37.

66. She was born in Puebla, the daughter of Navarran Martín Fermín de Larraínzar. AGNDDF, Protocolo de Andres Delgado Camargo, Mexico City, 1758.

67. Yraeta Papers, 2.2.4, August 29, 1770, October 31, 1770, June 5, 1771; 2.1.2, December 6, 1769, June 11, 1772, August 3, 1774; 2.1.3, January 1776, August 7, 1776; 2.1.4, August 7, 1777; and 2.1.5, July 15, 1778. In 1768, Aycinena was in arrears to the Oaxacan for some 211 pesos. In 1771 Sinande owed Aycinena 423 pesos, and 136 pesos in 1777. In 1768 Juan Fermín consigned some six zurrones of indigo to Sinande. Aycinena Papers, Inventories of 1768, 1771, and 1777.

68. Yraeta Papers, 2.1.6, May 31, 1780, June 28, 1780, August 16, 1780, September 13, 1780; 2.1.8, May 16, 1781, June 27, 1781.

69. See Yraeta Papers, 2.1.11, May 9, 1787; 2.1.16, August 18, 1790, January 19, 1791; 2.1.17, March 30, 1791; 2.1.25, April 25, 1795. Juan Fermín owed Magro 334 pesos in 1768 and 502 pesos in 1771. See Hamnett, *Politics and Trade*, 177, which documents the ties of trade and politics between Magro and Yraeta.

70. Juan Fermín owed Francisco José 1,179 pesos in 1768. Aycinena Papers, Inventory of 1768.

71. Aycinena Family Papers, Inventories of 1768, 1771, and 1777. Francisco Mendibal had a debt of 349 pesos in 1768, while in 1771 Aycinena owed Mendibal 811 pesos. In 1777 Aycinena owed Candido González Maldonado 1,378 pesos.

72. Yraeta Papers, 2.1.11, January 11, 1787, January 23, 1788; and the accounts in 2.2.6, July 24 and August 7, 1795, where Ojeda y Estrada charged 1,500 pesos on each occasion to Aycinena's account with Yraeta.

73. Antonio Sáenz owed Aycinena some 1,797 pesos in 1771, while Aycinena owed the Saenz Rico firm 95 pesos. Aycinena Family Papers, Inventory of 1771.

74. AGCA, A1.20, Leg. 973, Protocolo de M. V. Guzmán, 1765. Aycinena Family Papers, Inventories of 1768, 1771.

75. Yraeta Papers, 2.1.2, May 2, 1770.

76. Alberto Flores Galindo, "Aristocracía en vilo: Los mercaderes de Lima en el siglo XVIII," in *The Economies of Mexico and Peru during the Late Colonial Period, 1760–1810*, ed. Nils Jacobsen and Hans Jurgen-Puhle (Berlin: Colloquium Verlag, 1986), 253.

77. AGCA, A1.20, Leg. 1121, Exp. 9614, Protocolo de Francisco Márquez Rendón. In his stead, the powers were to be delegated to Isidro Aborea and Juan de Orobioquita y Aguirre, respectively.

78. Flores Galindo, "Aristocracía," 270.

79. Ibid., 261.

80. As of 1768 the Marqués de Negreiros owed Aycinena 290 pesos. The Conde de San Isidro owed him 1,984 pesos. And Sebastián de Urrutia owed him 1,498 pesos. At the same time, Aycinena owed Miguel de Olavide 3,485 pesos. In 1771 Olavide owed Aycinena 49 pesos. Manuel Lorenzo García, formerly of Realejo, Nicaragua, and formerly (or perhaps still) the owner of the merchant vessel *La Fama*, had increased his obligation to Juan Fermín de Aycinena to 15,695 pesos. The 514 pesos owed by Juan Josef Anbelaez had been written off. As of 1771 Aycinena owed the Conde de San Isidro 187 pesos, and Antonio Rodríguez, 449 pesos. Finally, in 1777 José de Zaldumbide owed Aycinena 6,630 pesos; Juan Baptista de Yrigoyen was in arrears 16 pesos; and Isidro de Abarco (Conde de San Isidro), 59 pesos. Aycinena Family Papers, Inventories of 1768, 1771, and 1777.

81. Benjamin Keen reminds us, "It must be stressed, however, that these reforms did not seriously weaken the dominant role of the Cádiz monopolists and their American agents in colonial trade. As late as 1790, more than 85 percent of the trade moved through Cádiz, thanks to its superior facilities for shipping, insurance, warehousing, and communication." Benjamin Keen, *A History of Latin America*, 4th ed. (Boston: Houghton Mifflin, 1992), 122 n. 2.

82. See Hamnett, *Politics and Trade*, 29–30.

83. Floyd, "The Indigo Merchant," 470.

84. Ordóñez Jonomá, "La Familia Varón de Berrieza," 575.

85. Ibid., 688. His brother, Pedro José Micheo y Barreneche, also became a powerful figure in Santiago and Guatemala City. Pedro José was the treasurer of the Santa Cruzada. He married his brother's sister-in-law, María Gertrudis Nájera y Mencos. Their daughter, Mariana Josefa Joaquina Micheo y Nájera, married Juan Fermín's second son, José Alejandro de Aycinena y Carrillo, in 1799. Ordóñez Jonomá, "La Familia Varón de Berrieza," 691.

86. Aycinena Family Papers, Inventory of 1768, 1771; Ordóñez Jonomá, "La Familia Varón de Berrieza," 571.

87. Hamnett, *Politics and Trade*, 29-30.

88. Ibid. Hamnett continues, "Intimately connected with the Cinco Gremios was the Casa de Uztáriz, an eminent joint-stock trading company, described by Arcila Farias as the strongest that existed in Spain, at least as regards Spanish trade to the Indies."

89. Cristobal Xavier Uztáriz owed Aycinena 126 pesos in 1777. Aycinena Family Papers, Inventory of 1777.

90. AGCA, A1.20, Leg. 570, Exp. 9063, Protocolo de Manuel Ignacio Carcamo. Landaburu was a business associate of Francisco Yraeta as well. Torales Pacheco et al., *Compañía de comercio*, 2:216. Landaburu was born in Durango, Viscaya. At the time of his marriage to Maria Alzaga Gorrosary in 1741, his worth was estimated to be 70,000 pesos. He joined the Consulado de Cádiz in 1748. See Fernández-Pérez, "Family and Marriage," 464, 544.

91. Aycinena Family Papers, Inventories of 1768, 1771, and 1777.

92. AGCA, A1.20, Leg. 1345, Exp. 9836, Protocolo de Antonio Santa Cruz.

93. AGCA, A1.20, Protocolo de Carlos de Figueroa, May 6, 1777.

94. Fernández-Pérez, "Family and Marriage," 465, 519. Larraín was born in Oyeregui, Navarre, in 1723. He joined the Consulado de Cádiz in 1757. He resided in

Benedición de Dios. His account with Aycinena showed him in arrears 70 pesos in 1768. Aycinena Family Papers, 1768.

95. Floyd, "Salvadoran Indigo and the Guatemalan Merchants," 233.

96. Fernández-Pérez, "Family and Marriage," 431, 509, 552. He resided in the Comisari José Artecona.

97. Aycinena Family Papers, 1768.

98. Fernández-Pérez, "Family and Marriage," 427 and 567. Later on, María Ignacia inherited a house from her parents worth 820,000 reales de vellón. She also purchased two houses that belonged to the patronato of the Flemish nation, auctioned off after the royal decree on disentailment of pious properties, worth 527,000 reales and 397,000 reales, respectively. Ibid., 283.

99. AGCA, Protocolo de Antonio Santa Cruz, December 27, 1788.

100. Yraeta Papers, 2.1.9, March 8, 1784.

101. Yraeta Papers, 2.1.15, November 27, 1790, September 29, 1791.

102. Some of these ties are suggested by the Aycinena estate inventories and the notarial records in Guatemala and Mexico City. Caro Baroja mentions a Salvador Aycinena who along with Miguel de Elizalde created a company to enter the wine trade of Chile in 1794. Caro Baroja, *La hora navarra*, 397 n. 102. The Larraín family of Chile achieved a dominance there similar to that of the Aycinenas in Guatemala. It is likely that the fellow Navarrans were related, given the prominence of the Larraín surname among Aycinena family members. Guatemalan merchant scion and politician, diplomat, and literary figure, Antonio José Irisarri, was intimately related to the Chilean Larraíns, whom he joined in Chile's struggle for independence. See Mary Lowenthal Felstiner, "The Larraín Family in the Independence of Chile, 1780–1830" (Ph.D. dissertation, Stanford University, 1970), and her groundbreaking article, "Kinship Politics in the Chilean Independence Movement," *Hispanic American Historical Review* 56, no. 1 (February 1976): 58–80.

103. Kicza, *Colonial Entrepreneurs*, 62.

104. Based on his analysis of the estates of a group of important Guatemalan merchants that did not include Aycinena, Fernández Molina ("Colouring the World in Blue," 297) questions the extent to which merchants dominated the provinces or monopolized indigo profits: "export merchants who became part of the colonial elite failed in their attempt to monopolize Central America's market . . . [and] remained dependent on Cádiz houses, which shared the profits of indigo trade with other European merchants." Elsewhere he writes, "Export merchants occupied a marginal and weak position within the imperial structure of trade, while they were far from monopolizing the supply of European merchandise to the Central American market" (p. 321). Given the extraordinary success of Aycinena and his profitable relations with numerous merchants outside of Spain, this view is perhaps subject to at least partial modification.

CHAPTER 6

1. AGCA, A1.23, Leg. 4633.

2. For example, Balmori, Voss, and Wortman, *Notable Family Networks in Latin America*, 64; and Ralph Lee Woodward, Jr., "Economic and Social Origins of the Guatemalan Political Parties, 1773–1823," *Hispanic American Historical Review* 46, no. 4 (November 1966): 546.

3. Ladd, *The Mexican Nobility at Independence*, 17.

4. AGCA, A1.23, Leg. 4633; A1.23, Leg. 2362, Exp. 17842.

5. AGCA, A1.23, Leg. 4633, "Libro de Reales Cédulas, 1782–1785," 232–43.

6. AGCA, A1.20, Leg. 1045, Exp. 9538, Protocolo de Lucas Martínez García, November 19, 1761; A1.20, Leg. 1069, Exp. 9562, Protocolo de Diego Milán, November 11, 1761.

7. Wortman, *Government and Society*, 314 n. 9.

8. AGCA, A1.23, Leg. 4633.

9. Floyd, "Salvadoran Indigo and the Guatemalan Merchants," 124.

10. AGCA, A1.23, Leg. 4633. The Omoa fortress, the largest fortification in Central America, had taken more than twenty years to construct, at a cost of more than a million pesos. It was promptly captured by British troops in its very first engagement in 1777.

11. For example, Floyd, "The Indigo Merchant," 481–82.

12. Burkholder and Johnson, *Colonial Latin America*, 164. "The use of government revenues for personal gain was common." In such cases, "access to institutional funds often gave officials a competitive advantage in the marketplace."

13. Ibid. "A *visita* conducted by the president of the audiencia of Guatemala in 1717 found that the *contador* of the local treasury owed the crown 30,000 pesos and that his predecessor owed 4,000. In . . . these cases, officeholders had invested public funds in private-sector enterprises or lent them to kinsmen or business associates."

14. According to Webre, "the revival of [Santiago] cabildo membership dates from the 1760s with the formation of a dominant family cluster under the leadership of don Juan Fermín de Aycinena, first marqués de Aycinena. . . . In the late eighteenth century and early nineteenth century, this group found monopoly of the cabildo to be essential to the maintenance of its political power against challenges from other elite elements organized in the newly-approved consulado (1794) and in the indigo growers society (sociedad de cosecheros de añil) of San Salvador." Webre, "Social and Economic Bases of Cabildo Membership," 314–15.

15. Ibid., 34.

16. Floyd, "Salvadoran Indigo and the Guatemalan Merchants," 122–26.

17. AGCA, A1.20, Leg. 1119, Exp. 9612, Protocolo de Francisco Márquez Rendón, August 9, 1769.

18. AGCA, A1.20, Leg. 1022, Exp. 9515, Protocolo de Manuel Laparte, June 21, 1773.

19. Ibid., May 20 and 28, 1774.

20. Balmori, Voss, and Wortman, *Notable Family Networks in Latin America*, 64.

21. Ibid., 65.

22. Manuel was named to these posts on September 4, 1775, and July 23, 1777, respectively. AGCA, A1.20, Leg. 1341, Exp. 9832, Protocolo de Antonio de Santa Cruz, August 5, 1776.

23. " . . . depositario[s] encargado[s] de colectar dinero para la construcción de la nueva ciudad de Guatemala, destruida por un terremoto del ano 1773." Torales Pacheco et al., *Compañía de comercio*, 1:55.

24. AGCA, A3.10, Leg. 200, Exp. 3652; A3.10, Leg. 204, Exp. 3696; A1.30. Leg. 206, Exp. 3716; A1.29, Leg. 2331, Exp. 17425; A1.2, Leg. 44, Exp. 1129.

25. Ordóñez Jonomá, "La Familia Varón de Berrieza," 607–11; Balmori, Voss, and Wortman, *Notable Family Networks in Latin America*, 62–63; Juarros, *Compendio*, 192–200.

26. The financial ties between Aycinena and royal officials that we do know of are drawn from the estate inventories found among the Aycinena family papers. This is not necessarily a complete list, because I do not have in my possession complete copies of the inventories.

27. Richard N. Adams, *Energy and Structure: A Theory of Social Power* (Austin: University of Texas Press, 1975), 10–20. Cited in Tutino, "Power, Class, and Family," 360 n. 2.

28. AGCA, A1.20, Leg. 1345, Exp. 9836, Protocolo de Antonio de Santa Cruz, November 28, 1789, and December 2, 1789. With respect to Troncoso, see A1.20, Leg. 1025, Exp. 9518, Protocolo de Manuel Laparte, May 10, 1794.

29. Aycinena Family Papers, Inventory of 1777.

30. AGCA, A1.20, Leg. 1346, Exp. 9837, Protocolo de Antonio Santa Cruz, 1791.

31. Fernández Molina, "Colouring the World in Blue," 239.

32. Aycinena Family Papers, Inventories of 1768, 1771, and 1777.

33. AGCA, A1.20, Leg. 1024, Exp. 9517, Protocolo de Manuel Laparte, September 2, 1779.
34. Floyd, "Bourbon Palliatives," 113.
35. Aycinena Family Papers, Inventories of 1768, 1771, and 1777. On the "housecleaning," see Floyd, "Bourbon Palliatives," 117.
36. AGCA, A1.20, Leg. 890, Exp. 9383, Protocolo de Sebastián González, 1765.
37. AGCA, A1.20, Leg. 892, Exp. 9385, Protocolo de Sebastián González, 1767.
38. AGCA, A1.20, Leg. 898, Exp. 9391, Protocolo de Sebastián González, May 14, 1773.
39. AGCA, A1.20, Leg. 1024, Exp. 9517, Protocolo de Manuel Laparte, February 5, 1776.
40. Aycinena Family Papers, Inventory of 1777.
41. Manzanares was married to Ana María Carrillo y Gálvez's first cousin, Antonia Elias. Ordóñez Jonomá, "La Familia Varón de Berrieza," 572.
42. AGCA, A1.20, Leg. 1121, Exp. 9614, Protocolo de Francisco Márquez Rendón.
43. AGCA, A1.20, Leg. 1000, Exp. 9493, Protocolo de José M. Guzmán, October 9, 1760.
44. AGCA, A1.20, Leg. 892, Exp. 9385, Protocolo de Sebastián González, October 28, 1767.
45. AGCA, A1.20, Leg. 1120, Exp. 9613, Protocolo de Francisco Márquez Rendón, October 15, 1771. As of 1778, Becerril owed Bernabé de la Torre the younger, who was an agent of Aycinena and his family, some 2,200 pesos. A1.20, Leg. 1342, Exp. 9833, Protocolo de Antonio Santa Cruz, March 25, 1778.
46. Fernández Molina, "Colouring the World in Blue," 167–69.
47. His wife, Petrona Tagle y Bracho, was the daughter of Simón de Tagle y Bracho. AGCA, A1.30, Leg. 205, Exp. 41403, "Testament of Bernabé de la Torre."
48. Wortman, *Government and Society*, 126.

49. He owned a hacienda named San José de la Bermuda in San Salvador. Ordóñez Jonomá, "La Familia Varón de Berrieza," 546–54.

50. His Salvadoran holdings included the indigo-producing haciendas San Nicolas, San Jacinto, and La Trinidad near San Vicente, all of which he rented out during his legal struggle. He also owned the hacienda San Antonio Tepeagua near Guisucán, which he purchased from Joseph Plazaola, and he had an interest in the hacienda Santa Eulalia. Plazaola was later a corregidor of del Viejo and a debtor to Juan Fermín de Aycinena. AGCA, A1.30, Leg. 205, Exp. 41403, "Testament of Bernabé de la Torre."

51. AGCA, A1.30, Leg. 205, Exp. 41403.

52. Rubio Sánchez, *Alcaldes mayores* 2:45–63.

53. AGCA, A1.20, Leg. 1120, Exp. 9613, Protocolo de Márquez Rendón, 1771.

54. Ibid.

55. Ibid., June 6, 1771.

56. Ibid., January 13, 1771.

57. AGCA, A1.23, Leg. 4633.

58. AGCA, A1.20, Leg. 1025, Exp. 9518, Protocolo de Manuel Laparte, 1796.

59. Melchor de Mencos Varón de Berrieza (1715–87) was the son of Lugarda Antonia Varón de Berrieza y López de Ramales (daughter of José Varón de Berrieza and sister to both grandmothers of Ana María Carrillo y Gálvez, first wife of Juan Fermín de Aycinena) and Bernardo de Mencos. Ordóñez Jonomá, "La Familia Varón de Berrieza," 747–48.

60. In this transaction Escamilla increased his debt to Juan Fermín de Aycinena to 11,440 pesos (goods and silver). Escamilla pledged to repay in indigo. AGCA, A1.20, Leg. 1119, Exp. 9612, Protocolo de Francisco Márquez Rendón, April 10, 1769.

61. Yraeta Papers, 2.2.6. "En 14 de Abl. [1795] cargo 10,000 pesos que é entregado en dinero efectivo Sor. D Juan Jose Villalengua consejero de SM en el de Indias en virtud de

su carta orn. que me entrgo dho sor. fha 23 de Octre. del ano prox pasado segun consta del recivo que me firmo."

62. Franklin Knight notes among the elite families of mainland Spanish America the "common eighteenth-century pattern ... of intermarriage and overlapping participation in the Church, bureaucracy, economy, and military." Franklin Knight, *The Caribbean: Genesis of a Fragmented Nationalism*, 2d ed. (Oxford: Oxford University Press, 1990), 232.

63. Alan Knight, *The Mexican Revolution* (Lincoln: University of Nebraska Press, 1990), 1:20.

CHAPTER 7

1. Van Oss, *Catholic Colonialism*, 183.

2. AGCA, A1.23, Leg. 4633.

3. Juarros, *Compendio*, 62, noted that there were more than thirty cofradías in Guatemala City alone. For Mexico City, Kicza, *Colonial Entrepreneurs*, 180, explains that "cofradías were popular with every sector of society, and merchants were no exception. Some belonged to sodalities which restricted membership to men of commerce, and some joined others which were less restrictive. Most commonly, they affiliated with one whose patron saint or sacred place was identified with their home province in Spain. It was seen previously that these cofradías regularly functioned as lending institutions, most often to their own constituents and countrymen."

4. María Teresa Aycinena Piñol (Carmelite) and Miguel Aycinena Piñol (Dominican), in their turn, became extremely prominent and controversial religious figures in the independence era.

5. Juarros, *Compendio*, 179.

6. Van Oss, *Catholic Colonialism*, 65.

7. Ibid., 163.

8. Cited in Van Oss, *Catholic Colonialism*, 173; also see p. 68.

9. Van Oss states that in rural areas priestly power greatly exceeded the "civil authority of officials such as alcaldes mayores and corregidores (especially through their control of villages)." Facility in Indian languages contributed especially to mendicant power. Royal officals (and secular clergy) did not command the requisite language skills to gain direct access to the Indian populations independent of mediation by the friars. *Catholic Colonialism*, 50.

10. Ironically, the transfer of Indian parishes from the mendicant orders to secular priests in the late colonial era weakened Spanish authority in the countryside by weakening the bonds between priest and parishioner. Van Oss, *Catholic Colonialism*, 141. Lest one have too idealized a picture of friar-Indian relations, however, Wortman in *Government and Society*, 134, reminds us that "long-standing abuses were described: creole friars with close family connections in nearby areas used Indian labor on their personal properties, paying money into community funds which they controlled."

11. Van Oss, *Catholic Colonialism*, 183.

12. Jones, *Guatemala*, 74–75.

13. Murdo J. MacLeod, "Aspects of the Internal Economy," in *Colonial Spanish America*, ed. Leslie Bethell (Cambridge: Cambridge University Press, 1987), 344. Wortman, in *Government and Society*, 279–83, provides estimates on tithe collections in late colonial Central America. See also Van Oss, *Catholic Colonialism*, 83–84.

14. Jones, *Guatemala*, 75.

15. Wortman, *Government and Society*, 61. According to Kicza, *Colonial Entrepreneurs*, 58, 180, in Mexico each church agency "collected and managed its own revenue with little interference from higher ecclesiastical authorities." Moreover, they "preferred to lend out their funds for a steady return of five percent annually rather than invest directly in enterprises or to establish their own businesses. Consequently they amounted to so many banking institutions available to the businessmen of the colony."

16. Wortman, *Government and Society*, 62. In 1665 and 1668 the administrator sent some 125,000 pounds of indigo worth 95,000 pesos and 17,175 pounds of cacao north to Mexico. Fourteen years later (i.e., 1682) it was estimated that the indigo shipped north defrauded the fiscal administration of 43,000 pesos in taxes annually, with additional frauds in Guatemala and other regions. The last transaction involved José Varón de Berrieza.

17. Wortman writes, "The Crown repeatedly called the attention of the audiencia to the activities of 'many pernicious and harmful' clergy who, led by ambition, took advantage of their position, trading with the Indians and making them keep and breed horses in their villages, selling them merchandise at inflated prices, and generally 'giving bad examples of themselves.'" *Government and Society*, 45, 154.

18. Van Oss, *Catholic Colonialism*, 155.

19. Ración and servicios required parishioners to provision resident and visiting clerics. See Van Oss, *Catholic Colonialism*, 85–89.

20. Van Oss, *Catholic Colonialism*, 106.

21. Ibid., 50.

22. Ordóñez Jonomá, "La Familia Varón de Berrieza," 546–54.

23. The reader may recall that Cristóbal de Gálvez was not only Cilieza's first cousin but also the husband of his sister, Luisa.

24. Ordóñez Jonomá, "La Familia Varón de Berrieza," 748; Juarros, *Compendio*, 192.

25. AGCA, A1.20, Leg. 889, Exp. 9382, Protocolo de Sebastián González, 1765.

26. AGCA, A1.20, Leg. 1344, Exp. 9835, Protocolo de Antonio Santa Cruz, December 5, 1785.

27. Torales Pacheco et al., *Compañía de comercio*, 1:27.

28. AGCA, A1.20, Leg. 1119, Exp. 9612, Protocolo de Francisco Márquez Rendón, December 26, 1769.

29. AGCA, A1.20, Leg. 1344, Exp. 9835, Protocolo de Antonio Santa Cruz, December 5, 1787.

30. AGCA, A1.20, Leg. 890, Exp. 9383, Protocolo de Sebastián González, May 9, 1765; A1.20, Leg. 1343, Exp. 9834, Protocolo de Antonio Santa Cruz, April 1, 1784.

31. See, for example, Yraeta Papers, 2.1.2, May 31, 1769.

32. AGCA, A1.20, Leg. 900, Exp. 9393, Protocolo de Sebastián González, August 16, 1775; A1.20, Leg. 1022, Exp. 9515, Protocolo de Manuel Laparte, September 7, 1776; A1.20, Leg. 1346, Exp. 9837, Protocolo de Antonio Santa Cruz, July 3, 1792.

33. AGCA, A1.2, Leg. 5551, Exp. 48052. Also see Ordóñez Jonomá, "La Familia Varón de Berrieza," 577.

34. Aycinena Family Papers, Inventory of 1771.

35. AGCA, A1.20, Leg. 890, Exp. 9383, Protocolo de Sebastián González, April 3, 1765.

36. AGCA, A1.20, Leg. 901, Exp. 9394, Protocolo de Sebastián González, 1776.

37. AGCA, A1.20, Leg. 1166, Protocolo de Francisco José Palacios, 1762.

38. AGCA, A1.20. Leg. 1341, Exp. 9832, Protocolo de Antonio Santa Cruz, 1774.

39. See the comments made by Archbishop Pedro Cortés y Larraz as a result of his famous visita of 1769–70, in his *Descripción geográfico-moral de la diocesis de Goathemala* (1771), (Guatemala: Biblioteca "Goathemala," 1958), 1:263.

40. AGCA, A1.20, Leg. 1120, Exp. 9613, Protocolo de Francisco Márquez Rendón, 1770.

41. AGCA, A1.20, Leg. 1121, Exp. 9614, Protocolo de Francisco Márquez Rendón, 1772.

42. The Aycinena estate inventories reveal that a number of Aycinena's creditors were men and women of the cloth. These included Josef Manuel de Iglesias of Comayagua (169 pesos), Matheo Cornejo of San Vizente (whose estate

Aycinena owed 8,770 pesos), and María Ana Rafaela Zeage, a nun of the Convent of Santa Catalina in Santiago (850 pesos). In addition, Aycinena owed Francisco Gómez Dighero, cura de Xalapa, 1,756 pesos, and Ambrosio de Gálvez 512 pesos. And, finally, as fiador of Nicolás de Obregón, Juan Fermín was liable for 2,200 pesos his late wife's cousin owed to the Monjas de Nuestra Señora de la Concepción of Santiago. The 1771 inventory reveals similar relations. As of 1771 Aycinena controlled 8,000 pesos belonging to Maestro Carlos Tunsin, cura of San Sebastián, along with 2,800 from Josef Mariano Barrientos of Santiago. The inventory continued to show the debt of 8,150 to the estate of Padre Matheo Cornejo of San Vizente. Finally, some 2,023 pesos had been placed in Aycinena's care for the Foundation of the Convent Nuestro Padre San Francisco in San Vicente.

43. "hipotecando generalmente todos sus bienes y especialmente el Pontifical." AGCA, A1.20, Leg. 1341, Exp. 9832, Protocolo de Antonio Santa Cruz, 1774.

44. AGCA, A1.20, Leg. 1046, Exp. 9539, Protocolo de Lucas Martínez García, June 20, 1766.

45. AGCA, A1.20, Leg. 893, Exp. 9386, Protocolo de Sebastián González, 1768. On Luceno, see Cortés y Larraz, *Decripción* 1:169.

46. AGCA, A1.20, Leg. 893, Exp. 9386, Protocolo de Sebastián González. On March 27, 1772, Juan Fermín was empowered to represent Francisco Antonio Machado, Cura Proprio Vicario y Juez Eclesiástico in Gracias a Dios. AGCA, A1.20, Leg. 1121, Exp. 9614, Protocolo de Francisco Márquez Rendón, 1772. Cortés y Larraz, *Descripción*, 1:191: "don Ignacio Villata, anciano escrupuloso y por esto inutil."

47. AGCA, A1.20, Leg. 882, Exp. 9375, Protocolo de Antonio González, November 1755. Suria also stated that he kept a house in Santiago.

48. AGCA, A1.20, Leg. 884, Exp. 9377, Protocolo de Antonio González, 1757.

49. AGCA, A1.20, Leg. 900, Exp. 9393, Protocolo de Sebastián González, 1775. On Perdomo, see Cortés y Larraz, *Descripción*, 1:269.

50. AGCA, A1.20, Leg. 892, Exp. 9385, Protocolo de Sebastián González, 1767. On Larrave, see Cortés y Larraz, *Descripción*, 2:239.

51. These included a hacienda in the valley of Jumaez, named Nuestra Señora del Refugio, which he purchased in 1758 from Father Gregorio de Almeida for 1,800 pesos. Zeage also owned the hacienda la Ascención del Señor, measuring some 22 1/2 caballerías, which he acquired in 1760 for 13,000 pesos. In 1780 he acquired from don Ignacio Muñoz y Barba "varias labores de pan llevar y pan sembrar" near San Agustín Sumpango. Finally, in 1784, he acquired the sugar mill of los Pastores y del Potrero de Palomo, near Santiago. AGCA, A1.20, Leg. 944, Leg. 9437, Protocolo de José Díaz González, March 1793. Also see Ordóñez Jonomá, "La Familia Varón de Berrieza," 559–60.

52. Cortés y Larraz, *Descripción*, 2:78–81.

53. AGCA, A1.20, Leg. 892, Exp. 9385, Protocolo de Sebastián González. On May 22, 1769, Aycinena transferred his power to Francisco Ortíz. A1.20, Leg. 1119, Exp. 9612, Protocolo de Francisco Márquez Rendón. As of 1771 Zeage owed Juan Fermín some 2,864 pesos; as of 1777, the amount was 486. Aycinena Family Papers, Inventories of 1768, 1771, and 1777.

54. AGCA, A1.20, Leg. 891, Exp. 9384, Protocolo de Sebastián González, 1766.

55. AGCA, A1.20, Leg. 1120, Exp. 9613, Protocolo de Francisco Márquez Rendón, 1770.

56. Ibid.

57. Ibid.

58. AGCA, A1.20, Leg. 1046, Exp. 9539, Protocolo de Lucas Martínez García, June 20, 1766.

59. AGCA, A1.20, Leg. 898, Exp. 9391, Protocolo de Sebastián González, April 15, 1773.

60. Cortés y Larraz, *Descripción*, 1:158.

CHAPTER 8

1. See, for example, Socolow, *The Merchants of Buenos Aires*; Kicza, *Colonial Entrepreneurs*; and Hoberman, *Mexico's Merchant Elite*.

2. Ladd, *The Mexican Nobility at Independence*, 52.

3. Caro Baroja, *La hora navarra*.

4. These letters are reproduced in del Cid F., *Origen histórico*, 47–52.

5. Ladd, *The Mexican Nobility at Independence*, 17.

6. Kicza, *Colonial Entrepreneurs*, 16. Fernández Molina, "Colouring the World in Blue," 363, relates that Cayetano Pavón refused the offer of a title.

7. AGCA, A1.23, Leg. 4633, "Libro de Reales Cédulas, 1782–1785," 232–43. Copies of the title may also be found in A1.23, Leg. 2362, Exp. 17842 (1784), which includes the formal acknowledgment of the grant by the appropriate colonial officials, and as part of the mayorazgo established by Juan Fermín de Aycinena before Manuel Laparte in February 1796, A1.20, Leg. 1025, Exp. 9518.

8. Ladd, *The Mexican Nobility at Independence*, 61.

9. Ibid., 60–61.

10. Ibid., 53.

11. Ibid.

12. Cited in Ladd, *The Mexican Nobility at Independence*, 58.

13. Ibid.

14. Caro Baroja, *La hora navarra*.

15. Ladd, *The Mexican Nobility at Independence*, 58.

16. Floyd, "The Indigo Merchant," 481.

17. Ibid., 483.

18. Ladd, *The Mexican Nobility at Independence*, 64.

19. Wortman, *Government and Society*, 162.

20. A paja is a municipal allocation of water flow, equal to one-eighth the area of a real. See Stephen Webre, "Water and Society in a Spanish American City: Santiago de

Guatemala, 1555–1773," *Hispanic American Historical Review* 70, no. 1 (February 1990): 57–84.

21. John Lloyd Stephens, *Incidents of Travel in Central America, Chiapas and Yucatan* (New York: Dover, 1969), 1:194.

22. Ladd, *The Mexican Nobility at Independence*, 64.

23. George A. Thompson, *Narrative of an Official Visit to Guatemala from Mexico* (London: John Murray, 1829), 191. Thompson estimated the Aycinena estate to be worth 750,000 pesos in 1825; he figured the Pavóns were worth 1.25 million (p. 521).

24. Stephens, *Incidents of Travel*, 1:206.

25. Juarros, *Compendio*, 179.

26. Tutino, "Creole Mexico," 221.

27. Ibid., 222.

28. Edith Couturier, "Philanthropic Activities of the Conde de Regla," *The Americas* 32 (July 1975): 15.

29. Ibid., 29–30.

30. See Mario Rodríguez et. al., *Applied Enlightenment: Nineteenth-Century Liberalism, 1830–1839* (New Orleans: Middle American Research Institute, 1972). Ramiro Ordóñez, Guatemalan attorney, genealogist, and director of the ecclesiastical archives in Guatemala City, has conveyed to me the prominence of Vicente de Aycinena as a compadre for numerous individuals in turn-of-the-century Guatemala City (based on Ordóñez's examination of baptismal records in the Archivo Eclesiástico). The Aycinena Family Papers are rife with requests by the destitute for personal charity from the second Marqués. As Tutino surmised for Mexico, the volume of those requests implies at least the presumption on the part of the many supplicants that alms were forthcoming. Similarly, Stephens, in *Incidents of Travel*, 2:132, tells us that Juan Fermín's youngest son, Maríano Aycinena, was the leading patron of the Hospital San Juan de Dios.

31. Handy, *Gift of the Devil*, 132–33. Other notable musings of the archbishop cited by Handy include the

following: "Rossell attacked all aspects of the government's reform. He argued that democracy was not necessarily good for Guatemalans because 'Sad experience shows that liberty left to the caprice of each individual only disorganizes [our people] into opposing bands, weakens them and begins to destroy them.'" Criticizing Juan José Arévalo's educational reforms, Rossell averred, "Books are too fragile a staircase for our Indians to climb to civilization. One does not need, as a first step, literacy for Indians. What is essential is to redeem them."

32. Ladd, *The Mexican Nobility at Independence*, 70.

33. Ibid., 71. Theoretically a mayorazgo represented seven-fifteenths of the founder's estate.

34. AGCA, A1.20, Leg. 1025, Exp. 9518, Protocolo de Manuel LaParte, February 29, 1796.

35. Ibid.

CHAPTER 9

1. Woodward, "Economic and Social Origins of the Guatemalan Political Parties," 547.

2. Cited in Mario Rosenthal, *Guatemala* (New York: Twayne, 1962), 15.

3. AGCA, A1.20, Leg. 1119, Exp. 9612, Protocolo de Francisco Márquez Rendón, January 1769.

4. Ordóñez Jonomá, "La Familia Varón de Berrieza," 608–11.

5. For detailed discussions of independence era politics in Central America, see Mario Rodríguez, *The Cádiz Experiment in Central America, 1808–1826* (Berkeley: University of California Press, 1978); Woodward, "Economic and Social Origins of the Guatemalan Political Parties," 544–66; and Louis Bumgartner, *José del Valle of Central America* (Durham: Duke University Press, 1963). See also the recent article by Timothy P. Hawkins, "José de Bustamante and the Preservation of Empire in Central America, 1811–1818," *Colonial Latin American Historical Review* 4, no. 4 (Fall 1995): 439–64.

6. In 1788 Vicente married Juana Nepomucena María Piñol y Muñoz (1763–1832). She was the daughter of the Catalan merchant José Piñol y Sala and the creole doña María Manuela Muñoz y Barba de Figueroa. Vicente's wife was the sister of Juan Fermín's third wife, Micaela Piñol y Muñoz; their brother, Tadeo Piñol y Muñoz, was the husband of Vicente's half-sister by Juan Fermín's second marriage, María Bernarda Aycinena Nájera.

7. David L. Chandler, *Juan José de Aycinena: Idealista conservador de la Guatemala del siglo XIX* (Antigua: CIRMA, 1989).

8. AGCA, A1.3, Leg. 1946, Exp. 12989.

9. Balmori, Voss, and Wortman, *Notable Family Networks in Latin America*, 62–63; Ordóñez Jonomá, "La Familia Varón de Berrieza," 607–8; Juarros, *Compendio*, 192–200.

10. José Alejandro married doña Mariana Josefa Joaquina Micheo in 1799, daughter of Navarran merchant Pedro José de Micheo y Barreneche and creole María Gertrudis Hermegilda de Nájera y Mencos. José Alejandro's mother-in-law was the sister of his father's second wife. His father-in-law, Pedro José Micheo, was treasurer of the Santa Cruzada, a post often held by members of the Gálvez Corral family. Pedro Micheo was the brother of Juan Tomás Micheo, yet another prominent Navarran merchant in late colonial Guatemala. In time-honored fashion, José's daughter, Dolores Aycinena Micheo, married Pedro de Aycinena Piñol, her first cousin and the son of Vicente de Aycinena.

11. He became prior of the consulado in 1807 and served as alcalde ordinario of Guatemala City in 1797, 1801, and 1805.

12. Ramón Salazar, *Mariano de Aycinena* (Guatemala: Biblioteca de Cultura Popular, 1952). At the same time, Mariano's first cousin (and the son of Pedro de Beltranena Aycinena), Mariano Beltranena y Llano, served as president of the federation.

13. Tobis and Jonas, *Guatemala*, 216–51.

Glossary

Abastecimiento (abasto de carne) - Provisioning license (license or contract to supply meat to a city)
Adelantado - Frontier ruler or expedition leader
Albacea - Estate executor
Alcabala - Sales tax
Alcalde mayor (alcaldía mayor) - District magistrate (area governed by alcalde mayor)
Alcalde ordinario - Annually elected member of city council (ayuntamiento) with judicial and administrative responsibilities
Alférez - Officer in militia; royal standard-bearer
Alguacil mayor - Chief constable (audiencia post)
Alhajas de plata - Silver furnishings
Añil (tinta) - Indigo (dye)
Apoderado. - Individual legally designated to act in the name of another

Arras - Endowment of bride by groom, theoretically not exceeding 10 percent of his fortune
Arriero - Muleteer
Asentista - Holder of royal concession (*asiento*)
Audiencia - Court of appeals, legislative and supervisory body of the jurisdiction of the same name
Aviador - Financier
Ayuntamiento - Municipal council. See *Cabildo*
Bascongada - Member of "Basque" party on Mexico City *consulado* (opposite of Montañeses)
Beneficiado - Beneficed clergy, head of a secular parish
Caballería - Unit of measure, roughly 104 acres
Cabildo - Municipal council (see *Ayuntamiento*)
Cabildo eclesiástico - Cathedral chapter (administrators of bishopric)
Caja de comunidad - Municipal treasury
Cajero - Commercial employee or apprentice, subordinate
Canónigo - Canon, position on cabildo eclesiástico
Capellanía - Chantry, prayer endowment
Casa solariega - Family household
Casta - Person of mixed race
Cédula real - Royal decree
Censo - Long-term real estate loan
Clérigo diácono - Secular priest
Cofradía - Confraternity, religious lay brotherhood
Colegio - School
Comerciante - Merchant
Comercio libre - "Free trade"
Compadrazgo - Godparenthood
Consulado de comercio - Merchant guild
Consul - Annually elected officer of consulado
Corregidor (corregimiento) - District magistrate (area governed by corregidor)
Cortes - Spanish provincial parliament
Cura propio - Beneficed clergy
Dependencias (activas, dudosas, perdidas) - Commercial debts (active, doubtful, lost)

GLOSSARY

Depositario general - Ayuntamiento officer, receiver of funds or property
Diezmo - "Tenth"; tithe, royal assessment to finance the church
Doctrina - Indian parish administered by friars
Encomienda - Grant of tribute-collecting rights, royal pension
Fiador - Guarantor of another's financial obligations
Fianza - Bond posted to assume office
Fiel ejecutor - Cabildo official, supervisor of weights and measures
Finca - Commercial estate
Fiscal - Royal attorney (audiencia post)
Fuero - Privilege
Futuro - Future claim to royal office
Generos de mercancias - Merchandise
Gobernador (gobierno) - Governor (area presided over by a gobernador)
Hacendado - Estate owner
Ingenio - Sugar mill
Jefe politíco superior - Political chief
Juez administrador (de alcabalas) - Administrator responsible for overseeing alcabala collections
Juez de milpas - Judge of plantings
Justicia mayor - Principal justice or magistrate
Ladino - In colonial era, a Spanish-speaking casta; in contemporary Guatemala, Spanish speaker (non-Indian)
Lanza - Feudal obligation of military service; in practice, a tax paid for royal title
Libranza - Bill of exchange
Maestre - Supercargo
Maestreescuela - Officer of cathedral chapter, supervisor of schools
Mayorazgo - Entailed estate, proprietor of same
Media annata - Officeholder's bond equal to half of year's salary
Montañeses - Those from the mountains (natives of Burgos, Spain); party within the Mexican consulado (opposite of Bascongadas)
Obra pía - Pious work

Oidor - Audiencia judge
Peninsular - Spanish-born person residing in the Americas
Plaza mayor - Central plaza of city
Poder cumplido - Full powers of representation
Poder para testar - Extension of powers to make a will
Presbítero domiciliario - Beneficed clergy
Prior - Presiding officer of consulado
Procurador (síndico) - Legal representative (city attorney)
Protocolo - Notarial record
Ración - Ration, customary payment to priest by parishioners
Radicado - Official "rooted" in the colony by business or family ties
Reales de vellón - Copper coins, worth 1/20 of a silver peso
Regidor (perpetuo) - Permanent member of ayuntamiento
Repartimiento - Compulsory labor system, primarily employed in indigo and mining
Repartimiento de efectos (mercancias, bienes) - System of forced trade (compulsory purchases or production)
Residencia (juicio de) - End-of-term judicial review of official's conduct in office
Riesgo de mar - Shipping "insurance"
Santa Cruzada - Agency that sells indulgences to finance Christian conquest
Servicio - Customary personal service rendered to priest by parishioners
Síndico procurador - City attorney; the cabildo's spokesman before the audiencia
Sinodal examinador - Officer of cathedral chapter, supervisor of priests' salaries
Teniente - "Lieutenant," subordinate of colonial official
Traslado - Transfer
Vara - Unit of measure, about 33 inches
Vecino - Citizen
Visita - Royal investigation
Visitador - Royal investigator
Zurrón - Cowhide case used to transport dyes, unit of measure, about 220 pounds

Bibliography

ARCHIVES

Guatemala City
Archivo General de Centroamérica (AGCA)
Most useful for this study were the notarial records (*protocolos*) of the numerous scribes (*escribanos*) active in Santiago and Guatemala City in the second half of the eighteenth century. In most cases, protocolos may be consulted by signature (A1.20) and the name of the *escribano* (scribe). Many protocolos are indexed. The following escribanos were examined.

    Manuel Ignacio Carcamo (1763–68)
    Pedro Alvarado y Guzmán (1776–81)
    José Díaz González (1781–1804)
    Carlos de Figueroa (1772–85)
    Miguel José Godoy (1755–56)
    Antonio González (1751–62)

Sebastián González (1764–76)
Francisco Antonio Guzmán (1756–62)
José Matías Guzmán (1754–60)
Miguel Vicente Guzmán (1751–65)
Manuel Laparte (1772–97)
Francisco Márquez Rendón (1769–73)
Lucas Martínez García (1761–64)
Diego Milán (1759–70)
Manuel Ordóñez (1755)
Francisco José Palacios (1756–63)
Pedro José Rendón (1781–90)
Antonio Santa Cruz (1771–92)
José Sánchez de León (1769–80)
Manuel Taracena (1749–68)

Aycinena Family Papers
   The private collection of Aycinena family papers belonging to the late Margarita Fortuny Nanne of Guatemala City consists of more than two dozen plastic bags filled with historical documents (correspondence, drafts of sermons and essays, broadsides, business records, newspapers, government documents, etc.) dating from the mid-eighteenth century. It is a remarkable but poorly organized collection. In November 1988 I managed to sort most of the documents by year. The most important documents for this study were three estate inventories taken in 1768, 1771, and 1777, respectively.

Mexico City

Archivo General de la Nación (AGN)
Archivo General de Notarias del Departamento del Distrito Federal (AGNDDF).
Yraeta-Yturbe Collection of Merchant Papers (Colección de Comerciantes), Universidad Iberoamericana
   This is one of the most complete collections of merchant records of any Spanish American or early Mexican family enterprise, spanning three generations of the Yraeta and Yturbe families of Mexico City. Additional parts of the

collection are housed at Princeton University and the New York Public Library. In Mexico City, I consulted all documents relating to the eighteenth century: copy books 2.1.1 through 2.1.33 (1769–1800) and account books 2.2.1 through 2.2.6 (1769–1800).

Oaxaca
Archivo General del Estado de Oaxaca (AGEO)
Archivo General de Notarias del Estado de Oaxaca (AGNEO)

Published Works

Acuña Ortega, Victor H. "Capital comercial y comercio exterior en Centroamérica durante el siglo XVIII." *Mesoamérica* 4 (December 1982): 302–31.

———. "La reglamentación del comercio exterior en América Central durante el siglo XVIII." *Mesoamérica* 1, no. 1 (January 1980): 7–55.

Adams, Richard N. *Energy and Structure: A Theory of Social Power*. Austin: University of Texas Press, 1975.

Altman, Ida. "Emigrants and Society: An Approach to the Background of Colonial Latin America." *Comparative Studies of Society and History* 30, no. 1 (January 1988): 170–90.

Bakewell, Peter. *Silver and Entrepreneurship in Seventeenth-Century Potosí: The Life and Times of Antonio López de Quiroga*. Albuquerque: University of New Mexico Press, 1988.

Balmori Diana. "Family and Politics: Three Generations (1790–1890)." *Journal of Family History* 10, no. 3 (Fall 1985): 247–57.

Balmori, Diana, and Robert Oppenheimer. "Family Clusters: Generational Nucleation in Nineteenth-Century Chile and Argentina." *Comparative Studies of Society and History* 29 (1979): 231–61.

Balmori, Diana, Stuart F. Voss, and Miles Wortman. *Notable Family Networks in Latin America*. Chicago: University of Chicago Press, 1984.

Barbier, Jacques. "Elite and Cadres in Bourbon Chile." *Hispanic American Historical Review* 52 (August 1972): 416–35.

———. *Reform and Politics in Bourbon Chile, 1755–1796*. Ottawa: University of Ottawa Press, 1980.

Bard, Rachel. *Navarra: The Durable Kingdom*. Reno: University of Nevada Press, 1982.

Bethell, Leslie, ed. *Central America since Independence*. Cambridge: Cambridge University Press, 1991.

———. *Colonial Spanish America*. Cambridge: Cambridge University Press, 1987.

Blank, Stephanie. "Patrons, Clients and Kin in Seventeenth-Century Caracas: A Methodological Essay in Colonial Spanish American Social History." *Hispanic American Historical Review* 54 (May 1974): 260–83.

Borchart de Moreno, Christiana R. *Los mercaderes y el capitalismo en la ciudad de México: 1759–1778*. Translated by Alejandro Zenker. Mexico City: Fondo de Cultura Económica, 1984.

———. "Los miembros del consulado de la Ciudad de México en la época de Carlos III." *Jahrbuch für Geschichte von Staat, Wirtschaft und Gesellschaft Lateinamerikas* 14 (1977): 134–60.

Brading, D. A. "Bourbon Spain and Its American Empire." In *Colonial Spanish America*, edited by Leslie Bethell, 112–62. Cambridge: Cambridge University Press, 1987.

———. *Miners and Merchants of Bourbon Mexico, 1763–1810*. Cambridge: Cambridge University Press, 1971.

Bumgartner, Louis. *José del Valle of Central America*. Durham: Duke University Press, 1963.

Burkholder, Mark A. "From Creole to Peninsular: The Transformation of the Audiencia of Lima." *Hispanic American Historical Review* 52 (August 1972): 395–415.

———. *Politics of a Colonial Career: José de Baquíjano and the Audiencia of Lima*. 2d ed. Wilmington, Del.: Scholarly Resources, 1990.

———. "Titled Nobles, Elites, and Independence: Some Comments." *Latin American Research Review* 13 (1978): 290–95.

Burkholder, Mark A., and Dewitt S. Chandler. *From Impotence to Authority: The Spanish Crown and the American Audiencias, 1687–1808.* Columbia: University of Missouri Press, 1977.

Burkholder, Mark A., and Lyman L. Johnson. *Colonial Latin America.* Oxford: Oxford University Press, 1990.

Cabat, Geoffrey A. "The Consolidation of 1804 in Guatemala." *The Americas* 28 (July 1971): 20–38.

Campbell, Leon G. "A Colonial Establishment: Creole Domination of the Audiencia of Lima During the Late Eighteenth Century." *Hispanic American Historical Review* 52 (February 1972): 1–25.

Cardoso Ciro, F. S., and Héctor Pérez Brignoli. *Centroamérica y la economía occidental (1520–1930).* San José: Editorial Universidad de Costa Rica, 1977.

Caro Baroja, Julio. *La hora navarra del XVIII (Personas, familias, negocios e ideas).* Pamplona: Diputación Foral de Navarra, Institución Principe de Viana, 1969.

Chance, John K. *Conquest of the Sierra: Spaniards and Indians in Colonial Oaxaca.* Norman: University of Oklahoma Press, 1989.

———. *Race and Class in Colonial Oaxaca.* Stanford: Stanford University Press, 1978.

Chandler, David L. *Juan José de Aycinena: Idealista conservador de la Guatemala del siglo XIX.* Antigua: CIRMA, 1989.

———. "Juan José de Aycinena, Nineteenth-Century Guatemalan Conservative: An Historical Survey of His Political, Religious, Educational and Commercial Careers." M.A. thesis, Tulane University, 1965.

———. "Peace through Disunion: Father Juan José de Aycinena and the Fall of the Central American Federation." *The Americas* 46 (October 1989): 137–57.

Chandler, Dewitt S. "Jacobo de Villaurrutia and the Audiencia of Guatemala, 1794–1804." *The Americas* 32 (January 1976): 402–17.

Chinchilla Aguilar, Ernesto. *Historia de Centroamérica*. 3 vols. Guatemala City: Ministerio de Educación, 1974–1977.

Cortés y Larraz, Pedro. *Descripción geográfico-moral de la diocesis de Guatemala*. 2 vols. Guatemala City: Biblioteca "Goathemala," 1958.

Couturier, Edith. "Philanthropic Activities of the Conde de Regla." *The Americas* 32 (July 1975): 13–31.

del Cid F., Enrique. *Origen histórico de la Casa y Marquesado de Ayzinena*. Guatemala City: published privately, 1969.

Dozier, Craig L. *Nicaragua's Mosquito Shore: The Years of British and American Presence*. Tuscaloosa: University of Alabama Press, 1985.

Estrada Monroy, Agustín. *Datos para la historia de la iglesia de Guatemala*. 2 vols. Guatemala City: Sociedad de Geografía e Historia, 1974.

Farriss, Nancy. *Crown and Clergy in Colonial Mexico, 1759–1821: The Crisis of Ecclesiastical Privilege*. London: Athlone, 1968.

———. *Maya Society under Colonial Rule: The Collective Enterprise of Survival*. Princeton: Princeton University Press, 1984.

Felstiner, Mary Lowenthal. "Kinship Politics in the Chilean Independence Movement." *Hispanic American Historical Review* 56, no. 1 (February 1976): 58–80.

———. "The Larraín Family in the Independence of Chile, 1780–1830." Ph.D. dissertation, Stanford University, 1970.

Fernández Molina, José Antonio. "Colouring the World in Blue: The Indigo Boom and the Central American Market, 1750–1810." Ph.D. dissertation, University of Texas at Austin, 1992.

Fernández-Pérez, Paloma, "Family and Marriage Around Colonial Trade: Cádiz, 1700–1812." Ph.D. dissertation. University of California, Berkeley, 1994.

Fisher, John R. *Commercial Relations between Spain and Spanish America, 1778–1796.* Liverpool: University of Liverpool Press, 1985.

Florescano, Enrique. "The Hacienda in New Spain." In *Colonial Spanish America,* edited by Leslie Bethell, 250–85. Cambridge: Cambridge University Press, 1987.

Flores Galindo, Alberto. "Aristocracía en vilo: Los mercaderes de Lima en el siglo XVIII." In *The Economies of Mexico and Peru during the Late Colonial Period, 1760–1810,* edited by Nils Jacobsen and Hans Jurgen-Puhle, 252–80. Berlin: Colloquium Verlag, 1986.

——— . *Aristocracía y plebe: Lima, 1760–1830.* Lima: Mosca Azul Editores, 1984.

Floyd, Troy S. *The Anglo-Spanish Struggle for Mosquitia.* Albuquerque: University of New Mexico Press, 1967.

——— . "Bourbon Palliatives and the Central American Mining Industry, 1765–1800." *The Americas* 18 (1961): 103–25.

——— . "The Guatemalan Merchants, the Government, and the *Provincianos,* 1750–1800." *Hispanic American Historical Review* 41, no. 1 (February 1961): 90–110.

——— . "The Indigo Merchant: Promoter of Central American Economic Development, 1750–1808." *Business History Review* 39 (1965): 466–88.

——— . "Salvadoran Indigo and the Guatemalan Merchants: A Study in Central American Socio-Economic History, 1750–1800." Ph.D. dissertation, University of California, Berkeley, 1959.

Fox-Genovese, Elizabeth, and Eugene D. Genovese. *The Fruits of Merchant Capital: Slavery and Bourgeois Property in the Rise and Expansion of Capitalism.* New York: Oxford University Press, 1983.

García-Baquero González, Antonio. *Cádiz y el Atlántico (1717–1778): El comercio colonial español bajo el monopolio gaditano.* 2 vols. Seville: Escuela de Estudios Hispano-Americanos, CSIC, Excelentísima Diputación Provincial de Cádiz, 1976.

Graham, Richard. "Political Power and Landownership in Nineteenth-Century Latin America." In *New Approaches to Latin American History*, edited by Richard Graham and Peter H. Smith, 112–36. Austin: University of Texas Press, 1973.

Greenow, Linda. *Credit and Socioeconomic Change in Colonial Mexico: Loans and Mortgages in Guadalajara, 1720–1820.* Boulder: Westview Press, 1983.

Grieb, Kenneth, ed. *Research Guide to Central America and the Caribbean.* Madison: University of Wisconsin Press, 1985.

Hamnett, Brian. *Politics and Trade in Southern Mexico, 1750–1821.* Cambridge: Cambridge University Press, 1971.

Handy, Jim. *Gift of the Devil: A History of Guatemala.* Boston: South End Press, 1984.

Haring, Clarence. *The Spanish Empire in America.* New York: Oxford University Press, 1947.

Hawkins, Timothy P. "José de Bustamante and the Preservation of Empire in Central America, 1811–1818." *Colonial Latin America Historical Review* 4, no. 4 (Fall 1995): 439–64.

Hoberman, Louisa Schell. "Merchants in Seventeenth-Century Mexico City: A Preliminary Portrait." *Hispanic American Historical Review* 57 (August 1979): 479–503.

———. *Mexico's Merchant Elite, 1590–1660: Silver, State, and Society.* Durham: Duke University Press, 1991.

Jacobsen, Nils, and Hans-Jurgen Puhle, eds. *The Economies of Mexico and Peru During the Late Colonial Period, 1760–1810.* Berlin: Colloquium Verlag, 1986.

Jones, Oakah L., Jr. *Guatemala in the Spanish Colonial Period*. Norman: University of Oklahoma Press, 1994.

Juarros, Domingo. *Compendio de la historia del reino de Guatemala, 1500–1800*. Guatemala City: Editorial Piedra Santa, 1981.

Keen, Benjamin. *A History of Latin America*. 4th ed. Boston: Houghton Mifflin, 1992.

Kicza, John. *Colonial Entrepreneurs: Families and Business in Bourbon Mexico City*. Albuquerque: University of New Mexico Press, 1983.

———. "The Great Families of Mexico: Elite Maintenance and Business Practices in Late Colonial Mexico City." *Hispanic American Historical Review* 62, no. 3 (August 1982): 429–57.

———. "The Role of the Family in Economic Development in Nineteenth-Century Latin America." *Journal of Family History* 10 (Fall 1985): 235–46.

Knight, Alan. *The Mexican Revolution*. 2 vol. Lincoln: University of Nebraska Press, 1990.

Knight, Franklin. *The Caribbean: Genesis of a Fragmented Nationalism*. 2d ed. Oxford: Oxford University Press, 1990.

———. "Origins of Wealth and the Sugar Revolution in Cuba, 1750–1850." *Hispanic American Historical Review* 57 (May 1977): 231–53.

Kuethe, Alan J. *Cuba, 1753–1815: Crown, Military and Society*. Knoxville: University of Tennessee Press, 1986.

Kuznesof, Elizabeth Anne. "The History of the Family in Latin America: A Critique of Recent Work." *Latin American Research Review* 24 (February 1989): 168–86.

Kuznesof, Elizabeth Anne, and Robert Oppenheimer. "The Family and Society in Nineteenth-Century Latin America: An Historiographical Introduction." *Journal of Family History* 10, no. 3 (Fall 1985): 215–34.

Ladd, Doris M. *The Mexican Nobility at Independence, 1780–1826.* Austin: University of Texas Press, 1976.

Langenberg, Inge. *Urbanisation und Bevolkerungsstuktur der Stadt Guatemala in der ausgebenden Kolonialzeit (1773–1824).* Cologne: Böhlau Verlag, 1981.

———. "Urbanización y Cambio Social." *Anuario de Estudios Americanos* 36 (1979): 351–74.

Lanning, John Tate. *The Eighteenth-Century Enlightenment in the University of San Carlos de Guatemala.* Ithaca: Cornell University Press, 1956.

Lindo-Fuentes, Héctor. *Weak Foundations: The Economy of El Salvador in the Nineteenth Century.* Berkeley: University of California Press, 1990.

Liss, Peggy K. *Atlantic Empires: The Network of Trade and Revolution, 1713–1826.* Baltimore: Johns Hopkins University Press, 1983.

Lockhart, James. "The Social History of Colonial Spanish America: Its Evolution and Potential." *Latin American Research Review* 7, no. 1 (Spring 1972): 6–46.

Lockhart, James, and Stuart B. Schwartz. *Early Latin America: A History of Colonial Spanish America and Brazil.* Cambridge: Cambridge University Press, 1983.

Love, Joseph L., and Bert J. Barickman. "Rulers and Owners: A Brazilian Case Study in Comparative Perspective." *Hispanic American Historical Review* 66, no. 4 (November 1986): 743–66.

Lovell, W. George. *Conquest and Survival in Colonial Guatemala: A Historical Geography of the Cuchamatán Highlands, 1500–1821.* Rev. ed. Montreal: McGill-Queens University Press, 1992.

Lovell, W. George, and Christopher H. Lutz. *Demography and Empire: A Guide to the Population History of Spanish Central America, 1500–1821.* Boulder: Westview Press, 1995.

Lugar, Catherine. "Merchants." In *Cities and Society in Colonial Latin America,* edited by Susan M. Socolow and Louisa Schell Hoberman, 47–75. Albuquerque: University of New Mexico Press, 1986.

Lutz, Christopher H. *Historia sociodemográfica de Santiago de Guatemala, 1541–1773*. Antigua: CIRMA, 1982.

———. *Santiago de Guatemala, 1541–1773: City, Caste, and the Colonial Experience*. Norman: University of Oklahoma Press, 1994.

Lutz, Christopher H., and W. George Lovell. "Core and Periphery in Colonial Guatemala." In *Guatemalan Indians and the State, 1540–1988*, edited by Carol A. Smith, 35–51. Austin: University of Texas Press, 1990.

Lynch, John. *Bourbon Spain, 1700–1808*. Oxford: Basil Blackwell, 1989.

McAlister, Lyle. "Social Structure and Social Change in New Spain." *Hispanic American Historical Review* 43 (1963): 349–70.

McCreery, David. "'An Odious Feudalism': Mandamiento Labor and Commercial Agriculture in Guatemala, 1858–1920." *Latin American Perspectives* 13 (Winter 1986): 99–118.

———. "Debt Servitude in Rural Guatemala, 1876–1936." *Hispanic American Historical Review* 63 (November 1983): 735–59.

———. "Guatemala." In *Research Guide to Central America and the Caribbean*, edited by Kenneth J. Grieb, 26–37. Madison: University of Wisconsin Press, 1985.

———. *Rural Guatemala, 1760–1940*. Stanford: Stanford University Press, 1994.

McKinley, Michael P., *Pre-revolutionary Caracas: Politics, Economy, and Society, 1777–1811*. Cambridge: Cambridge University Press, 1985.

MacLachlan, Colin M. *Spain's Empire in the New World: The Role of Ideas in Institutional and Social Change*. Berkeley: University of California Press, 1988.

MacLachlan, Colin, and Jaime Rodriguez O. *Forging of the Cosmic Race*. 2d ed. Berkeley: University of California Press, 1990.

MacLeod, Murdo J. "Aspects of the Internal Economy." In *Colonial Spanish America*, edited by Leslie Bethell, 315–60. Cambridge: Cambridge University Press, 1987.

———. *Spanish Central America: A Socioeconomic History 1520–1720*. Berkeley: University of California Press, 1973.

Markman, Sidney D. *Colonial Architecture of Antigua Guatemala*. Philadelphia: American Philosophical Society, 1966.

Martínez-Peláez, Severo. *La patria del criollo: Ensayo de interpretación de la realidad colonial guatemalteca*. Guatemala City: EDUCA, 1985.

Meneray, Wilbur. "The Kingdom of Guatemala During the Reign of Charles III, 1759–1788." Ph.D. dissertation, University of North Carolina, 1975.

Moore, John Preston. *The Cabildo in Peru under the Bourbons*. Durham: Duke University Press, 1966.

Mörner, Magnus. "Economic Factors and Stratification in Colonial Spanish America with Special Regard to Elites." *Hispanic American Historical Review* 63 (May 1983): 335–69.

———. "Spanish Migration to the New World Prior to 1810: A Report on the State of the Research." In *First Images of America: The Impact of the the New World on the Old*, edited by Fredi Chiappelli, 737–82. Berkeley: University of California Press, 1976.

Naylor, Robert A. *Penny-Ante Imperialism: The Mosquito Shore and the Bay of Honduras, 1600–1914: A Case Study in British Informal Empire*. Cranbury, N.J.: Fairleigh Dickinson University Press, 1989.

Ordóñez Jonomá, Ramiro. "La Familia Varón de Berrieza." *Revista de la Academia Guatemalteca de Estudios Genealógicos, Heráldicos e Históricos* 9 (1987): 523–826.

Palma Murga, Gustavo. "Nucleos de poder local y relaciones familiares en la ciudad de Guatemala a finales del siglo XVIII." *Mesoamérica* 12 (December 1986): 241-308.

Pinto Soría, Julio Cesár. *Centroamérica de la colonia al Estado Nacional (1800-1840)*. Guatemala City: Editorial Universitaria, 1986.

———. *El Valle Central de Guatemala (1524-1781)*. Guatemala City: Editorial Universitaria, 1988.

Rodríguez, Mario. *The Cádiz Experiment in Central America, 1808-1826*. Berkeley: University of California Press, 1978.

———. "Research Topics for Bourbon Central America, 1700-1821." In *Research Guide to Central America and the Caribbean*, edited by Kenneth J. Greib, 16-26. Madison: University of Wisconsin Press, 1985.

Rodríguez, Mario, et al. *Applied Enlightenment: Nineteenth-Century Liberalism, 1830-1839*. New Orleans, Middle American Research Institute, 1972.

Rosenthal, Mario. *Guatemala*. New York: Twayne, 1962.

Rubio Sánchez, Manuel. *Alcaldes mayores*. 2 vols. San Salvador: Ministerio de Educación, 1979.

———. *Historia del añil o xiquilite en Centro América*. 2 vols. San Salvador: Ministerio de Educación, 1976.

Russell-Wood, A. J. R. *Fidalgos and Philanthropists: The Santa Casa da Misericórdia, 1550-1755*. Berkeley: University of California Press, 1968.

Salazar, Ramón. *Mariano de Aycinena*. Guatemala: Biblioteca de Cultura Popular, 1952.

Schulz, Donald E. "El Salvador: Revolution and Counterrevolution in the Living Museum." In *Revolution and Counterrevolution in Central America and the Caribbean*, edited by Donald E. Schulz and Douglas H. Graham, 189-268. Boulder: Westview Press, 1984.

Schulz, Donald E., and Douglas H. Graham. *Revolution and Counterrevolution in Central America and the Caribbean*. Boulder: Westview Press, 1984.

Schwartz, Stuart B. *Sovereignty and Society in Colonial Brazil: The High Court of Bahia and Its Judges,*

1607–1751. Berkeley: University of California Press, 1973.

Seed, Patricia. *To Love, Honor and Obey: Conflicts Over Marriage Choice in Colonial Mexico, 1574–1821.* Stanford: Stanford University Press, 1988.

Sherman, William L. *Forced Native Labor in Sixteenth-Century Central America.* Lincoln: University of Nebraska Press, 1979.

Smith, Carol A., ed. *Guatemalan Indians and the State, 1540–1988.* Austin: University of Texas Press, 1990.

Smith, Robert S. "Forced Labor in the Guatemalan Indigo Works." *Hispanic American Historical Review* 36, no. 3 (August 1956): 319–28.

———. "Indigo Production and Trade in Colonial Guatemala." *Hispanic American Historical Review* 39, no. 2 (May 1959): 181–211.

———. "Origins of the Consulado of Guatemala." *Hispanic American Historical Review* 26 (May 1946): 150–61.

———. "Retail Stock of a Guatemala Store, 1780: An Entire Expediente." *Hispanic American Historical Review* 26 (1946): 60–65.

———. "Statutes of the Guatemalan Indigo Growers' Society." *Hispanic American Historical Review* 30 (1950): 336–45.

Socolow, Susan M. "Economic Activities of the Porteño Merchants: The Viceregal Period." *Hispanic American Historical Review* 55 (February 1975): 1–24.

———. *The Merchants of Buenos Aires, 1778–1810: Family and Commerce.* Cambridge: Cambridge University Press, 1978.

Socolow, Susan M., and Louisa Schell Hoberman. *Cities and Society in Colonial Latin America.* Albuquerque: University of New Mexico Press, 1986.

Stein, Stanley. "Bureaucracy and Business in the Spanish Empire, 1759–1804: Failure of a Bourbon Reform in Mexico and Peru." *Hispanic American Historical Review* 61 (February 1981): 2–28.

Stephens, John Lloyd. *Incidents of Travel in Central America, Chiapas and Yucatan.* 2 vols. New York: Dover, 1969.

Stern, Steve J. "Feudalism, Capitalism, and the World-System in the Perspective of Latin America and the Caribbean." *American Historical Review* 93, no. 4 (October 1988): 829–72.

Stone, Samuel Z. *The Heritage of the Conquistadors: Ruling Classes in Central America from Conquest to the Sandinistas.* Lincoln: University of Nebraska Press, 1992.

Thompson, George A. *Narrative of an Official Visit to Guatemala from Mexico.* London: John Murray, 1829.

Tobis, David, and Susanne Jonas. *Guatemala.* Berkeley: NACLA, 1974.

Torales Pacheco, María Cristina, et al. *La compañia de comercio de Francisco Ignacio de Yraeta (1767–1797): Cinco ensayos.* 2 vols. Mexico City: Instituto Mexicano de Comercio Exterior, 1985.

Tutino, John. "Creole Mexico: Spanish Elites, Haciendas, and Indian Towns, 1750–1810." Ph.D. dissertation, University of Texas at Austin, 1976.

———. "Power, Class, and Family: Men and Women in the Mexican Elite, 1750–1810." *The Americas* 39 (January 1983): 359–81.

Twinam, Ann. "Enterprise and Elites in Eighteenth-Century Medellín." *Hispanic American Historical Review* 59 (August 1979): 444–75.

———. *Miners, Merchants and Farmers in Colonial Colombia.* Austin: University of Texas Press, 1982.

Van Oss, Adriaan C. *Catholic Colonialism: A Parish History of Guatemala, 1524–1821.* Cambridge: Cambridge University Press, 1986.

———. "Central America's Autarkic Colonial Cities (1600–1800)." In *Colonial Cities*, edited by Robert J. Ross and Gerald Telkamp, 33–49. Boston: Leiden University Press, 1985.

———. "La población de América Central hacía 1800." *Anales de la Academia de Geografía e Historia de Guatemala* 55 (1981): 291–311.

Viotti da Costa, Emilia. *The Brazilian Empire: Myths and Histories.* Chicago: Dorsey Press, 1988.

Walker, Geoffrey. *Spanish Politics and Imperial Trade, 1700–1789.* Bloomington: Indiana University Press, 1979.

Webre, Stephen. "The Social and Economic Bases of Cabildo Membership in Seventeenth-Century Santiago de Guatemala." Ph.D. dissertation, Tulane University, 1980.

———. "Water and Society in a Spanish American City: Santiago de Guatemala, 1555–1773." *Hispanic American Historical Review* 70 no. 1 (February 1990): 57–84.

Williams, Robert G. *Export Agriculture and the Crisis in Central America.* Chapel Hill: University of North Carolina Press, 1986.

Woodward, Ralph Lee, Jr. "The Aftermath of Independence, 1821–c. 1870." In *Central America since Independence*, edited by Leslie Bethell, 1–36. Cambridge: Cambridge University Press, 1991.

———. *Central America: A Nation Divided.* 2d ed. Oxford: Oxford University Press, 1985.

———. *Class Privilege and Economic Development: The Consulado de Comercio of Guatemala, 1793–1871.* Chapel Hill: University of North Carolina Press, 1966.

———. "Economic and Social Origins of the Guatemalan Political Parties, 1773–1823." *Hispanic American Historical Review* 46, no. 4 (November 1966): 544–66.

———. "The Historiography of Modern Central America Since 1960." *Hispanic American Historical Review* 67, no. 3 (August 1987): 461–96.

———. *Rafael Carrera and the Emergence of the Republic of Guatemala, 1821–1871.* Athens: University of Georgia Press, 1993.

Wortman, Miles. "Bourbon Reforms in Central America: 1750–1786." *The Americas* 32 (October 1975): 222–38.
———. *Government and Society in Colonial Central America, 1680–1840.* New York: Columbia University Press, 1982.
———. "Government Revenue and Economic Trends in Central America, 1787–1819." *Hispanic American Historical Review* 55 (1975): 251–86.
Zilbermann de Luján, María Cristina. *Aspectos socioeconómicos del traslado de la ciudad de Guatemala (1773–1783).* Guatemala City: Academia de Geografía e Historia de Guatemala, 1987.

Index

Abad, Rafael, 121
Abarca, Isidro de (Conde de San Isidro), 126
Acapulco, Mex., 53, 115
Adams, Richard N., 143
Aguerrevere e Aycinena, Juan Angel de, 120–21
Aguerrevere e Aycinena, Juan Miguel de, 121, 125, 128–30, 180
Aguirre, Pedro de, 128
Alameda, Miguel de, 173
Alcabalas, 20, 32, 62, 133, 140
Alcaldes mayores, 26–27
Aldasoro, Juan Bautista, 122, 170

Aldecoa family, 41, 45
Almaceneros (wholesalers), 47
Almendro, Navarre, 104
Alvarado y Guzmán, Tomás, 167
American Revolutionary War, 96, 135
Anbelaez, Juan José, 126
Andino y Arce, Ambrosio, 175
Andino y Arce, Manuel, 94, 175
Antequera (Ciudad Juárez de Oaxaca, Mex.), 49–51, 54
Anzuola, Guipuzcoa, 113

Apastepeque, 84–85, 175
Aranjuez (hacienda, Oaxaca), 51, 53
Araurrenechea e Yrigoyen, Jorge de, 129
Archbishop of Guatemala, 31
Arechaga, Manuel, 52
Arizcun, Navarre, 43, 45
Arnais, Miguel, 146
Arroyo, Francisco, 146
Arzú, Tomás de, 180
Audiencia of Guatemala, 25–26, 31–32, 145
Aycinena, Ana María de, 72
Aycinena, Casa de, 101–31
Aycinena, Juan de (brother), 41
Aycinena, Juan Francisco de, 128
Aycinena, Salvador, 247n.102
Aycinena Alzualde, Juan Miguel, 41
Aycinena e Yrigoyen, Graciana, 41
Aycinena e Yrigoyen, Juan Fermín de: and American Revolutionary War, 96; arrives in Santiago, 14, 19; ayuntamiento member, 133–40; birth, 38; Bourbon Reforms, 30; cajeros, 103–105; children, 70, 199–202; commercial representatives, 107–10; consulado de comercio de Guatemala (prior), 35; control of church funds, 170–71; control of public funds, 146; credit system, 97–98; death, 195, 197; depositor general, 134; financier, 78–92; haciendas, 93; home, 153, 179, 185; indigo, 82–87; investment preferences, 89–92; landownership, 93–99; leaves Spain, 13; marriages, 15, 54, 68; mayorazgo, 191–96; mining investor, 87–89; municipal slaughterhouse, 68, 135; myth, 36; origins in Baztán Valley, 41; presence in Oaxaca, 50, 53; philanthropy, 188–91; power, 8; relations with Catholic Church, 29, 158–77; relations with church officials, 165–68; relations with the Gálvez Corral family, 64; relations with Mexico City, 118–23; relations with monastics, 168; relations with Peru, 125; relations with provincial officials, 147–55; relations with Spanish merchants, 126–30; relations with the state, 132–57; retirement from ayuntamiento, 180; shipowner, 92; Spanish emigrant, 7; testament, 54; title of Castile, 132; traslado

INDEX

administrator, 135; water commission, 135; wealth, 75–76; wholesaler, 77–78
Aycinena e Yrigoyen, Pedro de, 47–48, 54, 118–21, 124, 128–29, 140, 145
Aycinena family, 6–7, 211n.10
Aycinena family papers, 9
Aycinena home, 186
Aycinena y Carrillo, José Alejandro, 114, 141, 198–200
Aycinena y Carrillo, Vicente (second Marqués de Aycinena), 69, 114, 141, 191, 195, 198–200
Aycinena y Larraín, Pedro de, 41, 71, 103, 128, 139, 141, 145, 152, 170
Aycinena y Nájera, María Bernarda, 69, 200
Aycinena y Nájera, María Josefa, 71, 200
Aycinena y Nájera, María Micaela, 69, 200
Aycinena y Piñol, Antonio, 202
Aycinena y Piñol, José Ignacio de, 202
Aycinena y Piñol, Juan Fermín de, 201
Aycinena y Piñol, Juan José (third Marqués de Aycinena), 199, 202
Aycinena y Piñol, Mariano, 201–202
Aycinena y Piñol, María Teresa, 201
Aycinena y Piñol, Pedro de, 202
Ayuntamiento of Santiago, 16, 20–21, 26, 35, 60, 62, 98, 133–40. *See also* Cabildo

Balmori, Diana, 37
Banking, 74
Barcelona, Spain, 42, 69
Bargas, Blas de, 172, 176–77
Barreneche e Yrigoyen, Juan José, 48
Barrios, Justo Rufino, 8
Barrutia, Francisco, 71, 103, 134, 139
Barrutia, Juan Sebastián de, 170
Barrutia y Echeverría, Francisca, 71
Bascongadas, 122
Basque provinces, 37–38
Baztán Valley, Navarre, 38, 41–43, 45
Becerril, Francisco, 149–50
Beleña, Eusebio, 145
Beltranena, Martín, 71
Beltranena e Aycinena, Pedro de, 71, 83, 103, 140–41, 152, 170
Bergaña, Antonio, 103–104, 125
Berroeta, Navarre, 41
Beteta, Juan de, 103
Beteta, Tomás, 103

Borda family, 45
Bourbon dynasty, 30
Bourbon Reforms, 15, 21–22, 30–35, 87, 96, 162
Brading, D. A., 71, 94, 111
Bucareli, Antonio María, 114, 140
Bureaucracy, 25, 27
Burgos, Spain, 59, 127, 151
Bustamante, José de, 199–200
Busto y Bustamante, Francisco Nicolás, 148

Cabildo, 31. *See also* Ayuntamiento of Santiago
Cabrejo, Miguel, 168
Cacao, 60, 119
Caceres, Juan de, 172
Cadalso, Diego, 129
Cadalso, Manuela, 129
Cadalso Garay, María Ignacia, 129
Cádiz, Spain, 42, 46–47, 62, 69, 126
Caja de comunidad, 145
Camara Real, 43
Cañas, Francisco de, 86
Capellanías (chantries), 29
Captain general, 22, 25–26
Capuchinas, 159, 168–69
Caro Baroja, Julio, 42, 45
Carrera, Rafael, 7–8, 202
Carrillo y Gálvez, Ana María, 54, 58–59, 61–62, 67, 75, 77, 199
Carrillo y Mencos, Pedro, 55, 64, 77

Carrillo y Varón, Pedro de, 58–59, 62–63
Cartago, Costa Rica, 17, 23
Casa de Aycinena, 101–31
Casa de Contratación, 46
Casa de rescate, 34
Casa solariega, 41, 291n.14
Castas, 16–17, 19
Castilla, Benito de, 93–94
Cathedral chapter (cabildo eclesiástico), 161
Catholic Church, 27, 158–77; as agent of Europeanization, 28; economically active clergy, 29; education, 29; public services, 29; relations with state, 28, 163; wealth, 29
Cattle, 18
Cavello, Domingo, 148
Central America, 3, 5, 6, 21–22, 82; economy, 23; geography, 23; population, 16; provinces, 22; society, 18; strategic importance, 23. *See also* Kingdom of Guatemala
Cerro de la Avilla (hacienda, San Vicente)
Ceylon, 116
Chalatenango, El Salvador, 84
Charles II, King of Spain (Hapsburg), 42
Charles III, King of Spain (Bourbon), 15, 132–33, 181
Chiapas, 16, 34

INDEX

Chimaltenango, Guatemala, 22, 27
Chiquimula, Guatemala, 22
Ciga, Navarre, 38, 41, 48, 58, 71, 120, 129
Cilieza y Varón, Agustín, 151
Cilieza y Varón, Luisa Gonzaga, 64
Cilieza y Varón, Miguel de, 166
Cilieza y Velasco, Tomás, 60, 64
Cinco Gremios (Madrid), 45, 126–27
Cinnamon (canela) episode, 116–17
Ciudad Real (Chiapas), 22
Cochineal, 15, 49–50, 53–54
Cofradías, 28
Colegio de Cristo Crucificado, 159, 168–69
Colegios, 28
Colonial establishment, 56
Colonial merchants, 74, 79, 101, 211n.16
Comayagua, Honduras, 22, 34
Comerciantes (merchants) of Cádiz, 46
Comercio libre (free trade), 15, 32
Commercial deputation, 217n.44. *See also* diputación comercial
Compadrazgo, 190
Competition for offices, 27
Congregación, 28
Consejo Real (Navarre), 38
Consejo Real (Spain), 43
Consignment, 111–12, 115
Consulado de Comercio (Cádiz), 47, 129
Consulado de Comercio (Guatemala), 34–35, 141, 155–56
Consulado de Comercio (Mexico), 33, 48, 114, 118, 122
Core and periphery, 18, 28
Corregidores, 26–27
Corruption, 27
Cortes (Navarre), 38
Cortés y Larraz, Pedro, 29, 161, 174, 177
Costa Rica, 16, 22–23
Council of the Indies, 43, 60, 141, 155–56, 200
Couturier, Edith, 190
Creole establishment, 58
Creoles (criollos), 16
Crimin, George, 128

Defense, 23
Del Cid F., Enrique, 9
Dependencias activas (active dependencies), 79, 81
Diputación (Navarre), 38
Diputación comercial, 32. *See also* Commercial deputation
Doctrinas, 31
Domezaín, Ignacio, 148
Domínguez, Salvador, 146
Dominicans, 162
Dowries, 75, 77

Earthquakes of 1773, 21, 97
Ecclesiastical offensive, 31
Echandía, Pedro de, 150
Echandía family, 45
Economic integration, 23, 58
Economic Society, 141
Elite (Central America), 198
Elite (Guatemala), 7
Elite (Mexico City), 6
Elite historiography, 5
El Naranjo (hacienda), 187
El Salvador, 4, 16, 34, 65–66, 151
Elizalde, Antonio de, 125
Elizalde, José Matías de, 125
Elizalde e Aycinena, Fermín de, 120, 129–30
Emigrants, 46
Encomiendas, 25, 32, 217n.43
Endogamy, 46, 58, 72
Equizábal, Bartolomé, 170
Equizábal y Gálvez, Leonor María de, 127
Errazu, Navarre, 51
Escamilla, Tomás, 154
Escuintla, Guatemala, 22, 61, 66, 103
Estachería, José de, 144–45
Estrada Cabrera, Manuel, 8
Extremadura, Spain, 69

Fadrique y Goyena, Manuel, 65–66, 105, 154
Fagoaga, Juan José, 47
Ferdinand VII, King of Spain (Bourbon), 199

Ferdinand of Aragon, 37
Fernández Bobadilla, Juan, 148
Fernández Gil, José, 113
Fernández-Pérez, Paloma, 102
Fernandín, Antonio, 147
Fitero, Navarre, 104
Floyd, Troy S., 8, 82, 87, 103, 148, 184
Fortuny Nanne, Margarita, 9
Franciscans, 162
French Revolution, 15
Fuente, Antonio de la, 169
Fueros, 38

Gallardo y Varona, Juan Antonio, 170
Gálvez, Matías de, 96, 135, 144
Gálvez Corral, Bartolomé, 60, 63
Gálvez Corral, Cristóbal de. See Gálvez y Varón, Cristóbal de
Gálvez Corral family, 63, 151–52, 230n.28
Gálvez y Cilieza, Josefa Nicolasa, 66
Gálvez y Varón, Ana Micaela, 174
Gálvez y Varón, Cristóbal de, 59, 63–66, 105, 151, 155, 169
Gálvez y Varón, Francisca Antonia, 67
Gálvez y Varón, Manuela de, 58–59, 62–63, 173

INDEX

Gálvez y Varón, Manuel de, 64, 66
Gandiaga, Felipe, 122
Ganuza, Juan José de, 122, 167–68
Ganuza, María Josefa de, 113
Ganuza, Pedro de, 113, 122–23, 126
Garay, María Francisca, 129
García, Manuel Lorenzo, 92, 126, 174
García Bustamante, Paula, 129
García Goyena, José, 104–105
García Goyena, Rafael, 105
Gaztelu, Navarre, 126
Gobernadores, 26
González Batres, Juan José, 166–67
González Batres, Manuel, 139
González Maldonado, Eugenio, 124
González Rancaño, José, 149
Gortari, Juan de, 104, 125
Goyeneche y Echenique, Juan, 43–44
Goyeneche e Yrigoyen, Juan Francisco (Marqués de Ugena), 43, 45, 52
Goyeneche e Yrigoyen, Tomás, 43
Goyeneche e Yrigoyen, Xavier (Marqués de Belzunce), 43
Graham, Richard, 6
Granada, Nicaragua, 17, 23
Guaraquiche (hacienda, Chiquimula), 173
Guardia, José de la, 168
Guatemala (province), 4–5, 16
Guatemala City, 6, 9, 135
Guayaquil, Ecuador, 60, 105
Guazacapán, Guatemala, 61
Guzmán y Alvarado, Pedro, 167

Handy, Jim, 4
Havana, Cuba, 32
Hermanos Elizalde (Lima), 125
History of the family, 37
Holy Inquisition, 217n.37
Honduras, 16, 87
Hospital Real San Juan de Dios, 194
Huazolután, Oaxaca, 52
Humboldt, Alexander von, 183

Ibarra, Miguel de, 52
Indigo, 15, 18, 25, 27, 56, 64, 81, 83, 175, 215n.26, 234n.15
Indigo Growers' Fund (Monte Pio de Cosecheros de Añil), 34, 96
Inheritance practices, 41
Irungaray, Mateo de, 153
Irurita, Navarre, 71, 121, 129
Iturralde, Juan Bautista, 220n.21
Iturralde family, 45

Jacobs y Pellaert, Isabel, 128
Jalapa, Mexico, 121
Jáuregui family, 45
Jesuits, 31
Jewelry, 185
Jicayán (Xicayan), Oaxaca, 52
Juarros, Domingo, 159, 188

Keith, Minor Cooper, 8
Kicza, John, 6–7, 95, 100, 130, 182
Kingdom of Guatemala, 13, 14, 16, 31. *See also* Central America
Kingdom of Navarre, 14
Knight, Alan, 157

Labayru, Sebastián, 148
La Baztanesa (ship), 92, 129
Labor, 25
Labor, forced, 25
Lacayo, Gerónimo, 148
La Concepción (hacienda, San Vicente, El Salvador), 94
La Culebra (hacienda, Mixco, Guatemala), 66
Ladd, Doris, 179, 182–84, 191
La Fama (ship), 92, 104, 126, 174
La Familia, 7, 201
La Joya (hacienda, San Vicente, El Salvador), 86
Landa, Juan Lucas de, 88
Landa, Miguel de, 88
Landa brothers, 89

Landaburu, Matías de, 80, 128, 246n.90
Lara, Pedro Juan de, 104
Larraín, Juan Francisco de, 128
Larraín, Juan Miguel de, 128
Larraín, María de, 41
Larraín, Pedro de, 41
Larraín family (Chile), 247n.102
Larraínzar, Francisca Xaviera, 123
Larrasquito, Francisco José, 124
Larrasquito, José Ignacio, 124
Larrave, Matías de, 173–74
Larrazábal, Feliciano, 123
Larrazábal family, 55
Larrazábal y Barroeta, Simón, 55, 138
Larreta, Manuel de, 147
Lecároz, Navarre, 41
Lem, Buenaventura, 168
León, Nicaragua, 17, 22–23, 34, 85
Liberal Revolution of 1871, 7
Libranzas, 111–12, 115
Llano, Manuel Eugenio de, 72, 140, 182
Llano y Nájera, María Josefa, 72
Loaiza, Pedro, 134, 139
Lockhart, James, 210n.7
López, Diego José, 174–75
López de Ramales, Juana Antonia, 59, 61

López de Ramales, Pedro, 61
Luceno, Joaquín, 172

Madrid, Spain, 42–43, 46
Magro, Alonso, 124
Malaga, Spain, 63
Maldonado, Manuel, 103
Manrique, Felipe, 140
Manzanares, Matías de, 149, 170
María de Dutari, 51
Marquissate of Aycinena, 14, 181
Marriage laws, 59
Marticorena, Juan Bautista, 71, 201
Marticorena, Juan Vicente, 128
Mayan communities, 23
Mayorazgo, 14, 191–96
McCreery, David, 5
Mella, Manuel de, 149
Mencos, Bernardo de, 60
Mencos, Carlos de, 60–61
Mencos y Varón, Bernardo, 153
Mencos y Varón, Melchor de, 167
Mercederians, 162
Merchants, 23; in Cádiz, 102; and landholding, 94–95; in Santiago, 34–35, 58; in Spanish America, 8; in Veracruz, 51
Mexico, 6, 32, 47
Mexico City, 13, 49, 62
Micheo e Uztáriz, Domingo, 123, 126
Micheo y Barreneche, Juan Tomás, 127, 139, 150
Mier, Josefa Antonia de, 121
Miners, 23
Mining, 87–89
Miraflores (hacienda, San Salvador, El Salvador), 94, 175, 192, 194
Mirafuentes, Navarre, 167
Miskito Indians, 23
Molina, Pedro, 198
Monte Pío de Cosecheros de Añil 34. *See also* Indigo Growers' Fund
Montiel y Coronado, Pablo, 148
Mosquito Coast, 18
Muñoz y Barba, María Teresa, 201
Muñoz y Barba, Teresa, 69

Nafarrate, Leonardo, 121
Nájera, José Delgado de, 68, 138
Nájera family, 232n.37
Nájera y Mencos, Francisco, 68, 146
Nájera y Mencos, Josefa, 72
Nájera y Mencos, Juana María, 127
Nájera y Mencos, María Micaela, 68, 200
Nájera y Mencos, Ventura, 68, 134–35, 138, 140
Natural disasters, 30

Navarre, 13, 43
Navarre, Kingdom of, 37
Navarro, Francisco, 59–61
Negreiros, Marqués de, 126
Nejapa, Oaxaca, 50–52
New Granada, 32
Nicaragua, 4, 16
Nicoya, Costa Rica, 148
Nuestra Señora de la Soledad (ship), 125
Nuestra Señora de los Dolores (ship), 92
Nueva Guatemala, 17, 22. *See also* Guatemala City
Nuevo Bastán, Mina de (Yuscarán), 88

Oaxaca, 13, 48–49, 51, 62, 123, 222n.40
Obregón, Francisco, 55
Obregón family, 55
Obregón y Gálvez, Ana Eudocia, 127
Obregón y Gálvez, Nicolas de, 67, 138
Ojeda y Estrada, José, 124
Olavide, Miguel de, 126
Oliver, Luis Francisco de, 88
Omoa (fortress), 34, 96, 135, 146–47
Order of Santiago, 12, 14, 43, 99, 179, 184
Ortíz de Letona, Pedro, 139
Ortíz de Manzaneda, Andrés, 139

Palencia, Francisco José de, 171
Palomo, Bernardo, 173
Palomo, Fernando, 139–40
Pamplona, Navarre, 38
Panama, 16, 23
Pavón, Cayetano, 55, 69, 139
Pavón y Aycinena, Francisco, 202
Pavón y Gil, Cayetano, 201
Pavón y Muñoz, Manuel José, 201
Paz, Francisco Xavier de, 59
Peninsulars, 16, 56
Peña, Juan Antonio de la, 127, 149
Pereyra, Antonio, 86
Pereyra, Gertrudis, 86
Pérez, Luis, 104
Pérez, Rafael, 149
Pérez de Elizalde, Gabriel, 115–18
Peru, 32, 60, 125
Philanthropy, 188–91
Phillip V, King of Spain (Bourbon), 42
Piñol y Muñoz, Juana, 69
Piñol y Muñoz, Micaela, 68
Piñol y Muñoz, Tadeo, 69, 201
Piñol y Sala, José, 69, 201
Pinto de Rivera, Sebastián de, 128
Pirates, 23
Placencia, Guipuzcoa, 122
Planters, 23

INDEX

Plaza, Joaquín de, 145
Plaza mayor, Guatemala City, 6
Political rivalries, 23
Puebla, Mexico, 48, 51, 62, 124
Purchase of offices, 27

Quezaltenango, Guatemala, 17, 22, 66

Real Asiento de Negros, 69
Real Congregación de San Fermín de los Navarros (Madrid), 42–43
Real hacienda (Santiago), 60
Regalism, 31
Regionalism, 23
Regla, Conde de, 190
Regular clergy, 28, 162
Religious orders, 161
Reparaz, Conde de, 127
Repartimiento. *See* Labor, forced
Repartimiento de efectos, 84. *See also* Trade, forced
Revolution of 1871, 7
Rivera, Juan de, 149
Riviero, Manuel, 145
Rodríguez, Antonio, 126
Rodríguez, José, 85–87
Rodríguez, Mario, 8
Roma, Basilio Vicente, 170
Rossell Arellano, Mariano, 191

Royal Phillipines Company, 114
Rum monopoly, 32

Sacatepéquez, Guatemala, 22
Sáenz Rico, Antonio, 124
Sáenz Rico, Gaspar, 52–53, 62
Sáenz Rico, Hijo y Compañía, 119
Sáenz Rico family, 124
Sagasti, Francisco Ignacio, 128
Salazar, Pedro, 144
Saldias, Navarre, 127
Salgado, Antonio, 54–55
Salmerón y Gallo, Manuel, 173, 228n.18
Sandinistas, 4
San Francisco Barillas (hacienda), 86
San José, Costa Rica, 17, 23
San José de la Bermuda (hacienda, El Salvador), 66
San José el Obrajuelo (hacienda, Santiago Nanualco, El Salvador), 85
San Juan de Vista (hacienda, San Vicente), 94
San Lorenzo de Ciga, Navarre, 38. *See also* Ciga, Navarre
San Miguel, El Salvador, 17, 84
San Nicolás de la Majada (hacienda, Escuintla), 66

San Pedro Mártir (hacienda, Santiago Nanualco), 85
San Salvador, El Salvador, 17, 22, 85
Santa Cruzada (Guatemala), 60, 63, 93, 163
Santa Cruzada (Oaxaca), 55
Santiago de Guatemala, 13, 14, 17, 19, 20, 26, 49, 53, 56, 73, 78, 82
Santiago Nanualco, El Salvador, 85, 175
Santo Tomás, Guatemala, 34
San Vicente, El Salvador, 17, 61, 85
Secular clergy, 28, 161
Secularization, 31
Seville, Spain, 42
Silver, 18, 25, 27
Sinande, Fernando, 123
Smith, Carol, 5
Socolow, Susan M., 77
Soconusco, 60
Sololá, 22, 27
Sonsonate, 22, 60
Soto, Antonio Marcos de, 168
Souza, Pedro de, 85, 87
Spain, 37
Spanish immigrants, 56
Stephens, John Lloyd, 185, 187
Suchitepéquez, Guatemala, 22, 60
Suria, Ramón, 172–73

Tafalla, Navarre, 104
Tagle y Bracho family, 151
Talamanca, 169
Taranco, Juan de, 80, 94
Tecpan, Guatemala, 146
Tegucigalpa, Honduras, 88
Tenientes, 27
Teoría y práctica del comercio y de la marina (1724), 45
Thompson, George A., 186
Title of Castile, 6, 15, 133, 178, 182
Tobacco monopoly, 32
Torre y Tagle, Bernabé Santiago de la, 153, 183
Torre y Trassiera, Bernabé de la, 65, 97, 150–55
Totonicapán, Guatemala, 22, 27, 60
Trade, forced, 25. *See also* Repartimiento de efectos
Trade fairs, 34, 83
Traslado, 22, 97, 134–35, 140, 144
Trelles, Francisco, 47
Troncoso Martínez, Bernardo, 144–45
Trujillo, Honduras, 34
Tudela, Navarre, 41
Tutino, John, 95, 189–90
Tututepeque (Oax), 52

University of San Carlos, 20, 141
Urrutia, Sebastián de, 126
Uzelaz, Casa de, 128
Uztáriz, Casa de, 45, 126–27

Uztáriz, Cristóbal Xavier de, 128
Uztáriz, Gerónimo de, 45
Uztáriz, Juan Bautista de (Conde de Reparaz), 127
Uztáriz family, 45

Van Oss, Adriaan C., 158, 162
Varón de Berrieza, Francisca Antonia, 55–56
Varón de Berrieza, Francisca Rosa, 63
Varón de Berrieza, José, 59–61, 63–64
Varón de Berrieza, Juan Antonio, 63
Varón de Berrieza, María Manuela, 59, 64
Varón y López, Francisca Rosa, 59
Varón y López, María Manuela, 59, 64
Veitia, María Luisa de, 53
Velarde y Cienfuegos, Juan Antonio, 151
Velásquez de las Reyes, Domingo, 173
Veracruz, Mexico, 47, 52, 54, 62
Vera Paz, Guatemala, 22
Verganza, Antonio, 146
Vertical integration, 99
Viceroyalty of New Spain, 16
Villa Aliva, Ignacio de, 172
Villa Alta, Oaxaca, 50–52
Villalengua, Juan José, 156
Villamagan, Gregorio, 173
Villa Nueva, Guatemala, 97
Viotti da Costa, Emilia, 6

War of Jenkins's Ear, 15, 33
Water supply, 135
Webre, Stephen, 18, 61
Western Europe, 15
Wholesale merchants, 23, 32
Wholesaling, 74
Wortman, Miles, 8, 68, 82, 94, 135, 140, 211n.10

Xamiltepeque, Oaxaca, 52

Yaguatique (hacienda, San Miguel, El Salvador), 93, 183, 192
Yraeta, Francisco Ignacio de, 11, 112–18, 123–25, 140, 145, 156, 198
Yraeta, José, 242n.44
Yriarte, Antonio, 173
Yrigoyen, Juan Bautista de, 125
Yrigoyen, Pedro Bernardo, 48–49, 51–55, 102, 123
Yrigoyen, Pedro de (Errazu, Navarre, father of Pedro Angel), 51
Yrigoyen e Yturralde, Ana Antonia, 41
Yrigoyen family, 45
Yrigoyen y Dutari, Juan Lorenzo, 51
Yrigoyen y Dutari, Pedro Angel, 48–49, 51–52, 123

Yrigoyen y Echenique, Miguel, 50–51, 53, 55
Yrigoyen y Larrainzar, Juana, 51
Yuscarán, Honduras, 88, 236n.31

Zaldumbide, José de, 126
Zapotitlán, Guatemala, 60
Zeage, Francisco (father), 59, 174
Zeage, Francisco Nicolás (son), 174
Zemurray, Samuel, 8